上海外国语大学新闻传播学院
"国际新闻与数字传播"系列丛书

FEATURE WRITING

英语特写采访与写作

林岩 著

上海交通大学出版社
SHANGHAI JIAO TONG UNIVERSITY PRESS

内容提要

　　本教材聚焦英语特写采访与写作这一专业领域,系统性涵盖英语特写采访与写作的基本要点,并着重探索如何应对在中文环境下针对国际受众进行特写报道的挑战。本教材结合大量特写报道采写实例,在中国对外传播的框架下就该领域的基本知识点和技能点展开详细讨论,以期解决学习者和从业者在英语特写采访与写作中遇到的常见问题。本教材语言为英语,旨在帮助新闻学本科高年级学生和研究生进行系统学习,也可为英语新闻从业者提供专业参考。

图书在版编目(C I P)数据

　　英语特写采访与写作 / 林岩著. —上海:上海交
通大学出版社,2022.8
　　ISBN 978 - 7 - 313 - 26669 - 9

　　Ⅰ.①英…　Ⅱ.①林…　Ⅲ.①新闻采访-英语②新闻
写作-英语　Ⅳ.①G212

　　中国版本图书馆 CIP 数据核字(2022)第 041102 号

英语特写采访与写作

YINGYU TEXIE CAIFANG YU XIEZUO

著　　者:林　岩

出版发行:上海交通大学出版社　　　地　　址:上海市番禺路 951 号

邮政编码:200030　　　　　　　　　电　　话:021 - 64071208

印　　刷:上海新艺印刷有限公司　　经　　销:全国新华书店

开　　本:710mm×1000mm　1/16　印　　张:18.5

字　　数:373 千字

版　　次:2022 年 8 月第 1 版　　　　印　　次:2022 年 8 月第 1 次印刷

书　　号:ISBN 978 - 7 - 313 - 26669 - 9

定　　价:69.00 元

Preface

The first question that came to mind before I set out to prepare for writing this textbook was why it was needed. Long a staple of newspaper and magazine writing, feature writing is far from a novel genre and many textbooks have been written on the subject. I myself have used and referred to several well-written textbooks in the course of my teaching. These textbooks approach feature writing from different perspectives, but they all cover the topic comprehensively and each provides a unique and effective roadmap for learning. Hence the question arises: why a new one is needed?

The answer lies in the fact that while there are many textbooks around, few have been written from a Chinese perspective and for Chinese students learning the craft. Writing English-language feature stories for an international audience is quite different from reporting for the domestic market. In this sense, feature writing falls within international reporting and international communication. Therefore, in addition to discussing the basics of the genre, I intend the book to examine the specific requirements concerning Chinese international reporting. These requirements affect all important editorial decisions throughout the process of reporting and writing feature articles, from finding the right story idea to writing the final draft. The so-called sense of news, i.e., the judgement of what is important and what is not, also shifts when the target audience changes from at home to abroad. International reporting is supposed to be across borders not just physical but also cultural. From a technical perspective, the inevitable translation between Chinese and English and all the problems that may arise during the process have to be taken into account and handled with principled care. Moreover, on many occasions a feature writer aiming for the international audience has to consider how to reconcile her needs with those of her audience. The fine line is between the need of effectively telling China's stories to the world and that of meeting the often capricious interest of an obscure international readership. This challenge must be met with both tact and tactics, as there is an important distinction between pandering to the interests of readers and serving their needs. Another major concern of feature writers is how to make reading their stories a rewarding experience for readers, as it is impractical and unrealistic to force any audience to accept one's message amid the digital information overloading, not to mention an audience that is ambiguous and foreign. This concern requires feature writers to master and hone their craft every way they can; to compete in the sea of information, the very least they can do is to work hard to be good storytellers. This book will therefore explore the reporting and writing of feature articles within the framework of Chinese international reporting, dissect the thought that goes into "customizing" the feature stories for a culturally different audience, and offer possible solutions to problems in this crucial communication we call "telling China's story to the world."

This book contains ten chapters that track and outline both the reporting and writing process. The first chapter introduces the definition and characteristics of feature writing and discusses the genre in the context of international communication in the digital age. The next three chapters discuss the reporting process in its natural order: how to find and form an idea for a feature story, how to research that idea and how to conduct an interview. For chapter five and six, the book turns to the writing process, with chapter five focusing on leads and chapter six on story organization at length. Then, three more chapters (seven, eight and nine) move from a general discussion of how to cover and write feature stories (mainly news features) to an analysis of three specific types of feature stories: profiles, travel stories and reviews. The final chapter (the tenth one) presents a reporting and writing experiment involving my own class at the School of Journalism and Communication of Shanghai International Studies University and the Songjiang Convergence Media Center. This experiment involved writing features on suburban Shanghai for international audiences; many of the lessons my students and I learned in the process coincide with the key points raised in the first few chapters of the book. A careful examination of the knowledge and experience we gained seems to be a proper ending to conclude this book.

Special thanks to *Shanghai Daily*, The Sixth Tone, ShanghaiEye, and *China Daily*. All of the feature articles cited and analyzed in the book come from the English-language media in China, including *China Daily*, *Shanghai Daily*, Sixth Tone, and ShanghaiEye, where journalists and editors work diligently day in and day out to make China's voice heard around the world.

Contents

Chapter 1   What Makes A Feature Story

1.1   Defining feature writing

Feature stories are an important genre of articles that constitutes part of the multifarious contents of newspapers and magazines in their traditional or digital forms. What is feature writing? One professional feature writer believes feature writing enables readers, listeners, and writers to appreciate news, by involving their feelings as well as their minds, and to understand—not merely to know.[①] Another writer defines feature writing as a piece of deliberately structured writing for publication, usually running from 600 to 2000 words, which aims to inform, comment, persuade or entertain. More specifically, newspapers' feature articles, although they may not all relate directly to the news of the moment, normally have a topical peg of some kind. And in feature writing, content and audience come before methods. Once content (having something to say) is understood and shaped, and the audience identified, the writing will follow and will adapt.[②] Yet another defines features as the special portion of the periodicals that publish them. Feature writing goes beyond the levels of conventional straight news and hard news topics and approaches to be special. Feature writers employ some "license" or flexibility and emphasize the unconventional or the different. They seek out something or someone that's offbeat or entertaining.[③] William E. Blundell sums up feature writing as "make the truth as interesting to others as it is to us (reporters)." He emphasizes greatly on the inseparable flowing process of reporting and writing and urges others to treat reporting and writing as a cohesive whole.[④]

①   Louis Alexander. Beyond the Facts, a Guide to the Art of Feature Writing [M]. 2nd ed. Houston: Gulf Publishing Company, 1982: 1-2.
②   Brendan Hennessy. Writing Feature Articles, a Practical Guide to Methods and Markets [M]. 3rd ed. Oxford: Focal Press, 1997: Preface, 7.
③   Bruce Garrison. Professional Feature Writing [M]. 4th ed. Mahwah: Lawrence Erlbaum Associates, Inc., Publishers, 2004: 6-7.
④   William E. Blundell. The Art and Craft of Feature Writing based on the Wall Street Journal Guide [M]. New York: Plume, the Penguin Group, 1988: x-xii.

The above gems of wisdom on feature writing given by professional writers delineate the outline and reveal the essence of the cluster of stories called feature articles. Feature writing is beyond the news, though a feature article takes a news peg (a news event that forms the basis of the article). Feature writing favors the novel and the unique as the reporting subject. Feature writing is somewhere between the news writing and the short story writing, the contents being factual and newsworthy, the writing techniques literary. Features are journalistic articles that deal strictly with reality. It makes no room for any made-up or fabrication. Involving characters, plot and even conversations, feature articles are usually considered to be soft, in contrast to the hard news. Given its often oblique approach, longer form, and various borrowed literary techniques, sometimes when reading a feature article, a reader might have the impression that she is perusing a short story. In this sense, features share certain characteristics with subjective and creative writing. However, subjective and creative it may be, a feature story is first and foremost a piece of journalistic writing, which means everything in a feature story must be the fact that the reporter gathered firsthand or from credible sources. The writing is a natural following of the reporting. The approach and style of a feature story could and should be subjective, creative or original. The contents in the story must be objective, factual, or verifiable. Features are part of the news business and **factualness** is its most prominent property.

To sum up, broadly speaking, feature writing is an umbrella term under which various types of stories cluster. Narrowly speaking, features are journalistic articles that go beyond presenting the mere facts, but strive to show in details what happened and the how and why to a specific audience. In other words, feature stories focus on story-telling and usually appear in longer forms and deeply involve humanity. One more important point, compared to news writing, is that feature writing is more **audience-driven**: a feature story is written for a specific market. This book is to explore feature writing on China for the international market.

1.1.1　Beyond the facts

As we all know that news stories are all about facts. They monitor the world and alert the readers to what's happening here and now. Features sometimes do the same, especially when the stories are still young, presenting an all-round picture of the virgin news event to the readers. But on more occasions, features go beyond the facts; instead of reporting the barebones of what happened, features dig deeper and try to show in clear descriptive terms how and why it happened. With the burden of explanation, feature writers must be able to see through the event and discern the seemingly chaotic and random factors that contribute to the forming and developing of the event. At the same time, feature writers must foresee and write in anticipation of any impacts and consequences of a given event. Like news, features keep people informed; furthermore, by keeping people informed, features help people understand better. This is an innate service features provide. It is also an important one. Today, given the rise of the new media in our life and the ensuing media landscape ruled by divide and bigotry, this **explanatory** property of the feature articles has never been more valuable. Feature writers have never before had the urgency to guide people through the fleeting and elusive facts and arrive at truth and understanding.

1.1.2   Capturing the event

News stories report the event; feature stories capture it. In appearance, features are closer to short stories. Feature writers employ literary techniques and thus render their stories original and descriptive. They do not just give the facts of the news but take the reader there by capturing the feel and spirit of the reported event. As a result, feature writers need to develop an eye for details and a power of observation to get the ambiance and the mood of the event. Successfully capturing the event it is reporting, a feature story does not just inform, it entertains by allowing the readers to experience the event through carefully-described details. That's why a good feature story is heavy on **description and color**. It always shows, never just tells.

1.1.3   It can be late

Compared with news, features are less conscious of the time element. News is all about now. In today's digital world, news breaks all over the world literally every second; many important events are reported in a piecemeal manner as things are still unfolding. In contrast, features **lack that urgency** and it could be late. Often instead of on the very front of the frantic human scene, features take a step back and exam the scene with a cooler eye, for its main task is helping the readers get a grasp of life and hopefully live better through understanding its complexities and nuances. Also depending on the subject and length, features may take months to produce.

1.1.4　A nose for feature

One thing feature writers need to keep in mind is that despite its literary appearance, a feature story is a journalistic article in all aspects. News values still apply except for the element of timeliness as explained above. A feature story has to be newsworthy otherwise it is not worth to be written. Features root firmly in reality and report on issues and people of note. It still takes **a nose for news** or, in this case, a nose for feature to successfully report and write a feature story. The nose for news, or news sense, is the ability to tell what's important from what's not, the ability to tell what's worth pursuing from what's not, and the ability to tell what's going into the final story from what's not. Take pets for example. Everybody loves a puppy or a kitten so we may safely assume a story on pets may sell. However, if the story is about your dog or your neighbor's, however cute it might be, it is not a feature story unless the canine in your story happens to stumble into the spotlight in some way. But a story that takes a close look at the metropolitan pet market in Shanghai or some story that dissects the emotional tangle between pets and their lonely city owners as urbanization drives people increasingly apart, when adequately executed and written, makes a good feature story. The former could turn into a potential business story and the latter a human interest piece. The point is both contain news values.

1.1.5　Human interest

Of all the news values, human interest is most commonly seen in almost all feature stories. Human interest is defined as the quality that engages attention and sympathy by enabling a reader to identify readily with the people, problems, and situations described in a story. A feature story that is dripping with human interest involves the experiences of real people and explores the personal side of a news event. Feature stories can be roughly categorized into two types of articles and both kinds will not do without the human element. A feature story about a particular person is called a profile feature. This person could be a celebrity, a news maker, an odd ball or an ordinary person with an interesting story. An issue-based story, the other kind, focuses on an issue, but is still about people. Sometimes the issue is presented through depicting people directly involved. Often the issue is dissected to explain how the on-going problem is affecting people and how people are reacting to it. An issue-based story without human element will be drab, thin, and simply boring. "Get people talking. ... Nothing so animates writing as someone telling what he thinks or what he does — in his words," decreed William Zinsser.[1] Similarly, feature stories are also told through people, as one important trait of feature writing is the proper use of direct quotes.

1.1.6   Story-telling

News stories are traditionally written in inverted pyramid style, though many believe that the time-honored structure is collapsing in today's non-stop 24-7 news cycle. As journalism scholars notice, "news becomes more piecemeal; what were once the raw ingredients of journalism began to be passed on to the public directly."[2] News is delivered to the public in more innovative ways. Many news media have their reporters in the field send back sentences written down in their mobile phones as news is breaking and the reporters staying behind put the pieces together and in context as quickly as they can. For a complex and devolving subject, some journalists managed to create a portal into the far-reaching issue, taking advantage of "combined strengths of original reporting, data journalism, social media, maps, photos, video, and more."[3] However, in the confusing and shifting experiment of presenting one's findings to the digital-age audience, features remain structured more of the same as before; **a piece of narrative.** As long-form story opposed to the "piecemeal" information people were constantly bombarded with, features are developed in a more organized way to give a relatively comprehensive picture of the world. Much care and creativity are put into the organization of a feature story. The

---

[1]   William Zinsser. On Writing Well [M]. 5th ed. New York: HarperPerennial, 1994: 63.

[2]   Bill Kovach & Tom Rosenstiel. The Elements of Journalism: what newspeople should know and the public should expect [M]. 3rd ed. New York: Three Rivers Press, 2014: 64.

[3]   Bill Kovach & Tom Rosenstiel. The Elements of Journalism: what newspeople should know and the public should expect [M]. 3rd ed. New York: Three Rivers Press, 2014: 212.

exact form of the organization is free as long as it serves the content; but however it changes, it focuses on telling the story at hand, usually with a central message, a surprising angle, characters and a plot line.

1.1.7 A range of stories

Feature is an umbrella term under which a number of different types of articles cluster. The varied stories can be categorized according to the subject the story reports on (news features, profiles, travel stories, sports features), the service it provides (how-to stories, seasonal features, sidebars), the news values it plays up (human interest stories), the opinion it offers (reviews and criticisms), or even the person of speech (personal experience stories which are often told in the first person). There are other ways to pigeonhole this unruly group of colorful stories. For instance, feature stories can be sorted into categories of news features, profiles, spot features, trend stories, and live-ins. Spot features are sidebar stories mentioned before, a supplement to the main story on a big event. Trend stories refer to articles appearing in the lifestyle, fashion, cooking, high-tech, or entertainment section of a newspaper or a news website. These stories do a service for the readers by taking the pulse of the culture at the moment, finding out what's new, fresh, and exciting in art, fashion, film, music, architecture, high technology, cooking, and other areas. Live-in is an in-depth, often magazine-length article that paints a picture of a particular place and the people who work or live there. As the name suggests, live-in stories, which are often done by spending a lot of time soaking in the environment, offer an immersive experience for the readers and often appear in the lifestyle section of the paper or in a magazine that the paper publishes occasionally, such as once a week or once a month.

Whatever the names, whatever the medium, however categorized, the stories basically serve the readers by adding depth, humanity, color, and entertainment to the news of the day. The first six chapters of this book focus on the basics of feature writing, mainly using news features (an issue-based story) as example. However, the reporting skills and writing techniques apply to all types of feature articles despite the fact that each type of the feature articles has its own characteristics and specific reporting concerns. To address these specific concerns, the seventh, eighth, and ninth chapter of the book will explore three major types of feature stories apart from the news features, namely, the profiles, the travel articles, and the reviews.

Exercise

1. Features take different forms and different approaches. Sometimes features might even be entirely about something in the past. However, the journey down the past is made for the benefit of understanding the present. Thus, the so-called history features always tie in with the present in some way. Take the following story from *Shanghai Daily* on Fuzhou Road in downtown Shanghai①. The feature article, part of a series of nostalgic reports on the old Shanghai in modern times to commemorate the opening port of this Eastern metropolis, focuses on the bygone "wild days of newspapering." Please read the following story and explain how it anchored the readers' interest by bringing the story back frequently to various popular attraction sites in today's Shanghai, not least the "busy book street today" whose past is all the story about.

Wild Days of Newspapering and Print Battlefield of Ideas

By Yao Minji

It was 4a.m., an ordinary morning in 1930s Shanghai, and 10-year-old Gu Dagang tagged along with his uncle to get the newspaper on Wangping Street. Though it was just 200 meters long, it was packed with thousands of people waiting for the day's papers.

Time was everything for a newsboy. Gu grabbed a few dozen and quickly ran to his usual spot, the streets behind the Bund, to hawk the news. His uncle also grabbed a bundle and took off with his bike.

"Those were sensitive and unsettled times, when people worried constantly about the policies, the different battles, so papers were gone very fast," says 92-year-old Gu, who now lives near Nanjing Road E.

"Sometimes you had to fight over the paper, especially when there was an extra edition, or hao wai, which meant something big, often horrible, just happened," he says.

After he sold all the papers, Gu strolled down the street to buy a

---

① Yao Minji. Wild days of newspapering and print battlefield of ideas. Shanghai Daily[N/OL]. (2013-11-02) [2021-08-04]. https://archive. shine. cn/feature/art-and-culture/Wild-days-of-newspapering-and-print-battlefield-of-ideas/shdaily.shtml.

dumpling for breakfast from a street vendor.

At 2p. m., he and his uncle went back for the evening papers, and again the street was mobbed with distributors and anxious readers.

Famous journalist and writer Cao Juren (1900—1972) recalled in his memoir that Wangping Street "was vivid all day long. All the influential figures whose writings shook the times left their mark there."

The famous newspaper street was a small part of today's Shandong Road M. between Hankou and Fuzhou roads. The area expanded to accommodate newspapers, publishers, printers and booksellers.

At one time the area housed almost all the city's influential newspapers, Chinese and English. It was a buzzing center of rumor, information and disinformation, and a battlefield of printed ideas in the late 19th and early 20th century.

Fuzhou Road, then known as Fourth Street (Si Ma Lu) near Wangping Street, remains a busy book street today. The old Si Ma Lu area was half occupied by publishing houses, newspaper buildings and bookstores, while the other half was occupied by famous tea houses, entertainment venues and brothels. The phrase "a woman from Si Ma Lu" was the old term for prostitute.

In fact, some newspapers carried brothel advertisements and even promoted many competitions to choose the most delightful ladies, their charms extolled in verse; photos and sketches were often published. Readers would vote.

Newsmen have always liked their saloons, and Shanghai had plenty to choose from.

At Hankou Road and Shandong Road M. stands the former headquarter of the famous *Shun Pao*, or *Shanghai News*, published between 1872 to 1949. It was one of the earliest and most widely circulated Chinese newspapers. Today it's a commercial building.

After Shanghai's port opened in 1843, modern newspapers were early imports. At first they published shipping schedules and business news.

Many early papers were established by expats and published in English, French, Russian, Japanese, Portuguese and other languages.

The English-language *North China Daily News*, known as *Tzu Lin His Pao*, was one of the earliest modern newspapers. It was founded by British auctioneer Henry Shearman in 1850, published for more than a century and closed in 1951.

At first it was published weekly, featuring shipping and commercial news; it went daily in 1856, with a weekly supplement of current affairs, fiction and opinions. Editors and correspondents were mainly early settlers, or Shanghailanders, including Frederic H. Balfour (1871—1908), famous for his writings and translations of Taoist texts.

For a long time, the paper was the major information source for expats, especially British officials and merchants. Chinese officials and merchants also paid close attention to the paper to understand foreign attitudes. At its peak, daily circulation reached 7,817.

Its former 10-story building, No. 17 on the Bund, was designed as the tallest office building in the city in 1921, but when it was finished in 1924, the record was already broken.

The publisher of the *North China Daily News* launched a Chinese newspaper in 1861, one of the city's earliest Chinese papers.

That inspired a group of British merchants, including Ernest Major, to found *Shun Pao* in 1872.

In 1909, *Shun Pao* was sold to Chinese comprador Xi Yufu and became one of the three most influential papers in the city.

Its two major competitors were *Xinwen Bao* (literally News Newspaper) and *Shi Bao* (literally Times Newspaper), all in the Wangping Street area.

Xinwen Bao was co-founded by Chinese and foreigners. One of the major investors was merchant Zhang Shuhe, owner of the Zhang Garden, the famous public entertainment venue featuring short films, magic shows, cameras and roller coasters.

2. The following feature story, "Generation Z artists' perspectives of China explode on social media" from *Shanghai Daily*[①], reports on a piece of interactive illustration art work called "Out of Poverty: Not One Less" by Chinese generation Z artists posted on social media platforms home and abroad. Read the story carefully and then rewrite it into a piece of news within 150 words. Use your own language and try not to repeat the words and sentences from the original story. Take note of the choices you make during the rewriting process: what information is kept? What details are omitted?

---

① Ke Jiayun. Generation Z artists' perspectives of China explode on social media [N/OL]. Shanghai Daily. (2021-08-04) [2021-08-14]. https://www.shine.cn/news/in-focus/2108043122/.

And why? Do you need to begin and organize your story differently? Why? Is there a shift of focus from a feature story to a news story on the same subject? If there is, what is exactly the nature of the aforesaid shift? If there isn't, why?

Generation Z Artists' Perspectives of China Explode on Social Media

Ke Jiayun

Serbian twitterer "El maestro" left an enthusiastic comment in response to a video posted by a Foreign Ministry official that showed 24 illustrations depicting the well-off and happy lives of 56 ethnic groups in China.

"Guangdong, Jiangsu, Guangxi (Guangzhou, Foshan, Shenzhen, Suzhou, Nanning). I liked it a lot and for sure I'm coming back as soon as possible. Loved everything about China, the people, the food. I like how safe the country is," El maestro wrote in response to the question the official Zhao Lijian posed in his post: "China has wonderful land and hardworking people. Which provinces have you been to?"

The 24 illustrations form a long picture scroll called "Out of Poverty: Not One Less" that was created by local studio Fusion Era run by a group of Gen Z youth. They depict the culture, history, landmarks and people of different regions and ethnic groups in China.

The scroll also has an interactive treasure hunt game and is embedded with 100 surprises, including stories of China's poverty alleviation, the shining aspects of the Party's century-long history, and aspects of the Chinese nation.

It had attracted about 160 million views on more than 60 social media platforms at home and abroad as of 11am on July 27, of which more than 6 million users had participated in the treasure hunt.

The Fusion Era studio was established in 2019 and created works for films made by European and US companies and cooperated with domestic museums, main designer Hu Muyang said.

But last year the team had to work from home due to the coronavirus and decided to deliver something to the public through illustrations. At the time, China was dealing with "rumors and slander" from overseas.

"We also hoped with our works to counter the rumors and tell stories about the real China," Hu told *Shanghai Daily*. "We wanted the world to hear Chinese voices and insisted on showing Chinese society and culture from our own Gen Z perspectives."

Though the studio is based in Shanghai, the team members and their collaborators are from all over the country, including several from ethnic minorities like Miao.

Hu was once invited to a panel discussion organized by local government about young content creators' lives and the entrepreneurial environment in Shanghai. During the discussion, he brought up the idea of creating something to tell the sense of community of the Chinese nation and the nation's concept of eco-development, as well as the fruits of the poverty alleviation campaign.

"We used to see examples of students who could finally leave their hometowns in poverty-stricken mountainous areas purely through their own efforts, such as outstanding university entrance exam scores," Hu said.

"But now we've eliminated poverty. So we hope to say that people are leaving these areas with joy and pride toward their hometown and can return without fear of poverty. That's what we called rural revitalization."

Poverty alleviation has also helped to eliminate conflicts between people and nature because there's no longer a need to destroy the environment just for money, Hu added.

And these ideas are all reflected in the 24 illustrations which were completed within 41 days.

"Sometimes we had no time to sleep," Hu said. "The members in different provinces set the same alarm clock and slept two hours."

The team perfected their works by improving the detail. On the illustration of Yunnan Province, they decided to use the image of Zhang Guimei, a teacher who founded a high school and worked for female education in poverty-stricken mountainous areas. But there was debate about how to depict her facial expression.

Some team members thought Zhang should show her fatigue caused by hard work, as did her photos in some media. But Hu and others felt that, although Zhao had worked very hard, she had joy in her mind, so she should have a smile on her face.

Eventually, they referred to some old photos of Zhang when she was young and put a smile on her for the illustration. "This came about because we believed that Party members like Zhang are happy and have a passion to change a poor and less advanced area's condition with their hands. It's a great job."

Every illustration features more than 10 elements and every one of them had many such details needing to be carefully considered.

For the illustration of Henan and Shandong, one of the artists insisted on including the image of Jiao Yulu, a civil servant who sacrificed his life in 1964 while trying to alleviate poverty. The artist thought his inclusion would demonstrate that poverty alleviation had been pursued in China for seven decades.

Hu said the team planned to use multimedia to show more aspects of China and Chinese people, including animation, interactive games on the world's largest online gaming platform Steam, and picture books for children.

"Foreigners want to see a real China and high-quality cultural products. That's why Chinese rural lifestyle YouTuber Li Ziqi is so popular and Chinese animation and Chinoiserie fashion has risen in overseas markets," Hu said. "For us, we hope our content can be tested by the market."

Yang Ting, deputy editor of Shanghai Literature and Art Publishing House, is responsible for works on ethnic groups and China's folk culture. Her team was invited to provide expert professional advice to Fusion Era.

"We did lots of work selecting highlights from massive amounts of ethnic culture content," Yang said. "What impressed me was the love of these young people toward their motherland and their confidence in Chinese culture. Their great passion moved me."

Yang said her team will continue to work with Fusion Era, Bilibili and more new media to spread their research.

As "treasure guardians," the 24 content creator uploaded videos on Bilibili to tell stories about their designs to netizens at home and abroad.

They explained the "treasures," or "knowledge surprises," behind the long scroll, shared their feelings on how to tell Chinese stories, and how to interact and grow together with their peers in Gen Z.

Netizens can follow their dynamic hints and go to the long scroll to discover the wonderful content shared by these "treasure guardians."

"Generation Z is a generation of Internet natives and a generation of self-confidence," said Bilibilier Wang Xiao Albert, the "treasure guardian" of Tibet on the scroll. He said there are many touching stories in China's development waiting for content creators to dig out and tell in a way that is more familiar to young people.

He said "Out of Poverty: Not One Less" is very innovative and makes the process of treasure hunting interesting for netizens.

Another Bilibilier, Gao You Si, an Israeli is a "treasure guardian" of Yunnan and has been in China for more than 10 years. He started to tell China's stories through short videos and live streaming four years ago to help Gen Z around the world to increase their knowledge and understanding.

He said that what he saw and heard in Yunnan really made him feel the achievements of China's poverty alleviation. In the future, he would like to help more foreign friends come to China and explore the country through their eyes, their culture and their language.

(Yao Han contributed to this article)

Source: SHINE　　Editor: Xu Qing

1.2　Writing for the international market

1.2.1　Connecting with the world

Recent years have seen a rise and thriving of English-language media in China, a proactive effort on China's part to meet the great demands of understanding and being understood in return in the increasingly globalized world. It has always been the mission of Chinese journalists to communicate to the outside world by reporting China accurately and fairly. And the mission has never been more urgent than today as China ascends, not least economically, and owes the world her perspective on the issues perplexing the gradually polarized world. Plus, the new century is ruled by the vibrant yet chaotic new media where getting oneself across has become very difficult, if not impossible. Everybody is talking and no one is listening. Complex issues are routinely taken out of its context and presented to the audience in the loudest terms. The world is saturated with bits and pieces of information and yet effective communication across borders is rare and understanding rarer. Chinese reporters are faced with the mounting task of helping readers make sense of the fragments about China floating around and a possible means at disposal is feature articles. Feature stories are equipped with the proper space and scope that in-depth story-telling demands, and in the case of international communication, they are strategically positioned to provide depth and context that is essential to fostering understanding in foreign audience of the home country. Heavy on description and human interest, feature stories can provide that rare degree of immersion for any serious reader that not only want to know what happened but also wish to get the how and why.

1.2.2 The Chinese English-language media

The Chinese English-language media concentrate in such metropolises as Beijing and Shanghai. Beijing-based English-language media are mostly national conglomerates that cover all the traditional forms of media outlets: newswire, newspapers, TV and radio. The past few years have seen a drive of media convergence where the traditional media outlets have transformed into multimedia platforms. Let's take a quick look:

Xinhua News Agency, the national news agency, provides 24-7 cycle of news service in various forms ranging from textual to video in eight languages and it has established 180 correspondent bureaus around the world, which guarantees its unique position to put the world in Chinese perspective[①].

China Daily, the national English-language newspaper, is widely recognized as the official voice of China and is read and quoted widely. Established in 1981, *China Daily* has developed into a multi-media information platform combining newspapers, websites and apps with a strong presence on Facebook, Twitter, Sina Weibo and WeChat. Its official website gives the readership as more than 330 million all over the world and claims to be "a default choice" for people who have an interest in Chinese affairs.[②]

China Global Television Network originates from the English-language channel of CCTV which started its test run in 1997 and was officially launched in 2000. CGTN now owns six foreign language channels, three overseas stations, one video news agency, and one new media matrix. In 2018, the network was merged into the China Media Group.

China Radio International, the national multi-language radio service, was established in 1941 and broadcasts in 65 different languages including ten Chinese dialects and ethnic minority dialects. It has merged into China Media Group in May 2018.

Shanghai boasts 215,000 foreigners working in the city, accounting for 23.7% of the country's total and ranking first in the country, according to a

---

① 新华社简介[EB/OL].新华社. [2021-08-04]. http://203.192.6.89/xhs/static/e11272/11272.htm.

② About China Daily Group [EB/OL].China Daily. [2021-08-04]. http://www.chinadaily.com.cn/e/static_e/about.

2019 news report[①]. Accordingly，Shanghai-based English-language media consider local expats as their main audience and part of the news content is clearly tailored towards the expatriate interest and needs. *Shanghai Daily*，launched in 1999，is the first local English-language newspaper in China，and since 2005，its circulation has extended to the Yangtze River delta，the economic engine of China，and in 2013 the paper went online and the multi-media website https://www.shine.cn/ provides a solid news service in text，photos，graphs，audio，and video. The English-language newspaper caters to the English-speaking foreigners working and living in the metropolis，the lion share of its contents focusing on local and national news，story by story，to foster the goodwill towards the city and China. Recently，*Shanghai Daily* has launched a brand new "In Focus" section which offers news features in response to the increasing interest in China from the world. The daily also has a vibrant lifestyle section full of feature articles that help the local expats enjoy the rich cultural life of the cosmopolitan city.

International Channel Shanghai was launched in 1992 and quickly became the only successful local English-language TV channel in China. During its heyday，ICS boasted a dozen original programs apart from a solid news service. Then the programs were gradually reduced to six with the rise of the new media spearheaded by short videos and the consequential fall of TV as the young audience have migrated online. However，the channel still broadcasts 19 hours daily with 7.5-hour first-run programs. Shanghai Live and Money Talks，two news programs of ICS，offer local news and the city's view on national matters.

Shanghai established her own English news website in 2014，the multi-device Sixth Tone. "There are five tones in Mandarin Chinese. When it comes to coverage of China，Sixth Tone believes there is room for other voices that go beyond buzzwords and headlines to tell the uncommon stories of common people,"[②] says the website，explaining its rather unusual appellation. Different from other English-language media in the same city，Sixth Tone is devoted to reporting China to the world and offers a strong feature service，with articles following the trending issues of the country as well as some fringe ones. Divided into five categories（tones），the website is dedicated to "tell the uncommon stories of the common people" of China. Stories by the Sixth Tone are

① 上海成为外籍人才眼中最具吸引力城市，逾 21 万外国人在沪工作[N/OL]. 解放日报. (2019-01-16) [2021-08-04]. http://www.cnr.cn/shanghai/tt/20190116/t20190116_524484010.shtml.
② ABOUT US [EB/OL]. The Sixth Tone. [2021-08-04]. http://www.sixthtone.com/about-us.

characteristically human-centric and the news subjects are chosen for the conflict he or she represents that reflects the "the nuances and complexities of today's China."①

Besides the aforementioned major English media both at national and local level，there are other news services targeting the English-speaking audience. Among the many publications，Yicaiglobal，a Shanghai-based multi-device website，offers business and finance news and features in English. *Global Times*，the English version of the synonymous Chinese newspaper which is known for its nationalist stand and large readership，offers a small yet exemplary English-language news service both in print and online.

1.2.3　Telling China's stories to the world

It is important to acknowledge that news that crosses national borders usually comes with an agenda；like it or not，international news has an impact，often far-reaching，on serious issues such as national image，international relations and the global economy. Substandard international reporting is costly. And of all the concerns one should take into consideration when writing for the international audience，the most important one is providing the necessary context and background information in one's story so that anyone who encounters the subject for the first time will gain a clear and correct picture of the issue at hand. The key is not just for the reader to know what has happened but to understand why this could happen. Remember the "why" always counts more than all the other four Ws in feature writing for an international market.

Context is defined as the parts of a discourse that surround a word or passage and can throw light on its meaning.② Without context，the meaning will be unclear，obscure，and even misleading. In international communication，the importance of context，at least in theory，is universally recognized，but in practice，context is rarely provided and chaos reigns. As discussed above，thanks to its length and depth，feature articles are uniquely positioned to provide the lost context when telling stories of China to the world. Moreover，English features by Chinese writers are most effective because the stories offer an original native perspective that is lacking in China reporting which has long

---

① ABOUT US［EB/OL］. The Sixth Tone.［2021-08-04］. http：//www.sixthtone.com/about-us.

② Merriam-Webster Dictionary［EB/OL］［2021-08-04］. https：//www.merriam-webster.com/dictionary/context.

been dominated by foreign correspondents. Chinese reporters can tell China's stories better by providing the necessary context and explaining the Chinese aspects of the story that root in traditions and customs and often have no ready equivalents in English language. This explanation, which distinguishes a successful feature story from a failed one, takes more than simple translation. The following factors must be taken into consideration: firstly, a deep understanding of the situation of one's mother country is needed to lend authority and authenticity to one's story. Secondly, a cultural sensitivity that encompasses cultural and racial differences, a sort of anthropological view, is needed to render the story the kind of interpretation that helps understanding. Thirdly, language skills based on English proficiency are a must to guarantee the language quality of the story. There's already enough misinformation and barriers of all kinds in the world of international communication. China's effort at talking to the world should not be hampered by simple language errors.

1.2.4　An example: explaining TCM to foreign audience

Traditional Chinese medicine (TCM) is a culturally distinctive discipline. The purely Chinese character fostered by its long history and tradition makes it a challenge to report effectively on the issues involved. How can the issue of the TCM be discussed in a language and manner that English-speaking foreigners understand? The following story from the *Shanghai Daily* about the role of TCM in the fight against the COVID-19 pandemic is a good example of how these culturally specific topics and terms should be handled.

TCM is not a new topic, but this story contains a news peg, the approval of clinical use of TCM in the war on COVID-19, which makes the story relevant and current. Discussing TCM in the urgent context of the COVID-19 pandemic, the story highlights two facts (see paras. 25-31). One is historical: in China's long history, TCM has had its own experience of dealing with pandemics; the other is about the present: some of the "front-line" doctors who successfully treated patients in Wuhan hospital were actually TCM specialists. Linking TCM to pandemics, this TCM story contains real substance and has an immediacy not normally found in TCM discussions. The combination of a long history and current practice lends legitimacy to both TCM and this story.

One difficulty in dealing with a story like the TCM one is how to explain and interpret specific terms from Chinese culture, some of which have no ready equivalent in English. TCM has many components and combinations that would confuse most Chinese people, and few foreign readers would be able to understand these components or combinations. In this story, the reporter solves this dilemma by not specifying or naming each ingredient, but by using a general term, product (paragraph 1), and talking about TCM in broad terms such as system, virus and immunity (paragraph 8) that are familiar and easily understood by foreign readers. This solution may make the story less precise, but the result is that the story is comprehensible, which is the ultimate aim of any story.

As the saying goes, we learn about the world through metaphors. Comparisons, especially when it comes to familiar objects or terms, will help in understanding unfamiliar subjects, or subjects from other cultures. Traditional Chinese medicine treatments and their theories may seem mysterious to a layman, let alone a foreign reader. In this story, the journalist uses acupuncture and kung fu in the same context when referring to TCM treatments (para. 4), terms that overseas audiences are already familiar with and understand to some extent, so that the audience can gain some idea by relating unspecified TCM treatments to something they are familiar with. Later in the story (para. 15-18), the journalist explains some of the principles involved in TCM by citing the example of washing the face. By following this advice, readers, foreigners and natives alike, can begin to understand the basic ideas of TCM by doing a routine that all people do every day.

Another good example of explaining a complex Chinese concept is found in the tenth paragraph. *Jun chen zuo shi* is a principle in formulating the traditional Chinese medicine. Roughly, *jun* (the emperor) *chen* (the minister) *zuo* (the assistant or advisor) *shi* (the errand-runner) respectively represent four kinds of ingredients in terms of its therapeutic function. The idea is that for any combination of ingredients, a practitioner should consider the ingredients in the four function groups to complement one another and to form a perfect whole. This concept is derived from classical texts and has been studied and argued ever since. To explain this deeply esoteric jargon to a foreign audience is no easy task. In this piece, the journalist has chosen to use a dramatic analogy: the different functions of the components of TCM are compared to the various characters in a drama. As a result, most foreign readers will be able to understand the concept without much difficulty.

In the 23rd paragraph, the story comes to another key TCM concept zhiweibing. This underlying principle of TCM is even more mysterious than the above-mentioned *jun chen zuo shi* if analyzed in its whole. So the reporter has chosen to play up the preventive aspects of the concept and tie it to the COVID-19 battle by highlighting the role of a strong immunity. Thus, this "strange" concept could be understood and even accepted by the western audience.

Feature story usually does a service for the reader. The TCM story ends with tips from doctors who have first-hand experience in battling COVID-19. The tips involve theories and practices of TCM treatment, and the writer again uses a language that the foreign reader is familiar with to explain TCM. For example, *Ba Duan Jin*, a routine exercise popular among Chinese aged groups, is identified with "*kung fu*" and compared to "*tai chi*", both terms are familiar to a western reader. Also, when explaining Moxibustion, the writer suggests using "a golf ball" in the massage, an object few Chinese will use but common to a foreigner reader, if the exact position of the acupuncture point is hard to be found.

Here is the complete story by reporter Yao Minji from *Shanghai Daily*[1]. The paragraphs of the major part of the story are numbered to aid the above discussion.

TCM a Key Player in the War Against COVID-19

Yao Minji

(1) For the first time this week, the Chinese medical authorities announced that they had approved the clinical trial of **a traditional Chinese medicine product** for potential use in the treatment of COVID-19 cases.

(2) There is currently no cure for the novel coronavirus pneumonia in either Chinese or Western medicine though the global medical community is optimistic after recent test results.

(3) TCM treatment has been widely used in China's battle against the invisible virus. Official reports show more than 90 percent of COVID-19 patients in China — more than 74,000 patients — used **TCM medicines in various forms.**

(4) "Clinical trials under strict regulations are under way and results are still inconclusive, but TCM treatment, along with **acupuncture and traditional wellness '*kung fu*,'** has been widely used by our team at the front line in

① Yao Minji. TCM a key player in the war against COVID-19 [N/OL]. Shanghai Daily. (2020-03-26) [2021-08-04]. https://www.shine.cn/news/in-focus/2003265075/.

Wuhan and here in Shanghai," Huang Haiyin, a senior respiratory physician from Yueyang Hospital of Integrated Traditional Chinese and Western Medicine, told *Shanghai Daily*.

(5) "Our experiences showed that these treatments have been effective in many cases."

(6) TCM treatment is included in the latest editions of the official guidelines for treating COVID-19 released by both the central and Shanghai governments. TCM medicinal products were also sent to virus-battling Italy.

(7) Huang said many remedies consist of a proper combination of **antiviral, detoxication and lung-improvement ingredients** that have been used for centuries.

(8) TCM treats the body as a sophisticated and interconnected system as a whole. Rather than just killing the virus, it tries to reach an overall balance — treating diseases and improving immunity.

(9) It is also rooted in traditional Chinese culture — philosophy, daily habits, classic texts and martial arts — thus finding an easy reach and acceptance in Asian societies.

(10) For instance, the idea of junchen zuoshi, the appropriate arrangement of main ("emperor") and assisting ("minister") ingredients, can also be found in other forms of traditional Chinese culture with slight changes in wording. In simple terms, you need a protagonist and many supporting ones, all in their right places, to achieve optimal results.

(11) With the crisis spreading globally, billions of people are being told to stay at home — self-isolate and maintain social distancing.

(12) "Since you are being advised to stay at home, why not use the time to reboot your own body and take control of your wellness management?" Professor Qian Hai of Shanghai University of Traditional Chinese Medicine suggested.

(13) "Whether you believe in TCM or not, there are some ideas and practices that you can work on to improve your health with no side effects. So why not?"

(14) He added that wellness depends on habits — "change little by little every day and you will feel the difference in your body in days."

(15) Qian cited his daily face-washing routine — one he "stole" from a veteran TCM practitioner. It is divided into three steps:

(16) * Use cold water for the nose and area near it to gradually improve the endurance of the nostril to deal with outside temperature. It can help in

preventing one from catching cold easily and fighting allergy brought by temperature changes.

(17) * Use a cold towel to clean the face and apply mild force on some of the acupuncture points around eyes and noses — organs that rule the five senses on the face are respectively linked to the five internal organs in TCM.

(18) * Warm towel on the back of the neck with mild force applied on the acupuncture points to relieve internal blockage that causes body pain or headache among people who spend too much time working on computers or mobile phones.

(19) Chinese front-line doctors are now among the much sought-after by their foreign colleagues. Media reports show TCM ingredients selling out and acupuncture demands rising sharply in cities like New York and Melbourne.

(20) Hu Bijie, a Western medicine practitioner who helped pen Shanghai's guidelines, recently told local media that TCM is essential to "Shanghai Plan," especially "in helping to relieve symptoms such as high fever, constipation and diarrhea, among others."

(21) Hu, who is director of the infectious diseases and infection control departments at Zhongshan Hospital, said TCM also helped improve patients' immunity.

(22) With no immediate vaccine or treatment for COVID-19, immunity is globally acknowledged as being essential in the prevention and recovery from the new virus.

(23) Other experts have also cited the significance and relevance of a key TCM idea — zhiweibing, literally translating into "treating the undiseased," and in the case of COVID-19 — prevention method for the healthy from getting infected and those with mild symptoms from getting severe.

(24) The number of critical cases is key to the mortality rates as inflow of very severe patients, whose lives depend on ventilators, would crush any medical system in the world.

(25) "Classic TCM texts have many theories and treatments on epidemic diseases. It's been with us for thousands of years of history, accumulated experience and group wisdom," Huang of Yueyang Hospital explained.

(26) "It is also clear on how to go about fighting it.

(27) "First of all, you avoid it — that means avoid gathering and wear masks. Secondly, positive energy trumps evil energy — improve your immunity to fight the virus. Thirdly, TCM therapies are always individualized because it strives to reach internal optimal balance for each individual body."

（28）There are classic therapies for many diseases and situations，Huang said. Doctors revise these therapies according to individual cases. In cases of urgency with mass patients，a broad therapy that applies to the most common body types is used.

（29）Huang's front-line colleagues have also experimented with the wide use of acupuncture and mild "kung fu" exercises，some of them targeting the heart and the lungs. Both methods were popular with the patients at Wuhan's Leishenshan Hospital.

（30）Medics from Yueyang Hospital，among the nearly 5,000 TCM health workers sent from all over the country for medical assistance in Wuhan，left home as early as on January 23，the eve of Chinese New Year.

（31）Many are still there treating patients although many have returned home and are under a 14-day quarantine.

Dr Huang's tips on overall wellness management

（1）Follow your daily routine，eat well and sleep well.

（2）Sanitation habits are key，especially with regards to hands.

（3）Keep the spirits up — classic TCM texts on staying healthy insist on keeping spirits up，which work better than food therapy and medicines.

（4）Exercise according to individual condition — Liu Zi Jue（particularly good for heart and lung and applicable for all including those weak），Ba Duan Jin（a general "kung fu" exercise similar to and less complex than tai chi），biking or jogging（if condition allows）. Exercise also helps you stay positive.

（5）Moxibustion，or massage on acupuncture points，helps improve positive energy，such as the acupoint zusanli（below the knee on the tibialis anterior muscle）. If you are worried about not hitting exactly on the acupoint，you can massage it with a golf ball，which covers more areas.

（6）For food therapy，a pear is generally good for lungs，congee with jujube and pearl barley helps with appetite and removes internal humidity （many with mild symptoms might have excessive internal humidity and experience lack of appetite）.

（7）TCM remedy — it is not essential for healthy people to take medicines. If you want to take TCM remedy，there are classic prescriptions against catching a cold or flu，such as Yu Ping Feng San. It is an ancient therapy with three main ingredients — huangqi（astragali radix）to improve immunity，baizhu（atractylodis macrocephalae rhizome）to help with appetite and remove internal humidity，and fangfeng（saposhnikoviae radix）to prevent from catching a cold. It should be taken according to individual conditions.

Dr Qian's guidance on self-protecting against COVID-19

(1) Don't panic or be anxious — body and mind are connected.

(2) Listen to your body — it gives you signals.

(3) Do not take medicine blindly, whether TCM or Western. In terms of TCM, the body type and internal optimal balance are a dynamic one rather than static. It changes as your situation — diet, daily routine, location and season — changes. What your doctor told you years ago may not apply to your body type today.

(4) Tea in spring, soup in summer, congee in fall and medical wine in winter as an overall seasonal wellness tip.

(5) Avoid any potential contact with the virus — no mass gathering, wear masks — no matter how healthy you think you are. Nobody is immune to this new virus. Plenty of healthy and young patients are in critical condition.

(6) Do not share utensils when dining with others.

(7) No need to take medicine if you are not sick, otherwise you might not have the endurance for some medicine when you really need it. Food therapy is preferred. For instance, put chenpi (aged sun-dried tangerine peel) in boiled water to help regulate and balance internal energy in general.

Exercise

1. Rewrite the following sentences and replace the Chinglish from the sentence.
   (1) Shanghai is famous as a never night city around the world.
   (2) He had no sight communication when he talked with other people.
   (3) They don't want to limit themselves in a small county town, but look forward to a broader platform and more promising development space.

2. Translate the following terms into English, explain when necessary.
   (1) 微博
   (2) 上海
   (3) 饭圈
   (4) 君臣佐使
   (5) 治未病

1.3 The English-speaking reader

A peculiar challenge arises in English feature writing in a Chinese environment: the question of readership, who am I writing for?

1.3.1 Beware of your audience

"On the question of who you're writing for, don't be eager to please. If you consciously write for a teacher or for an editor, you'll end up not writing for anybody. If you write for yourself, you'll reach all the people you want to write for," advised William Zinsser in his "*On Writing Well*."[①] Students who are new to feature writing often take the advice whole-heartedly in a wrong sort of way. They wrote for themselves: their stories are self-involved, concentrating on their lives or the limited world bounded by their personal interest and perception. Their favorite topics are the food of the school cafeteria, the stray cats roaming on campus, some young entrepreneur who happens to be their friend. All these are legitimate topics. Frisky felines are on the top of the list of what readers like. Canteen food is ever a source of interest on campus. Success stories of young college students or college graduates will surely inspire. However, these topics may not work in feature writing with a foreign audience in view.

To reach an international audience, the fledgling feature writers need to venture out of their own world and become aware of their true audience: readers from the English-speaking world. Is the reader an expat living in Chinese metropolises like Shanghai? Is the reader a foreigner who is outside China and knows little about the country? Is the reader from the West or the non-western world? Or is the reader actually one of the Chinese English-learners who, interestingly, make up a considerable share of the readership of the Chinese English language media?

Different readerships require different stories or different treatments of stories. As discussed in the first section of this chapter, feature writing is audience (market) driven. To be precise, exploring the nuances of her potential readers is not just a writer's humour. It is an exploration that will illuminate the

---

① William Zinsser. On Writing Well [M]. 5th ed. New York: HarperPerennial, 1994:97-98.

kind of stories that might be effective and thus worth pursuing. When it comes to international markets, thinking about audiences also implies a reconsideration of journalistic values. What constitutes news to a foreign audience? Is this the same or different from the value of news when it comes to domestic audiences? How can you reconcile the interests of your audience with your own reporting agenda?

1.3.2　Understanding the western audience

Readers from the West undoubtedly make up the bulk of the target readership of most Chinese English-language media. There is a long and biased tradition of Western interest in China that looks for the weird, the opposite and the abnormal in stories about the "Oriental". In the traditional Western perception of China, it is believed that everything about China is the opposite of the West. A Chinese bride will wear red at her wedding, rather than the white of the West. A Chinese person would wear white to the funeral of a beloved person rather than the black of the West. This oppositeness used to be interpreted as something strange and abnormal when the West considered itself a role model of what was right and normal during its colonial period. This perception has heavily influenced the Western media's coverage of China in the past. Even today, a quick glance at the headlines of the now defunct ChinaWire, a once-popular foreigner-run news app on WeChat, shows that this tradition is still very much alive. "19 Year Old Tries to Sell Her virginity to Save Her Brother." "Exotic Bird That Looks Like Trump Goes Viral in China." "Man Wrestles with a Panda to Impress Girls." "Woman Buys a House after 20 Boyfriends Each Gave her an iPhone 7." And so on so forth.

One of the reasons why this prejudiced tradition has been so difficult to extinguish may be that it brings benefits. It feeds the western stereotype of China and Chinese people, the "Oriental Other" on whom the western eye places its patronizing look. More importantly, this bizarre approach is sure to attract the attention of today's readers, which is fleeting and scarce. A headline promises a story where a woman scams each of her 20 boyfriends out of an iPhone will surely get that precious "wow" from its internet-jaded readers. And the number of the page-views and the enthusiastic comments at the end of the story suggests that the story gets it. The above-mentioned story get 30,976 page views while a thorough story published about the same time headlined Xian Air

Quality Station Accused of Tampering with Sensors from the SIX TONE (on its WeChat app) only gets 587.

When covering China, present Western media tend to adopt two frameworks of story-telling: economy-driven or ideology-driven, or both. China is the second largest economy in the world and the world's factory floor. Stories viewed through the economic lens will find a natural audience from the West whose economy has become increasingly co-dependent with the Chinese one. Studies on America, German and French media find that they publish more stories on Chinese economy than any other topics.

In addition, a consumption of stories on China by Western media will show that a skeptical undertone prevails. Whatever the topic is, an almost universal ideological frame is used when presenting China to the home audience. The frame is biased and skews the story from the truth. It keeps shedding old light on the new events, resisting to see what's really happening. China is often seen as a monolithic whole and is thought in terms from long-fixed reporting agenda. These biased stories foster prejudice among the readers and in turn, this readers' prejudice encourages more biased stories.

This entrenched and persistent bias of the western media pollutes every story they did on China and the result is bigotry, indifference and misunderstanding. Consequently, the task the Chinese English-language media face is a daunting one. What they have to deal with is an audience that has already had a fixed bias cultivated by the western media towards China. So they must go out of their way to get across to the world.

1.3.3 Proximity

China is a huge country in a historical period of transition. Of the countless events that take place in China every day, which should be reported to an international audience? The answer lies in proximity. Of course, all news values apply when deciding what is news. But proximity plays a special role in news reporting across borders. It has been said that in the age of globalisation, borders have blurred and an event in one country can be an international event. However, in order to attract an international readership to read a story willingly, the event being reported must still have an impact that transcends national borders or contain some universal element that most people can identify with. In other words, the event must be somehow relevant to the reader's life. It answers the question that most readers, whose lives are overwhelmed by information, will ask: If this has nothing to do with me, why should I bother to read it?

1.3.4   Getting out of the cultural box

One of the problems with a novice feature writer is that, in her eagerness to make the world aware of her country and bridge the gap between East and West, she tends to choose topics associated with Chinese culture. Her thinking was that foreign readers would be excited by any story about China's indigenous culture. Certainly, anything that has withstood the vicissitudes of five thousand years of human history will be of interest to foreign readers. However, this line of reasoning ignores the key news value, namely proximity. A story that is simply about a different culture may appeal to a few curious souls, but it is stories that involve the reader as a human being on some basic level that will reach the readers' heart. It is therefore best to be culturally aware, but not bound by your own culture. It is better to think outside the box of one's own culture and look for stories that readers from completely different backgrounds can identify with.

1.3.5   An example: serving the foreign reader

As mentioned above, it is important to raise one's awareness of readership. But we must distinguish between serving the needs of our readers and pandering to their interests. The former is a service provided by responsible, quality journalism, while the latter is a short-sighted shortcut taken by cheap sensationalism. Reporting the truth carefully and accurately is the ultimate service that any journalist does to his or her audience. But sometimes, serving the reader simply means being mindful of the reader's needs in reporting and writing.

Here's an example of how to serve the needs of foreign readers in a real way. In early May 2020, Shanghai was to host a literature and art translation competition, which was covered by the city's English-language media. Here are three reports on the same topic from the *China Daily*, *Shanghai Daily* and ICS news website ShanghaiEye respectively. In all three stories, the news event is reported clearly and comprehensively. On further consideration, however, we find that for the reader the event itself is news, but not necessarily news that everyone will care about. For news such as the opening of a translation competition, the interest of readers who want to sign up should be taken into account, otherwise why publicise it widely. Accordingly, the story on the contest should not stop at reporting the event itself, but provide relevant registration information aimed at an overseas audience. The journalist should consider the story from the reader's point of view: what steps need to be taken and what problems might there be if they want to sign up? What particulars are note-worthy? The *China Daily* story gives a telephone number. The other two local media reports give the website where readers can find and download an application form if they are interested in entering the competition. The *Shanghai Daily* report also gives tips on how to submit the application form. By providing the address of the competition website and related tips, these stories provide a real service to readers. Ms. Yao, the reporter for the *Shanghai Daily* story, suggested in an interview that journalists need to put themselves in the reader's shoes and think about what the reader wants, and ask the ultimate question of why the reader should read the story. Here, the translation award story alone is just a news story that may not mean as much to the average reader. With detailed information about the application process, the story becomes relevant to the reader. It is no longer just a piece of news, but an event that they can attend in person.

Shanghai Literature and Art Translation Awards now accepting submissions[①]
By Zhang Kun in Shanghai | chinadaily.com.cn | Updated: 2020-05-07 14:54

The inaugural Shanghai Literature and Art Translation Awards is now accepting submissions.

Translators of literary works and performing arts creations that were officially published, performed or broadcast for the first time between Jan 1, 2014 and Dec 31, 2018 are eligible for nomination.

The awards will only accept nominations by institutions instead of individual translators. Publishers, producers or performing arts companies and other relevant authorities and organizations can also submit nominations.

① Zhang Kun. Shanghai Literature and Art Translation Awards now accepting submissions[N/OL]. China Daily. (2020-05-07) [2021-08-04]. https://www.chinadaily.com.cn/a/202005/07/WS5eb3b0a2a310a8 b241153fbe.html.

All nominated works must have official copyrights. The awards are now open to translators with registered resident status in Shanghai only.

Artworks translated from Chinese into other languages must be created by Shanghai-based authors in order to qualify for the competition.

The deadline of the submission is Aug 31.

Jointly hosted by the Shanghai Federation of Literary and Art Circles, the Shanghai Writers' Association and the Shanghai Translators' Association, the Shanghai Literature and Art Translation Awards was established under the guidance of the publicity department of the CPC Shanghai Committee.

The triennial event will honor 10 translated literary works and 10 translated performing art projects starting from 2020.

The Awards have been designed to further boost the literary and art translations in Shanghai, create a new platform for cultural exchange and mutual understanding between China and other countries, according to the opening announcement.

The Awards will be granted to translators who are alive at the time of their nomination. The candidates will be divided into two categories: literature and performing arts, which includes theater productions, films and TV projects.

Five works translated from Chinese into other languages and another five translated from foreign languages into Chinese will be selected for each category.

For the competition of literature awards, only seven languages are eligible: English, French, German, Japanese, Russian, Spanish and Arabic. The performing arts category is open to other official languages used in countries neighboring China too.

For inquiries about the competition, please contact 021-62473142.

News / Metro
Shanghai Translation Awards Open for Submissions[①]

Yao Minji

16:24 UTC+8, 2020-07-14

Organizers in Shanghai are calling for global submissions of both literary and performing arts works for a new translation award.

The deadline for the inaugural Shanghai Literature and Art Translation

---

① Yao Minji. Shanghai Translation awards open for submissions[N/OL]. Shanghai Daily. (2020-07-14)
[2021-08-04]. https://www.shine.cn/news/metro/2007142108/.

Awards is August 31. Publishers, producers, performing arts troupes and other relevant organizations can submit literary works or performance projects translated from or into Chinese language that were officially published, performed or broadcast for the first time between January 1, 2014 and December 31, 2018.

Up to five award winners in the performance and literary categories will be honored for works translated from a foreign language into Chinese. There will be another five for Chinese works translated into a foreign language. Awards will only be presented to translators who are alive at the time of application.

For literature awards, seven languages are eligible: English, French, German, Japanese, Russian, Spanish and Arabic.

The awards, to be held every three years, are jointly hosted by the Shanghai Federation of Literary and Art Circles, Shanghai Writers' Association and Shanghai Translators Association.

The awards aim to further boost literary and artistic translations in Shanghai, create a platform for cultural exchange and mutual understanding between China and other countries, as well as to promote publications of translation works that bring to light the beauty of civilization.

Applications and required materials need to be delivered both in paper and electronic version. Application forms and more details can be found at http://www.shwenyi.com.cn/renda/2012shwl/service/node16092/u1ai6259693.html.

Source: SHINE　　Editor: Xu Qing

Translators — The First Shanghai Literature And Art Translation Awards Are Waiting For You! [1]

2020-07-15 11:48 am

The first ever Shanghai Literature and Art Translation Awards have been unveiled and are now taking submissions!

Shanghai, being a city of rich cultural and historical heritage, will be hosting this celebration of literature and art. The newly launched event aims to become one of international acclaim to promote the development of Shanghai's literary and artistic translation. Planned in collaboration by the Shanghai Federation of Literary and Art Circles, the Shanghai Writers' Association and

[1]　Translators — The First Shanghai Literature And Art Translation Awards Are Waiting For You[EB/OL]! ShanghaiEye. (2020-07-15) [2021-08-04]. https://www.shanghaieye.com.cn/translators-the-first-shanghai-literature-and-art-translation-awards-are-waiting-for-you/.

Shanghai Translators' Association, the event is scheduled to be held once every three years. Through this, the organizers also hope to "create a platform for cultural exchange and mutual understanding between China and foreign countries".

Submissions for this year's Translation Awards are limited to works produced, published, or performed between Jan. 1st of 2014 and Dec. 31st of 2018, and the submission deadline is August 31st. The two award categories are the Literature Translation Award and the Performing Arts Translation Award. For the inaugural ceremony, up to 10 works/translators per category (5 from Chinese to Foreign Language, and vice versa) can be awarded in a range of languages other than Chinese: English, French, German, Japanese, Russia, Spanish, and Arabic. Other than published literature/art, contestants can submit work in other creative mediums such as design exhibitions, performances, films, music, paintings, and even sculptures!

For more details or to apply, visit: http://www.shwenyi.com.cn/renda/2012shwl/service/node16092/u1ai6259693.html

Good luck!

Exercise

1. Who am I writing for? This is a question that most writers ask themselves at some point in their writing careers. With English feature writing, we at least know that we are writing for international audiences. Now, imagine a reader of your story and paint a portrait in words of this fictional reader of yours. Please keep this to 200 words or less.

2. Background information provides the context for the story, without which the story will make little sense to a reader that encounters the subject for the first time. Background information usually includes any story element that doesn't actually push the story forward; observations, explanations, descriptions, and points of instruction or analysis are all essential contextual elements. The following story[①] is a seasonal feature on green dumplings, a delicacy in the south of the Yangtze River that are popular among the local people during the Qingming Festival in spring. In this article there are many

---

① Yuan Tianyun. Chinese Green Dumplings: spring delights & poignant memories[EB/OL]. 上海松江. (2021-03-19) [2021-08-15]. https://app.sjmedia.net/App/content/detailshare.html? contentId = 5354424&appId=110139&projectId=12&shareAppId=110139&channelType=4.

terms and concepts related to traditional Chinese culture. Please read the article carefully and underline the background parts. Do you think these cultural terms and concepts are explained clearly? At the end of the article, the legend of the Cold Food Festival is narrated. The Cold Food festival entails a long tradition across several dynasties, and in this article, only a dramatic legend from the Spring and Autumn period is accounted; do you think this is a wise choice? If you were to introduce the Qingming Festival and the Cold Food Festival, how would you do it?

3.

Chinese Green Dumplings: Spring Delights & Poignant Memories

By Yuan Tianyun

Songjiang News

2021-03-19 09:30:00

On March mornings, the smell of grass emanates from the Fang Song Community Cafeteria as the pastry chef concentrates on making green dumplings for spring. Feng Lei is skilled in all steps of the process, from juicing grass to frying paste. "I make green dough from morning to night. At the end of the month, when sales reach several thousand a day, we have a dozen chefs working together," Feng said, his hands kneading the red-bean paste.

A specialty from southern China, green dumplings are a snack made from grass-like plants, such as mugwort and wheat seedlings. These plants sprout fresh in spring. Skilled chefs then squeeze them into green juice, mix the juice with glutinous rice and stuff it with various fillings. Fragrant and full of flavor, the saying goes that when you eat a green dumpling, you embrace the warm and fragrant spring of southern China.

Green dumplings are also connected to Chinese medicine. In the *Compendium of Materia Medica*, a classic text of traditional Chinese medicine, mugwort is recorded as "a warm, bitter herb that can used as a medicine for rheumatism". In southern China, mugwort sprouts fresh and damp in spring. According to the *Compendium of Materia Medica*, eating green dumplings is good for internal health, and provides warmth to tendons and veins, protecting people from catching a cold.

"I've been making green dumplings since I was seven or eight years old," said Feng. "Every March and April, I would go with my siblings to pick green grass in the wilderness next to our house. At that time, my grandmother did everything by hand, from juicing the grass to chopping the fillings." Having learnt the traditional recipe from his grandmother, Feng Lei now serves green dumplings to people in Songjiang.

When making the dumplings, the grass juice plays a vital role. Every March and April, Feng and other chefs go to Punan to harvest wild green grass, which they soak before adding it to the glutinous rice flour. "Certain specific types of green grass, rather than mugwort or wheat seedlings, give the dough a turquoise green color. You just can't get that color with other ingredients," Feng said.

While following tradition, Fang Song Community Canteen is also introducing some dumpling innovations. Apart from traditional sesame bean paste, the canteen has also introduced salted egg yolk and meat puff as fillings in green dumplings, to cater to the taste of young people.

In Songjiang, many people eat green dumplings in spring. Wu Xianghua, the manager of Fang Song Community Cafeteria, said that daily sales of green dumplings in the canteen topped 1,000 just three days after the first batches went on sale. On some days, sales reach 8,000. "My family all like green dumplings," said Hu Wu, a Fang Song Community Cafeteria customer. "Eating green dumplings is a kind of ritual for welcoming spring each year."

A traditional delicacy, green dumplings are also a must-have item for people who wish to pay respect to their ancestors. The Qingming Festival, a traditional Chinese holiday to mourn ancestors, takes places in early April. Traditionally associated with mourning and honoring ancestors, green dumplings have a role to play at Qingming.

Legend has it that in the Spring and Autumn Period (BC770-BC476), Jie Zitui, a high official, helped his exiled prince Chong Er in his struggle to regain his throne but refused to serve in the court when Chong Er succeeded. Jie went to live on a mountain and died in a fire set by the prince to force him from his hermit life. When he heard the news of Jie Zitui's tragic death, the prince decreed that, in remembrance of the noble minister, no cooking fire should be lit and only cold food should be eaten. That legend generated a tradition. Today the tradition is chiefly kept in the form of the green dumplings, which are served cold.

People no longer observe the cold food tradition, but they still enjoy eating green dumplings around the time of Qingming Festival. And the ancestors are not forgotten. "Some people take green dumplings to the cemetery as an offering," Wu said.

Photos and video by Shu Zhengyu

Editor: Lin Yan

1.4 Long-form articles in digital age

The digital age is marked by short attention spans. With the development of mobile networks, the pace of life continues to accelerate. Impatience becomes the mood of the age. The scarce of eyeball time has spawned Twitter and Twitter-like platforms featuring short texts, short videos and memes when even short texts are too much trouble. Feature articles are known for its length which provides the necessary room for the development of the line of logic and the supply of necessary context, both of which have become scarce commodity in the universal fragmentation of information. In an age that ever craves the quicker and the shorter, length becomes both the strength and the weakness of feature writing. Feature articles are often the product of much legwork, logical thinking, diligent reporting, and deliberation of the language. In fact, many long-form articles are charged for a fee in recognition of the efforts and resources put in the original product. In contrast, news and other piecemeal information flooding the Internet every day are easily accessible and can be read for free. Moreover, the ubiquitous camera-equipped mobile phone makes everyone a potential witness/journalist. As a result, the line between news and raw material has blurred and raw video with crude subtitles floods the news market, suggesting a decline in both the cost and quality of news. Thus, in the midst of widespread fragmentation, a hallmark of the digital age, the need for contextualized and logical holistic completion is very real. But equally real is the lack of attention in the information explosion. Therefore, in order to adapt to the rapidly changing media landscape and the capricious habits and tastes of readers, feature articles need to be innovative in order to stay in the game. Here are some innovative web-based ways to improve the reading experience of feature stories.

Firstly, web-based presentation of feature articles frequently uses links embedded in the text of the stories. These hyperlinks enrich the reading experience and make connections for the readers by recycling old stories in an innovative way. A web of knowledge is weaved together by the hyperlinks. The single story functions as a portal, from which the reader can take on a journey of learning. It is no longer a one-way communication，but an **interactive** activity making use of the very nature of the world wide web.

Take the Sixth Tone，the Shanghai-based English news website，for example. Many articles from its feature service boast the embedded links where the linking words are marked in red coloring. The links will take the readers to both stories in English of the relevant topics on the same website and articles in English or Chinese from other media outlets. The point is to provide a service for curious readers who are keen for information beyond this single story. For example，in the story titled "From Factory Towns to Facebook，China's Livestreamers Take On Exports"①，13 links can be found. The story tells about the contingent plans amid COVID-19 disruption of business adopted by Chinese manufacturers by hiring livestreamers to hawk goods directly to global buyers. The 13 links go to a variety of stories from a variety of publications. One link even goes to a PDF of the summary of a relevant company's half-year report in 2020. If a reader is to pursue all the links，she will probably not only know about the livestreamers profiled in the story but also the ins and outs of the whole industry.

Secondly，it has become a common practice for photos and videos to accompany the feature stories. Visual stories as the photos and videos tell will add to the understanding and raise the interest level. In feature production，the collaboration actually starts at the interviewing stage. It has become frequently the case for the new media reporters and the feature writers to do the legwork together to cover the story. As a result，almost all feature stories are published alongside with adorning photographs which break up the long text and give breathing space as well as additional information. For the web-based publication，a short video (several minutes long) often serves as a sort of promo trailer before or alongside the posting of the story. The short video touches upon the key points of the story briefly or presents an interview with the key subject of the story，allowing the reader to have a visual perception of the story，in addition to the textual coverage.

The use of short videos and photos is not to replace the long-form texts，but to complement it. Short videos whose contents are more a piling of raw materials lack the logic on which a feature story is planned and built. There's

---

① 　Wang Lianzhang and Wu Ziyi. From Factory Towns to Facebook，China's Livestreamers Take On Exports[EB/OL]. The Sixth Tone. （2020-12-21）［2021-08-15］. https://www.sixthtone.com/news/1006577/from-factory-towns-to-facebook%2C-chinas-livestreamers-take-on-exports

neither room for the necessary context which is essential for the readers to truly understand what's going on. In this compound，the textual story is the main dish，the short video a side one. The purpose of the multi-media presentation is to make sure the intended message of the story is delivered by meeting the different needs of readers.

Thirdly，besides videos and photos，sometimes a feature story is published alongside an audio version of it. Reading literature aloud has long been a popular tradition for radio. However，for an audio to accompany the feature story is a relatively recent development. Podcasting has been widely used in news and feature services in an assisting role. A ten-minute podcast that sums up the daily headlines may be offered at the end of the day. An audio version of a long detailed feature story can be played while the audience are driving or doing household chores，retiring the eyes from the various screens. However，at home，up until very recently，this combination is more seen on media platforms featuring Chinese-language non-fiction writing. In 2021，Sixth Tone launched a new column called the "×" which "features translations and cross-publications from respected Chinese and international media outlets，as selected and edited by Sixth Tone." In this new column，some long-form translated articles are posted alongside an audio version of it. For example，a story[1] titled "Peter Hessler's Last Class" is posted with a 22-minute audio version of it.

---

[1] He Yujia. Peter Hessler's Last Class[EB/OL]. The Sixth Tone. (2021-7-19) [2021-08-15]. https://www.sixthtone.com/news/1008025/peter-hesslers-last-class

How New Jersey's First Coronavirus Patient Survived

James Cai's case was completely new to his doctors. When he grew severely ill, he tapped a network of Chinese and Chinese-American medical colleagues who helped save his life.

By Susan Dominus

Published April 5, 2020
Updated April 27, 2020

f　🐦　🔖　💬 539

Listen to This Audio
Audio Recording by Audm

▶　Listen　37:54

To hear more audio stories from publishers, like The New York Times,
download Audm for iPhone or Android.

Access more of The Times by creating a free　　⋀

In the screenshot，a 6000-word plus feature story from *New York Times Journal* on the first confirmed case of COVID-19 in New Jersey is accompanied by a piece of audio running nearly 40minutes that could be downloaded. *New York Times* was seeking to further its podcasting ambition by attempting to acquire the Serial Production，the maker of the hit podcast "Serial"，according to a report by *Wall Street Journal* in July，2020.[①]

Exercise

Pick a feature story that's above 2000 words from the media and make an audio recording of it. Then invite a friend to listen to the audio and another to read the textual story. Ask them to tell you how they like both the story and the listening and reading experience.

---

① Benjamin Mullin. New York Times to Acquire Serial Productions [N/OL]. Wall Street Journal. (2020-07-22) [2021-08-04]. https://www. wsj. com/articles/new-york-times-reaches-deal-to-acquire-serial-productions-11595452716.

Chapter 2   Story Ideas

Like many other endeavours in life, feature writing starts with an idea. In fact, reporting and writing a feature story involves a systematic thinking process of finding a story idea, shaping it, executing it and finally turning it into a full story. And it all starts with the germination of a story idea, which is a thinking process in itself. This chapter will look at what constitutes a viable story idea, where to find such an idea, and how to shape it once we have it.

2.1   What makes a good story idea

2.1.1   Specificity

In determining whether an idea for a story is feasible, we must first clarify the difference between a subject/topic and an idea. A subject is what forms a basic matter of thought, discussion, or investigation, while an idea is a thought or suggestion as to a possible course of action. A subject is much broader than an idea, which is usually specific and on a smaller scale. For example, "Waste Separation in Shanghai" is a subject on which a book or a series of news stories or features could be written. A story idea under the broad subject of "Shanghai's rubbish sorting" would have to be much narrower to work. A feature story should only focus on one aspect of the waste separation campaign in Shanghai. If you want to write about more aspects, write more stories.

The year 2020 marked the first anniversary of Shanghai's efforts to sort garbage. *Shanghai Daily*, like many other media of the city, had launched a series of articles examining a year's worth of garbage sorting. "The regulations on garbage sorting that came into effect on July 1 last year in Shanghai have brought changes and challenges to both residents and authorities; but we've made them work in the past year with input from the government, residents, volunteers, communities, businesses, researchers and inventors. *Shanghai Daily* visited some of them recently to see how they have helped turn trash sorting into second nature and make Shanghai a better city," says the editor's note of one major news feature①. These series of articles under the section called "trash talk" are all on the same subject: the trash sorting in Shanghai. But each individual article assumes a specific angle, gives a scrutinizing look at one aspect of the common subject, and is developed from a particular and unique idea.

One article titled "Imaginative ideas to reduce the drudge of garbage sorting" on July, 7② is clearly born out of a specific idea. Garbage sorting has been in practice for a year in Shanghai and one problem emerged from the front-line experience is the "drudge" of such a massive project. This article focuses on the idea of reducing the drudge by giving three related examples, a teenager designing special bags to deal with dumping wet garbage, a local university working with a Singapore one to develop an in-situ kitchen waste-processing system, and another joint team between the two universities working on making use of shell waste. On an apparently dry topic, the story is surprisingly fun to read for it is packed with interesting details tied together by the same unique angle. The success can be fairly attributed to **the specificity** of the story idea.

2.1.2 Hard fact

As discussed above, for a story idea to work, **it must contain a specific angle**. By definition, an angle is the point or theme of a news or feature story. It's the lens through which the writer filters the information gathered. The right "slant" or theme makes the subject tie together neatly.

However, sometimes the angle can be too specific. The story idea is too narrow and can be easily explained in a few lines. The inexperienced writer barely thinks past the event that is actually the news peg and pads the story up with empty quotes (comments) from bystanders far removed from the central event. The result is what we call a talky piece, a piling of opinions that contain no substance. Or the student reporter failing to see the interconnectedness between things focuses on a single incident standing alone which by itself contains little news value. The result is a repetitive story so thin that it barely fits for a campus newspaper, not to mention a publication aiming for the

---

① Yang Meiping, Song Yiyang. Imaginative ideas to reduce the drudge of garbage sorting [N/OL]. Shanghai Daily. (2020-07-07) [2021-08-04]. https://www.shine.cn/news/in-focus/2007071630/.

② Yang Meiping, Song Yiyang. Imaginative ideas to reduce the drudge of garbage sorting [N/OL]. Shanghai Daily. (2020-07-07) [2021-08-04]. https://www.shine.cn/news/in-focus/2007071630/.

foreign audience. Of course, story idea is not the only thing to blame for a watery story. Many things can go wrong. Subpar reporting, for instance, will surely lead to a substandard story. But a meaty idea, one that contains **hard fact**, is a key contributor to the success of the finished story. A story idea that is informative usually examines beyond the news event that's the topical peg and focuses on the how and why and on the impact and consequence. A substantial story idea also shows the connection the single event may have with other similar incidents and considers the possible common cause behind.

2.1.3 Appeal and news values

A workable story idea usually appeals to the readers. Even at the incubation stage, the concept must be alluring to the reader in some way. Targeting the English-speaking audience, the story ideas we are concerned with must be attractive to the foreign readers. This attractiveness can be narrowly defined as being novel or entertaining, or it can be broadly interpreted as a practicality: the story is of interest to the reader because it can help the reader in some way or the story is of significance to the reader because it matters in the reader's life somehow. In other words, the story idea fascinates because it is of use to the readers somehow. In either case, the appeal of a story idea is in fact created by the news values contained in the idea.

Impact, timeliness, prominence, proximity, bizarreness, conflict, currency, and human interest. These news values create a significance for the story to justify the reader's attention. A significant matter that has far-reaching impact is naturally riveting. Conflict and drama lend an intensity that makes compelling reading. Prominent people occupy the spotlight for people like to see the mighty fall or otherwise engaged. Strange and novel things pique the curiosity. People are naturally interested in other people and human interest is the inherent characteristic of feature articles. Proximity, the most important factor in determining what is news for a foreign audience, answers the so-what question (Your news is all very interesting. But so what? Why should I pay attention to it?) a reader might ask. Equipped with one or more of these news values, a story idea possesses appeal as well as the potential to compete in the sea of information.

2.1.4 Something new

Compared with news stories, feature articles are not as timely. Often a feature story takes weeks or even months to prepare. But this does not mean that the topic or story idea does not need to be fresh. On the contrary, freshness or novelty is the key news value for feature articles. A feature story must offer something new, new information, latest development, emerging trends, or fresh perspectives. Even a feature story focusing on the past must tie to some new happening of the present. Freshness is the sole criterion that justifies the writing of any feature stories. So when giving the story idea a proper scrutinizing in testing its feasibility, the first element that mustn't be missed is the one of novelty. Readers love the unexpected and take delight in being surprised. A feature story full of rehashed information and idle talks is a turn-off.

2.1.5 The human element

A good story idea often involves an appropriate human element which will embody the idea. This story has to be told through life examples of the chosen subject/subjects. The challenge is often to find the right subject whose story illustrates the central theme of the story. The key word is typicality. The subject must be representative of the core issue. If the issue represented by the subject is not universal but incidental, the story will not succeed because it lacks depth as well as relevance. Conversely, universality gives importance to the experience or issue being described, thus making the idea of the story legitimate.

Often the effectiveness of the human element is determined by whether the people directly involved in the core issue are accessible. You can't write about, say, a trending issue you noticed on Weibo while you the writer have no way to get in contact with the people who are right in the center of the storm. The story idea will not pan out, no matter how many "experts" you've lined up ready to comment on the issue. You lack crucial original content involving the key human element. The resulting article will be a rehashed one just repeating what has already been covered by other media.

2.1.6   The local angle and the international slant

Localization is an effective device to generate new story ideas and to narrow a story idea down when it is too big. The news value "proximity" is implicit in the consideration of the local stand of a given issue. People naturally want to know what it means to them when something significant happens. In view of writing English feature stories in a Chinese environment, the local angle also means giving the story idea **a concrete purchase** when presenting China to the world. Huge and complicated, China as a subject is difficult to report. Sometimes reporters may feel like the fabled blind men who try in vain to get the whole of the elephant. One solution to effective reporting of such an immense subject lies in localization: to take foothold in microcosm illustrations from the local level and to tell the country's story through concrete examples rather than flat generalizations. In other words, the local angle provides the story with diversity as well as renders it unique by adding the native color.

In addition to the local angle, the international angle should also be taken into account when developing story ideas, especially when the target audience is foreigners. Here again, the news value of "proximity" plays an important role. The international angle connects the story to the reader, giving them a clear understanding of what what happens in China means globally, and vice versa. Therefore, when considering the conception of a story, ask the following questions. Is there a global element to the story? If so, what is it? Does what is happening globally affect my issue? Or does my issue have a global impact? Are there any specific examples or hard facts that can be used to illustrate the global aspect of my issue? The answers to these questions will make your story idea more substantial and valuable.

To sum up, a good story idea is neither too big nor too small. It is specific with a unique angle yet broad enough to allow a complete and clear presentation of the central issue. A good story idea is informative, developed on hard facts instead of empty talk. It is supposed to be irresistible to both the readers and the writer herself. A good story idea is driven by news values and often composed of an indispensable human element. It must be about something new though feature story sometimes lacks the urgency of a news story. A good story idea is endowed with the local color while at the same time gifted with a global point of view.

Exercise

1. Read the following story[①] from *Shanghai Daily* and try to answer the following questions: The story is of the broad subject "environment protection", but what is its specific focus? In which paragraph is it stated? Is there a Shanghai angle in the story? If so, what is it? Is there an international angle? If so, what is it? How the local angle and the international slant contribute to the story?

Coming of Age: Protecting the Environment Becomes Big Business

Yuan Luhang

15:33 UTC+8, 2021-01-29

Shanghai Select

Long Jisheng, chairman of Shanghai-based SUS Environment, an industrial leader in Chinese environmental protection, said it's wrong to compare the growth of the industry to that of a person.

People mature and eventually die, but the industry will live beyond its days of maturity, he said.

His company, founded in 2008 in Qingpu District, provides integrated solutions for greenhouse-gas reduction, increased recycling, burning rather than burying garbage, and cleaning up contaminated sites.

"Within five years," says Long, "we will double the scale and revenue of the company, and set up overseas SUS Environment branches."

The company is now the second-largest in China's waste-incineration industry, after China Everbright Environment Group Ltd, a state-owned company based in Hong Kong.

SUS now says it will achieve its 12-year goals in five years.

"The company grew at its fastest pace in the last five years, and that will not slow because China is resolved to address environmental problems," Long said. "That offers us great opportunities in waste incineration."

The environment protection industry in China, essentially launched in 2005, has exploded as the government continues to ramp up its

---

① Yuan Luhang. Coming of age: Protecting the environment becomes big business [N/OL]. Shanghai Daily. (2021-01-29) [2021-08-04]. https://www.shine.cn/news/in-focus/2101294044/.

commitment to cleaner air, cleaner water, cleaner industry and cleaner communities.

In the 10 years to 2015, annual industry revenue grew between 26 percent and 31 percent. By 2016, the industry had revenue of 1 trillion yuan (US$154.48 billion), even as growth slowed to between 14 percent and 20 percent.

"Overall, growth may be cooling a little, but that may not be the case for every company in the industry," Long said. "In our early stages, SUS Environment only sold waste incineration facilities. As the company accumulated capital, we began investing in building and operating incineration plants."

Before 2020, the Chinese government largely focused on solving immediate environmental problems, like air pollution, but now it has the capability, time and determination to expand that focus to repairing the damage of the past.

China's rapidly growing economy in recent decades has caused some environment problems, among them urban smog and polluted waterways. As population grew, so did household garbage, straining the capacity of landfills.

Since 2019, the Chinese government has rolled out a series of new and tougher environmental laws, providing expanded opportunities for industry players like SUS Environment and even foreign rivals.

In mid-January, Suez, a France-based utility company operating in water and waste management sectors, bought out the stakes of two former Chinese partners and expanded its footprint in the nation.

"Competition in the industry is fierce," says Steve Clark, chief executive officer of Suez Asia. "More Chinese capital is pouring in. Some companies entered the sector after seeing business opportunities. Recently, there have been many mergers and acquisitions. Chinese companies are not only strong competitors in the domestic market but also in overseas markets."

But he added, "There are still huge opportunities for us. We will more focus on businesses such as complex water treatment, industrial park projects, hazardous waste treatment and soil remediation, which demand more advanced technology."

He said China's need for repairing soil degradation is probably the biggest in the world.

"In Shanghai, many industrial companies have moved to industrial parks, so the sites they left behind were more or less polluted," Clark said. "We have established one team based in Shanghai and one in Chongqing to do soil remediation."

The environmental protection industry can be classified into six main segments: air quality, water treatment, waste treatment, soil remediation, noise abatement and environment monitoring and supervision.

In a 2019 survey, 92 percent of 11,229 companies in the industry were found to be engaged in air, water and waste treatment, and environmental monitoring and supervision. Less than 2 percent specialized in soil remediation, according to *the 2020 China Environmental Protection Industry Report* from the China Association of Environmental Protection Industry.

Water and waste treatment contributed to the bulk of industry revenue and profit, the survey found.

In 2019, China's first law on soil protection came into effect, signaling the government's commitment to addressing historical problems.

Long said SUS Environment plans to expand into soil remediation.

"In China, there is 10 times more industrial waste than household waste," he said. "We are developing facilities to co-process household and industrial waste, trying to recycle as much industrial waste as possible."

The company is also looking to expand overseas, particularly in Southeast Asia and Africa.

"Like anything else, waste from different countries is different," Long said. "For example, waste produced in China is wetter due to dietary habits. It usually contains 10-20 percent water. European waste, on the other hand, generally has less than 5 percent water. So we have to develop different methods to treat different types of waste."

Southeast Asia is fertile ground for expansion, he added, because economic development and waste characteristics there are similar to China's.

"China's environmental services will probably be another star export for the nation, just like high-speed rail and smart phones," Long said.

In 2019, the SUS Environment signed a series of contracts with foreign investors, including French Public Investment Bank, to co-develop waste treatment projects in Asia and Africa.

That same year, the company received a US $100 million loan from the Asian Development Bank to finance projects in Taiyuan, capital of Shanxi Province, and the city of Zhuhai in Guangdong Province.

"I think the best years are ahead of us," said Long.

2. Examine the following story ideas and determine whether it is workable. Explain why. If the story idea won't work, can you improve it in any way to make it feasible?

(1) After receiving loads of complaints about noise on the subway, the city of Shanghai banned subway riders from using speakers on their electronic devices, including mobile phones, with effect from Dec.1, 2020. Against the backdrop, the story wants to examine the use of loudspeakers on the passengers' electronic devices on public transport in Songjiang District of Shanghai.

(2) The campaign against telecom fraud in Songjiang University Town of Shanghai.

(3) In September of 2020, the school was back in session in Songjiang University Town. As the campus reopened after closing for an entire semester owing to the prevention of the pandemic, the economy of the college town, as that of the nation, has recovered. The story is to find out about the revival of food-delivery industry in Songjiang University Town.

(4) The Third China International Import Expo is a major event the city of Shanghai hosted in Sept. 2020. College students are a main source of volunteers that contribute to the success of the event. The story is to examine one college student who has volunteered her service to CIIE for the third time.

(5) "Stopping the Period Shame" had been a trending hashtag on China's social media since a student from a Shanghai-based college installed for the first time a box full of free sanitary pads outside a woman's toilet on her campus in Oct. 2020. The story is to examine the difficulties various sanitary napkin box projects encounter and ways to improve.

(6) With the pandemic lurking around, all colleges in Songjiang University Town have a strict access control system in place. This story is to focus on the fact that students from one university face inconvenience when entering dormitory due to uncoordinated access control rules between their university and a neighboring one.

2.2　Where to find story ideas

In journalistic practice, story ideas are usually generated from the following places: assigned by the editors, from the media (both domestic and foreign), from readers' feedbacks, and from the daily life.

In most media, reporters work on stories assigned by the editors. There's not much to say about this, except that feature stories produced by different English-language media have different preference of topics. For example, *China Daily*, as the national media, covers more "hard" stories like poverty relief and revitalization of Chinese villages. *Shanghai Daily*, targeting more the expat groups working and living in the metropolis, reports more on the local matter, the myriad stories happening in the city. *Sixth Tone*, on the other hand, though based in Shanghai, includes the whole country under its reporting purview and tells the nation's stories to the world.

2.2.1　Finding the story idea in the media

On more occasions, a reporter has to take initiative and pitch her own story ideas. Where to get them? A place that will yield most ideas is the media, both domestic and foreign. Feature stories always take a news peg which is a news event that forms the basis of the news story and thus worth further pursuit. Take the Twitter-like Sina Weibo which are crowded with such news stories every day. These trending hashtags on the most popular social media platform in China often point to interesting stories. These bare-bone news story, sometimes briefly presented without any context, begs for further digging. However, not all hot topics are newsworthy in terms of international journalism. Those that possess elements a foreign audience can somehow relate to have better chance to be turned into a feature article for the English-language media. As discussed in the first chapter, relevance to the foreign reader is the most important criterion in determining whether the topic is worth further pursuit.

For example, entertainment celebrities frequently make Weibo trending hashtags, but they are not suitable subjects for English-language feature writing unless their story can somehow touch upon the foreign reader's life. In 2020, Sisters Who Make Waves, a reality show produced by Hunan TV, took the country by storms for its unusual participants who are middle-aged female performing artists all above 30 years old, the oldest being 52. The show and the "sisters" attending it quickly became trending hashtags on China's social media and the topic was picked up by various media. For instance, both *Shanghai Daily* and the Sixth Tone did feature stories on the program and the buzz it generated. Why this topic is considered to be newsworthy in terms of telling China's story to the world? The reason lies in relevance. The individual celebrity attending the show, whatever fame she enjoys in the country, is not newsworthy to a foreign audience. However, the issue of age discrimination against women in the entertainment industry that the program raises is a general issue that foreign audiences can identify with. And it's no coincidence both stories focus on addressing the issue, albeit from different perspectives.

The *Sixth Tone* story titled "Middle-Aged' Celebs Are Vying to Become China's Next Girl Group" remains skeptical about the progressiveness of the program. "The show fails to address the real issues women face, including employment discrimination in the entertainment industry. Instead, it uses the participants' popularity to attract viewers, just like other television shows," says the story from the news website, quoting a commentator on gender issue.[①] The *Shanghai Daily* story titled "Middle-aged sisters make waves in new reality TV show", on the other hand, paints the show in glowing terms. After citing a poll numerating the problems facing the middle-aged women including low salaries, limited upward mobility and pressure from younger generations, the newspaper article goes on to present the show in a most favorable light: "Enter the Sisters, tough industry veterans who flout the rules, challenge cameramen, argue and talk back to judges, which many middle-aged women find comforting and gratifying."[②]

Apart from the trending hashtags on social media, other topical events covered by domestic media are also a valuable source of possible story ideas. Some of the Chinese stories were almost readymade for the international market, only need to be translated and edited into English ones. Others are viewed more as a worthwhile topic and a start point, to be developed into full-

---

① Cai Xuejiao and Zhang Wanqing. Middle-Aged' Celebs Are Vying to Become China's Next Girl Group [EB/OL]. The Sixth Tone. (2020-07-20) [2021-08-04]. https://www.sixthtone.com/news/1005808/%E2%80%98Middle-Aged%E2%80%99%20Celebs%20Are%20Vying%20to%20Become%20China%E2%80%99s%20Next%20Girl%20Group.

② Tan Weiyun. Middle-aged sisters make waves in new reality TV show[N/OL]. Shanghai Daily. (2020-07-17) [2021-08-04] https://www.shine.cn/feature/entertainment/2007172378/.

length features with further interviews and additional research.

2.2.2　Story ideas from international media

International media，especially its coverage on China，is another fertile field where feature story ideas can be found. First，the coverage on China by international media indicates a ready interest in the topics and issues that are central to the coverage. Second，the coverage on China by international media is often unfortunately skewed or biased，sometimes even downright wrong，fortifying not understanding but stereotypes and prejudices. This habitual "malpractice" creates a void for fair and high-quality reporting on China in international communication that Chinese English-language media are particularly positioned to fulfill. In this sense，story ideas evolving from the international media are all the more necessary to put right an incorrect report on China.

During the coronavirus pandemic，the coverage on the related stories in China by the foreign media is rife with mistakes，bias and disinformation. It falls on the Chinese English-language media to present to the world the true picture of the great efforts made by Chinese government and Chinese people against the horrible plague. Many such stories are produced，from a simple reporting need as well as an obligation to set right what's wrongly reported. Here is one of such stories that serves as a particularly effective rejoinder to the pervasively prejudiced reporting from the Western media.

The following story[1] titled "Chinese medicine：defenders and doubters" from *Shanghai Daily* tells how the traditional Chinese medicine is used，quite successfully，to treat the COVID-19 patients. The news peg — an incident narrated in the lead where a Paris family of four infected with the nova coronavirus sought help from the TCM doctors from China via Internet and got it — is a particularly effective choice to base the story on because the incident at the very beginning of the story connects the TCM with the cure of the COVID-19 of a family outside China. The group of TCM doctors the story centers on offer their service to the patients both at home and outside China with a surprising success rate. During the battle against COVID-19，the TCM

---

[1]　Yao Minji. Chinese medicine：defenders and doubters[N/OL]. Shanghai Daily. (2020-04-12) [2021-08-04]. https://www.shine.cn/news/in-focus/2004126175/.

treatment has been playing a very real role and the Chinese experience has been crucial in the battles to "ending the global pandemic," especially as there is still no decisive cure. In addition, one of the strengths of the piece is that it does not shy away from presenting the controversies and doubts that have loomed over the traditional Chinese medicine since the COVID-19 outbreak: "many young Chinese consider herbal treatments to be slow-working and only health supplements at best," says the story. At the end of the story, it is reported that a TCM is approved for clinical trials after telling the readers about the urgent needs for clinical trials of both Western and Chinese cures.

Chinese Medicine: Defenders and Doubters

Yao Minji

15:16 UTC+8, 2020-04-12

When June Pigeon, her husband and two children first developed symptoms of fever, headache, body pain, nausea, cough and stuffed noses, the Paris family was told to stay at home, take paracetamol, drink water and call back if serious respiratory problems developed.

Feeling anxious amid the novel coronavirus outbreak, she turned to friends in China for help. They put her in touch with traditional Chinese medicine doctors who had been treating COVID-19 patients since the end of January.

Free of charge, the doctors wrote out individualized prescriptions — different for each member of the family — and instructed them how to use acupoint massage until their package of herbal medicine arrived.

The family of four recovered.

"I'm Chinese Singaporean and grew up drinking herbal soups and mixtures, but it was not something I turned to for a quick remedy," Pigeon told *Shanghai Daily*. "Seeing the quick effects of the traditional medicine came as a surprise to me."

Traditional Chinese medicine supplier Herba Sinica, based near Nuremberg in Germany since 1996, has been working overtime since the end of February filling out orders for Chinese herbs.

Many sought-after herbs are traditionally used for cold and flu prevention, lung heat treatment or boosting energy — herbs like mulberry leaf, reed rhizome and radix astragali.

Similar orders are flooding into Chinese herbal stores around the world as people grasp at straws for treatment of a virus that has yet no known proven therapy. Most clients are local Asians, but the number of those trying traditional medicine for the first time is on the rise.

Herba Sinica founder Zhong Wenjun, who has a doctorate in plant nutrition, is connecting TCM doctors with the Munich-based International Society for Chinese Medicine, founded by Professor Manfred Porkert in 1978.

"I hope that by connecting the doctors, we can find ways to help those in need overseas, especially those unable to get into a hospital," Zhong said.

"If we use the metaphor of defending a city to the case of fighting the novel coronavirus, traditional Chinese medicine is to build up your wall to defend against it," he explained. "No matter who the enemy is and how strong they are, your wall is your defense line. Western medicine seeks to identify the enemy and attack accordingly. In the case of COVID-19, the enemy is still not fully known to us."

Half of the world is now home-bound due to the pandemic. Many with mild symptoms are unable to get into overwhelmed hospitals or, in some countries, to even get a coronavirus test. In many countries, health-care systems are treating only the most serious cases.

Doctors and researchers remain puzzled why some patients deteriorate more quickly than others. Many people like Pigeon, who show mild symptoms, become anxious because they aren't sure whether they will recover at home.

Chinese front-line doctors in the fight against the pandemic are sought out by peers overseas to share their experience via video conferences. Free digital handbooks on prevention and treatment of the novel coronavirus by Chinese doctors have also been translated into many languages.

Chinese Internet giants like Alibaba and JD. com have initiated multilingual tele-medicine platforms to connect Chinese doctors with patients overseas. According to JD. com, its platform, launched on March 17, was visited more than 5 million times in the first 10 days. It evoked more than 100,000 inquiries — 5,000 on the English version.

The Chinese experience has encountered resistance due to bias and other factors. Foreign media have reported how some patients of Chinese ethnicity, including the first New Jersey patient, had to fight with their doctors to refer them to Chinese advice on treating the disease.

The official Chinese guidelines on COVID-19 also include TCM methods, which are little understood and generally dismissed by Western medical establishments.

Even in China, traditional medicine had its doubters where novel coronavirus is concerned.

Zhang Boli, a traditional medicine expert on China's COVID-19 team, who spent two months in Wuhan, former epicenter of the outbreak in China, recalled in a TV interview how some patients refused to take traditional medicine at first.

Many young Chinese consider herbal treatments to be slow-working and only health supplements at best.

Wu Pinglu, director of the respiratory department at a traditional medicine hospital and a member of the COVID-19 expert team in the city of Xianning in hard-hit Hubei Province, told *Shanghai Daily* through an assistant that foreign patients simply don't know how traditional Chinese medicine can help them.

"We desperately want to contribute to ending the global pandemic, but it is very difficult to have our voice heard," Wu said.

Wu comes from a family of four generations of traditional Chinese medicine practitioners and chose to follow in their footsteps after graduating in Western medicine. He has founded the group Tang Po Xue, which communicated with Paris-based Pigeon via tele-medicine.

The name means "like thawing snow with hot water," which describes how effectively traditional medicine can treat disease if used accurately. The group comprises about 10 doctors from various hospitals, along with many volunteers.

In addition to their hospital duties, the team of doctors has been trying to help COVID-19 patients since late January, free of charge and many by remote diagnosis. The group said it had treated 491 patients in China by the end of February. Of those all but 56 who didn't get their deliveries of medicines beat the virus.

The group now wants to help other heavily hit areas. Using a combination of acupuncture and herbal remedies, they are finding ways to reach overseas patients.

Doctors from Tang Po Xue can help tele-medicine in English via WeChat (tangpoxue095) or Skype (tangpoxue@126.com).

Wu gives some general tips for those suffering mild symptoms: Avoid chicken if you are coughing, eat Chinese dates for diarrhea and refrain from sex life when taking traditional medicines.

"The essence of traditional Chinese medicine is individualized prescriptions," Wu said. "That's difficult to apply on a large scale in the situation of pandemic, so some common prescriptions with differences for individuals and easy-to-learn acupoint message can help effectively and quickly."

He added, "We have also modified prescriptions using substitutes for ingredients unavailable in some countries. There's often a delay in packages arriving. In the meantime, patients can easily learn acupoint message, which has proven effective in relieving the symptoms until their medicine arrives or they gain access to an acupuncture practitioner."

While Chinese sources teem with articles about the use of traditional medicine in treating symptoms of novel coronavirus, there has been little professional discussion in the West on the subject since the outbreak of the new virus.

There is no cure yet, Western or Chinese medicine, as the esteemed British medical journal *Lancet* paraphrased in March the World Health Organization as saying: "WHO has made it clear that there are currently no known effective treatments for COVID-19... Care should be taken to not give patients drugs of unknown efficacy. Clinical trials are urgently required in this context."

Clinical trials of existing drugs are undergoing around the world, including one traditional Chinese medicine approved of the clinical trial by Chinese medical authorities in late March.

Source: SHINE   Editor: Shen Ke

2.2.3 Finding story ideas in the readers' feedback

Thanks to the interactiveness of the new media, today readers'/users' feedback is instant and highly visible. This provides a pool of story ideas for feature writers. A point that needs to clarify, a misunderstanding to clear up, and a concern to address, all of these could be turned into a feature story that serves the interest and need of the audience. But it must be remembered that catering to the readers' require is completely different from fawning on the readers' taste. The new media is pervaded by a popular taste manifested by a favor for the loudest voice, regardless of the opinion contained, and the ensuing page views. Besides, readers' interest is notoriously capricious. So it is not advisable to base one's story ideas entirely on possible page views, which are often as unexplainable as it is unpredictable. Just remember a legitimate story idea should have all the news values in place. In picking a story idea, a writer should trust her own judgment and at the same time, tailor the story to serve her readers in some real way.

2.2.4　Finding story ideas in daily life

The digital new media is becoming increasingly polarized. It has been observed that internet users often live in a bubble of information filtered by affirmative bias. Genuine curiosity has become rare, as people trapped in information cocoons seek only information that is consistent with their existing politics and avoid information to the contrary.[①] However, a serious journalist, or a diligent student of journalism, must try to muster up enough curiosity to get out of this stagnant bubble to read about different points of view and, more importantly, to talk to real people, especially those who hold views different from their own. The freshness of colliding with different viewpoints may inspire ideas that have been elusive within one's own cocoon.

A reporter can always resort to daily life when running out of story ideas if she is willing to step out of her own cocoon. "Be curious and not judgmental," as the poet Whitman says. All she needs to do is to observe and listen. A writer on assignment opens her senses and monitors her surroundings. A writer on hunt for a story idea might do the same: look beyond the obvious for anything unusual that might be worth further investigation, and listen for people's concerns and troubles, even though much may appear to be trivial and petty. And workable ideas do come from the apparently mundane life. For example, smart phones have become ubiquitous in our daily life. The inseparable device brings great convenience yet greater distraction that causes problems in time management and self-control. This issue with the smart phone is clearly not any individual's particular problem but a general one. With a suitable news peg (a recent news story that concerns the smart phone), a story idea on the issue could be developed into a full story.

The following story titled "Balanced view urged for parents on digital life" from *China Daily*[②], one of the many that explore the effects, good or bad, of

---

①　Sunstein, C.. Infotopia [M]. Oxford: Oxford University Press, 2008.

②　BELINDA ROBINSON. Balanced view urged for parents on digital life [N/OL]. China Daily. (2020-02-25) [2020.07-30]. https://global.chinadaily.com.cn/a/202002/25/WS5e548092a31012821727a0f8.html.

the device that has become almost the extension of our body, presents a worldwide debate on the impact of mobile phones on children. The discussion reported in the story, though mostly limited to the concerns for children from their parents, is significantly current in the backdrop of the pandemic-stricken world in 2020 when people are forced to stay isolated and many aspects of their life have migrated online and the smartphone becomes the literary lifeline to a world that remains connected.

Balanced view urged for parents on digital life

By BELINDA ROBINSON in New York

| China Daily | Updated: 2020-02-25 10:04

Reject fears, experts say, citing benefits of smartphones and internet for children

Children who were born in the past 20 years will never know a world without smartphones or the internet.

The iGen — those born from 1995 to 2012 — have had their childhoods transformed by devices such as mobiles, tablets and laptops when compared with their parents and grandparents.

This shift raised initial concerns after the launch of Apple's iPhone in 2007. In 2011, the American Academy of Pediatrics released a paper warning that Facebook could give children depression.

But by 2016, they amended their findings, acknowledging that the digital world and its effects on children were constantly evolving.

Today, experts are torn on whether smartphone and internet use by children is harmful.

Adam Pletter, a child psychologist in Bethesda, Maryland, and creator of website "iparent101", told *China Daily*: "In my professional experience, there is a clear correlation (relationship) between increased time, consuming digital content, and increased mood, anxiety and attentional challenges for all humans, especially children and adolescents, given their stage of development.

"Humans are designed to seek out information (which helps us survive), and social media, games and ease of access to it all pulls us into the never-ending loop. The internet does not end. There is always more amazing content to scroll through. This...frequently has an impact on developing social skills and mental health."

In the United States, 53 percent of children aged 11 own a smartphone, and by the age of 12, 69 percent of them own their own mobile device, according to a report by Common Sense Media, a nonprofit organization that assists families in promoting safe technology and media for children.

In China, more than 90 percent of teenagers up to the age of 18 access the internet through a mobile phone, according to the *Bluebook of Teenagers* published by the Chinese Academy of Social Sciences. And 85 percent of all teens use social networking site WeChat.

Jordan Shapiro, an assistant professor at Temple University and author of *The New Childhood: Raising Kids to Thrive in a Connected World*, believes there is unnecessary "paranoia" and "fear" about children's use of smart devices.

"As a parent, I am constantly nervous. I recognize that changes in technology represent even larger cultural, economic and political changes. But deep down I know my kids will be fine … Computers are doorways that open into magical, limitless connected worlds," he writes in his book.

Suggestion by WHO

The World Health Organization advised in 2019 that children under one year old shouldn't be exposed to an electronic screen, and those between the ages of 2 and 4 shouldn't have more than one hour of "sedentary screen time" each day.

For parents, smartphones have created a new frontier to monitor old problems like bullying, sexual predators and bad behavior. The Pew Research Center found in 2016 that 60 percent of parents of teens between the ages of 13 and 17 had checked their children's social media and browser history.

Bark, a parental-control monitoring app, said in 2018 that it scanned 900 million messages among 2.6 million school-issued accounts in the US. The scan tracks e-mail accounts, children's texts and social media, and alerts parents if they find content with drug or alcohol use.

Pletter adds: "The amazing and concerning thing about smartphones is that they are all-in-one devices, so this complicates the parenting landscape for well intentioned, modern parents, many of whom are digital immigrants raising digital natives."

Yet children can still dodge their parents' spying eyes by using a burner (paywall) phone or creating a finsta, a fake Instagram account that contains risque content that they would prefer to hide.

Parents should resist monitoring and blocking potential harm, says

Pletter. Instead, he advises that they "set enforceable limits aimed at teaching children the importance of self-regulation so these children can be the future adults they need to be".

Pletter said it's important that parents are mindful of how they use their own cellphones because children learn by observing them.

International research into smartphone-usage has recently shifted from assessing the amount of time teens spend on them to the relationship they have with the devices. A November 2019 study by researchers at Kings College, London, examined data from 41 studies involving 42,000 participants across Europe, the US and Asia.

They found one in four children had "problematic smartphone usage" such as neglecting chores to be on it or anxiety if the phone wasn't available. Teenage girls struggled the most with this.

Nicola Kalk, co-senior author of the study from the London-based Institute of Psychiatry, Psychology and Neuroscience, said in a statement: "Smartphones are here to stay, and there is a need to understand the prevalence of problematic smartphone usage. We don't know whether it is the smartphone itself that can be addictive or the apps that people use."

Exercise

1. Keep an idea file.

Ideas come and go. It is fleeting. You may have an epiphany anywhere, but if you don't write it down, it could be gone in the next moment. Many feature writers keep a daily diary, or create a file of ideas that includes reading notes, thoughts and ideas, story ideas, sketches, snippets from newspapers, and anything else that catches their interest. We encourage you to keep such a diary. The diary can take the form of a small notebook that you carry with you or a memo in your smartphone. You can use subject headings to organize the idea file. An essential ability for journalists is the ability to quickly learn about, well, everything. Cataloguing the accumulated facts will help you understand the myriad of topics more effectively. Of course, you can organize the idea file in any other way you like. Any way will do; the important thing is to keep one. It will be your secret source of inspiration and you can rely on it whenever you are running out of ideas for a story.

2. Weibo hashtags.

Read the following top ten trending hashtags on Sina Weibo on Feb. 27,

2021. The trending hashtags on Weibo are updated every ten minutes. The following is only one version of the same day. Discuss them with your classmates and then decide which ones are story ideas worth further pursuit and which ones aren't. Why? Remember that the key here is the English-language feature articles we write for a foreign audience. Therefore, please take into account the needs and interests of the audience in your evaluation.

(1) Stephen Chow said he couldn't accept the death of his former acting partner.

(2) These acts will violate the penal code starting from March 1.

(3) Wu Mengda died.

(4) Don't call me Uncle Da, call me Brother Da.

(5) The box office of the movie "Hi Mom" ranked third in domestic market.

(6) The top five box office films in China's history are all domestic.

(7) Should parents teach the older siblings to give way to younger siblings?

(8) China becomes the biggest buyer of Thai Durian in the world.

(9) The current situation of contemporary young people buying funds.

(10) We will never see Wu Mengda and Stephen Chow working together again.

2.3   Giving shape to story ideas

A story idea, however promising, is still an idea and is still a long way from the full story. Like all ideas, it is vague, untested and undeveloped, running the risk of being too narrow and eventually coming to nothing or too broad and more suitable for bigger projects like a book. It is obvious that there are steps to be taken to turn this ambivalent concept into a clear story. And the first crucial step is to give shape to the shapeless thought in the head.

Story ideas, as ideas, are sprawling by nature. Giving shape to the story idea means to contain it by putting a fence around it. To do that, you need to orbit the issue at heart to recognize perspectives involved and define people or organizations embroiled. An issue worth examining is often complex and in some ways unbalanced. If your goal is to provide a complete and fair picture, you may need to examine a number of viewpoints. Of course, you must not take sides, but try to glimpse the issue from different positions to gain an understanding of the possible range of your ideas. And there are usually an equal number of people or organizations involved, with different interests and different propositions. There are not only heroes and villains, but also victims and beneficiaries. Make a list of them and determine whether they are worth pursuing as interviewees based on relevance to the central idea of the story, as well as resources, access and time allowed.

You must also consider the issue central to your story idea in terms of cause and effect. Cause and effect is a type of relationship between events whereby a cause creates an effect. In many cases, an effect can result from many causes and vice versa, so the exact nature of these relationships can be difficult to determine. You may draw a cause and effect diagram to help in your brainstorming. What you draw is actually a logic map, a systematic visualization of the relationships entangled in the construction of the issue. As the author, you must have a clear understanding of the logical chain of events, showing why and how it happened, what it all means, and what the implications are.

The above brainstorming advised for your story idea will help you shape the idea as well as make plan for the next stage of your reporting, the researching and interviewing. Before you move on to the next stage, there's one more thing you must do: get your story idea on paper. Writing thoughts down is a crucial step of clarifying it. Only when put on paper, words start to assume logic. A concise statement of a couple of lines helps you to focus, to see clearly your own thinking. This short statement of the story idea will also guide the subsequent interviews and research and keep you on track.

Exercise

1. The following story[①] from *Shanghai Daily* is one of a series of articles commemorating Pudong's 30 years of opening-up and development. The story tells about the crucial role the Shanghai Stock Exchange Science and Technology Innovation Board, a "Nasdaq-style market," has played in the development of hi-tech companies in Pudong, Shanghai. Read the following article carefully and try to discern the perspectives present in the story. Is the issue only viewed through the standpoint of the market? Or there are other points of views presented? What are they? Why are the other perspectives necessary? Make a list of the people and organizations present in the story.

---

① Zhu Shenshen, Huang Yixuan. Sci-tech companies bask in the glow of the STAR Market[N/OL]. Shanghai Daily. (2021-08-13) [2021-08-15]. https://www.shine.cn/news/in-focus/2108133535/.

Who are they respectively? What are their interests and claims? How they are reported? What are the relationships between the different groups of people and organizations? Is there a clear chain of cause and effect of events in the story? If so, what does it look like and can you draw a map showing these relationships?

Sci-tech companies bask in the glow of the STAR Market

Zhu Shenshen Huang Yixuan

Shanghai's STAR Market, which marked its second anniversary on July 22, has proven to be a popular and successful channel for investors to buy shares in the future of science and technology, such as advanced semiconductor chips, vaccines, green cars, cloud computing, artificial intelligence and robotics.

The Nasdaq-style market, officially named the Shanghai Stock Exchange Science and Technology Innovation Board, is now home to over 300 companies, which have raised about 380 billion yuan (US $58.8 billion) in initial public offerings.

Chip designer Shanghai Fudan Microelectronics is a recent example of the market success. Its share price surged eightfold on its August 4 debut. The company was already listed on the Hong Kong exchange.

"It's a milestone for Fudan Microelectronics, embarking on a new journey with this listing," Jiang Guoxing, chairman of the Fudan Microelectronics, said at the debut.

The company, which started out as a laboratory at Fudan University and went corporate in 1998, raised 747.6 million yuan by issuing 120 million shares priced at 6.23 yuan each. They closed their first day of trading at 55.9 yuan.

The Chinese government authorized the creation of STAR Market to provide a fundraising channel for creative companies in vanguard sectors of science and technology.

On its second anniversary, the market's value was estimated at around 4.95 trillion yuan, accounting for about 5 percent of all Chinese mainland-listed stocks. Companies related to major technology industries accounted for almost 75 percent of all firms listed.

Just over a third of companies are engaged in the new generation of information technology, such as cloud computing and artificial intelligence. Biotechnology companies account for 23 percent of listings.

In announcements to-date of first-half results, 67 of 100 companies predicted growth in operations.

It's not just the strength of companies like Fudan Microelectronics that mark the first two years of STAR. The market itself is undergoing changes to strengthen its performance.

STAR plowed new ground by allowing startup companies without profitable balance sheets to go public. It also has conducted a trial program allowing companies to list through a registration system rather than the usual approval procedure of vetting by stock regulators.

In April, China's securities regulators stipulated that research and development employees must account for 10 percent of staff in companies seeking IPO on STAR. It has also banned IPO by companies related to finance or real estate and signaled that STAR will become the first mainland board to introduce a market maker system to provide more liquidity.

In a recent guideline supporting further development of the Pudong New Area, China also announced it would pioneer a new program on STAR, allowing qualified foreign institutional investors to use yuan to participate in stock offerings.

With the Pudong-related policy support and the long-term strategy to build Shanghai into a global financial center on par with New York and London, the STAR Market's "position and essence in the capital markets will be significantly improved," according to Dongxing Securities.

Moreover, with Chinese technology IPOs under tighter scrutiny in markets like New York, STAR is well positioned to attract more of those listings, analysts said.

TOP 10 FIRMS ON INNOVATION AND PATENT IN THE STAR MARKET

Rank	Firm	Industry	Market Value (bn yuan, by Friday)	Code
1	SMIC	Core electronics	461.3	688981
2	AMEC	Core electronics	106.3	688012
3	Appotronics	Core electronics	15.4	688007
4	Kingsoft Office	New software and service	160.3	688111
5	Qi An Xin	New software and service	64.5	688561
6	China Railway Signal & Communication	Next generation network	54.0	688009
7	Cambricon	Artificial Intelligence	39.9	688256
8	China Railway Construction Heavy Industry	Railway and transportation equipment	28.2	688425
9	IVO	Core electronics	23.3	688055
10	Traffic Control Technology	Railway and transportation equipment	5.0	688015

Source: PatSnap and Shanghai Daily

Eight STAR-listed companies currently have market value of 100 billion yuan or more, including Semiconductor Manufacturing International Corp, with a market value of 461.3 billion yuan; online tool provider Kingsoft Office, with a value of 160.3 billion yuan; and vaccine maker CanSino Biologics, with a value of 117.9 billion yuan.

Since its inception in 2020, the STAR Market 50 component index has risen from 1,000 to 1,587 points.

STAR-listed firms have shown themselves at the vanguard of innovation, receiving 16,300 new patents in 2020, according to the Shanghai Stock Exchange.

PatSnap, a patent data and analytics service provider, said STAR-listed firms have rich pools of patents, covering industries such as information technology, high-end equipment manufacture, biomedicine and electric cars. That indicates a high level of research.

Kingsoft Office, the No. 2 STAR-listed firm, a company aiming to break the monopoly of Microsoft Office in China, spent 711 million yuan on research last year, accounting for a third of its revenue. It has a research team of 1,923 people.

The company now offers services to 100 million overseas users. Its flagship product WPS Office is doing particularly well in countries included in China's Belt and Road Initiative, Kingsoft said.

Fudan Microelectronics spent 490.5 million yuan, or a third of its revenue, on research in 2020. It employs a research team over 800 people.

Another star on STAR is CanSino Biologics, which is producing one-shot COVID-19 vaccines in Shanghai. The company said its annual production capacity will hit about 200 million units.

In addition to the STAR 50 Index, another index for the market will debut on August 16. It will track share performance in the information technology sector.

The new index, called the STAR Next Generation Information Technology Index, or STAR Next Generation IT, will cover the performance of 50 companies with relatively high market value and businesses in fields such as next-generation information networks, electronics, emerging software and cloud computing, big data and artificial intelligence.

The success of the STAR Market is gaining international recognition.

Swiss-based seed and pesticide firm Syngenta plans to list on the market in the first group of international company to sell shares in Shanghai.

Global index compiler MCSI has announced the inclusion of several new stocks listed on the STAR Market in its indexes, which will take effect later this year.

As of February, companies listed on the STAR Market could be included in the "stock connect" trading program that links mainland exchanges with Hong Kong. Stock connect provides a channel for overseas investors to gain access to mainland stocks.

In May, KraneShares unveiled the first ETF in Europe tracking the STAR 50 index. It's listed on the London Stock Exchange.

2. With regard to the scope of the story, it has been said that a good feature story is a limited story that is well told. The appropriate limits to the scope of the story can be determined by identifying perspective involved and identifying the people and organizations that are affected. Suppose you notice that many of your fellow students at college borrow money from various online lending platforms, whether legitimate or dubious, in addition to their monthly pocket money, and that they tend to overspend and even live on credit. You think this might be an issue worth exploring as it is current, important, and close to young people. Young people's spending habits and financial management styles certainly have many implications, especially as today's economy is heavily dependent on consumption. Please research this issue and do some preliminary research to identify the perspectives involved and the people and groups affected and write down three story ideas/theme statements based on the different perspectives defined. You could draw an idea map showing the logical relationships between the different groups of people to help you think.

Theme Statement 1:

Theme Statement 2:

Theme Statement 3:

Chapter 3　Researching For Feature Stories

3.1　Research shows

A story idea, however seemingly viable, is still a long way from the actual story. Sufficient research and careful interviews need to be conducted to gather the necessary materials to flesh out the idea into a real story. Research is a crucial step in any serious writing. Without it the writing will be impetuous and arbitrary, a guesswork. Though often in the end the writer might only use a small part of the materials turned up by the research, the authority that comes from knowing the subject thoroughly will infuse through the article. A confident story from a writer who knows her stuff is charming, winning, and convincing.

Moreover, a most common beginner's mistake that leads to weak feature stories is the meagre reporting. The story is simply thin, just a few examples strung haphazardly together, and read as repetitive and lengthy, lacking of perspective and insight. What is absent are the telling details and the meaningful contextual information. All of this comes from adequate reporting, which is the foundation of a good story. For a beginning journalist, it's best to do more reporting than is actually needed.

Conducting research for a feature article is a bit like solving a mystery. As a journalist, your role is similar to that of a detective. Getting to grips with the subject matter in question or dissecting the issues involved is about getting to the bottom of things. Every detail is important, and every new piece of information discovered could be that missing piece of the puzzle. Admittedly, researching for accurate information can be difficult and sometimes frustrating. But it is also surprisingly rewarding. It can give you both confidence and credibility as a writer. In reporting and writing feature articles, you are also acting as a communicator, and the least you can do is to make sure you know what you are talking about.

3.2　Starting with a plan

Once you've decided on your story idea, the serious research begins. In the process of coming up with the idea and shaping the idea，you must have done some preliminary research and have gained some idea about the subject or issue you are to report. But that is far from enough. Once you've made your decision with the reporting subject or issue，and you must task yourself with learning everything you can find about the subject/issue. You must become a temporary expert in a rather short time. To achieve that effectively and efficiently，it is highly advisable that before embarking on the arduous task you make a research plan to identify your wants and needs. The plan can serve as a road map in your trip of information hunt. It will help you stay focused and organized.

There are as many ways to plan the research as there are different writers. Here，as journalists，we can borrow the five Ws and one H from news writing to delineate the research outline.

- **Who** is to be investigated? And **what** information are to be gathered? All feature stories are stories about people：their achievements and their failures，their laughter and their tears，their concerns and their problems. Your story，too，must involve people and organizations they are in. Who are they? Or who will they be? What roles are they going to play? How important each one of them will be in your story? What information do you need? What types of information do you need?

- **Why** do you do the research? What is the central issue? What do you need to know about it? How much have you already known? What kind of information is to be gathered? How will the information collected add to the story?

- **Where** are the best places to search? Where to get the information needed? Are the sources credible? Is access a problem? Access is an important factor you must take into consideration. No original sources，no original story. The availability of the sources will determine whether the story idea is viable. Here the sources include both human sources and material sources.

- **When** did the events or news to be searched occur? When was the study or research that contains crucial statistics released? Are they current enough? Time is an important element in feature writing. In actual writing，clear time sequence will help anchor the story and keep the reader orientated. At the researching stage，conscious of the time element，a writer needs to make sure the information gathered around the event is relevant and current.

- **How** much research should be done? Can be done? Skipping on research is a common temptation. But one can over-research, too, and get so obsessed with the process of tracking down elusive facts that more time is spent on it than is really required. The trick is to hit a workable balance. Be practical.

3.3　The first place to look

Rarely is a feature story idea about something completely new. Most story topics have been covered by the media before, and a so-called new story is nothing more than presenting the latest development of a well-established event or looking at an old topic from a new perspective. In order to research the "new" story, it is advisable to identify stories on the "old" subject or with angles that had already been explored. Indeed, a search of existing media coverage often yields two results. On the one hand, this search helps the writer to get a quick grasp of the subject matter; the knowledge gained may not go directly into the story, but it establishes the authority the writer needs to gain full control of the story. On the other hand, it tells the writer whether the story idea under contemplation is worth pursuing and whether the new perspective is truly novel. This is why the media usually tops the list of go-to places for information hunting. Indeed, many journalists spent much time browsing the media every day.

Writers may encounter difficulties akin to "finding a needle in a haystack" when searching for valid data in today's explosion of information flooding the media. Of course, if the purpose of reading the media is simply to understand the subject matter and read background information, then the main issue may be how to set a reasonable limit on what can be mined. After all, there is a limited amount of time available and the purpose of the story should be limited as well. More often than not, however, the skill of searching for information in the media lies in what data to believe. Generally speaking, official media with fact-checking standards are more trustworthy, although lapses in official media in relaying false information from dubious sources can be seen every day. A study[①] of fake news in 2019 by *The Paper*, a Shanghai-based news app, showed that the number of fake news stories in Chinese media did not appear to have increased compared to the previous year. However, unfortunately, this does not mean that things are getting better. Rather, it means that the definition of fake news continues to be blurred and that the performance and influence of mainstream media continue to decline. As a result, be particularly careful of reposts, which are becoming more prevalent on various digital platforms as high-quality original content declines. Furthermore, the act of retweeting news does not imply an endorsement of its credibility. Far from it, the careless retweeting of information is merely a symptom of the great rush of the digital age, in which everything is being retweeted at a rapid pace. Therefore, if this information is crucial to the story, the writer is strongly advised to find the original posting and also to verify it from other sources.

3.4　Survey, study findings, and press conferences

Survey and study often produce solid findings that are valuable information to a feature writer. Think tanks, research institutes, universities, and industry consultancies all release survey and study findings, of course, the credibility of which usually depends on that of the publisher. Important findings are often picked up and dutifully reported by the media and nowadays most academic and research institutions have their own media outlets and publish their findings in a timely manner. So keeping an eye on media reports and the websites of these academic and research institutions will help you get valuable and relevant information. Survey is conducted to get the popular opinion on something. Sometimes the reporter can conduct a survey herself but she needs to identify the size of the surveyed sample in the story to allow the reader to decide on its reliability. Media platforms like Sina Weibo also conduct survey on a myriad of topics. Survey results from these online platforms sometimes find their way into a feature article. Again the identity of the survey conductor must be identified so that readers will understand that it is a fairly cursory poll and should not be taken too seriously.

Merriam Webster defines a press conference as an interview or statement

---

① 2019 年虚假新闻研究报告:专业媒体仍在持续生产错误信息[EB/OL]. 澎湃. (2020-01-15)[2021-08-04]. https://www.thepaper.cn/newsDetail_forward_5524167.

made by a public figure to the media by appointment. Press conferences are held regularly by government officials to announce government decisions, disseminate information on public affairs and explain official positions, especially in times of crisis. Press conferences are also held by large companies, mainly for public relations purposes, and the media are sought and invited to attend.

There is no doubt that press conferences are a valuable source of information. A whiff of the latest policy and up-to-date figures of any significance can be found there. However, press releases, especially from corporate press conferences, should be taken with a pinch of salt, especially when the one-way dissemination of information smells of spin. As for more credible information from official press releases, journalists must quickly scan through the press release and discern key points that may not be the announcement points on the official announcement. In addition, note that a press release is just another piece of information, the raw material for a feature story, and is never a story in itself.

For professional journalists, attending press conferences is part of the job. But for freelance journalists and writers who have little access, an alternative may be to follow the news closely and have press clippings on paper or digitally. Here, it is a good idea to place the clippings under subject headings. Proper indexing is important for quick retrieval. It's like having your own mini-encyclopedia on the current events.

3.5　Libraries and reference books

It is said that a library is a good place to go when you feel bewildered or undecided, for there, in a book, you may have your question answered. For a bewildered or undecided feature writer, the library is also a good place to go. Library takes many forms in the digital time. Apart from the mortar-brick ones, various commercial online databases offer a variety of reliable and solid information. The ability to making use of and navigating these electronic resources to find the information needed is now one of the essential aptitudes today's journalists must acquire.

Reference books, such as almanacs, yearbooks, encyclopedias, atlases, or other books focusing on statistics, are practical tools that will assist the investigation for feature stories. Trade magazines, academic periodicals, and any other information-rich publications are all good resources. And the status of being published officially indicates that the information contained has been checked officially.

3.6　The Internet

For most people the World Wide Web is the first place to go for information. However, surfing online to find useful facts on deadline amid the sea of information is a huge challenge for reporters and writers. Even if the required information is located, there's still the problem of verification. Is the piece of information to be trusted? Is the website that contains the information reliable? This is an age of never-ending news and in the rush for updating, the Internet is congested with information, misinformation, disinformation, and gossipy gibberish. Even for a credible website, the probability is high that information that's inaccurate, unreliable, or plain fake, can be found. So in the struggle to distinguish between what is real and what is false, what is information and what is disinformation, and what is to be trusted and what is to be discarded, here are a few suggestions.

3.6.1　Checking the server extension

A server extension ending in.com usually means it is a commercial website. Be wary of information coming from commercial sites. Of course, much reliable and useful information can be found there. However, for profit, such sites may not make fact-checking their priority. Official websites, on the other hand, including those operated by government agencies, think tanks and research institutes, non-profit organizations and foundations, colleges and universities, and other institutions, may use extensions other than .com. These official websites often provide accurate and important information that is difficult to find elsewhere.

In addition, another easy way to gauge the reliability of a website is to consider how it looks. Beware of an amateurish looking website with a poor layout and content full of typos and bad writing; the information there is likely to be substandard as well. Of course, this doesn't mean that a website with a professional look is a guarantee of credible information. Impostors can be dressed up to look smart. The key is that all information that will go into the final copy should be verified through multiple sources.

Because of its authoritative status, government publications are an indispensable source of information for journalists. Whatever the topic the feature writer is writing about, it doesn't hurt to have a look at the laws and policies on the subject. Nowadays, all levels of government have their own websites, and it has become customary to publish decrees, working reports, announcements and many other useful documents on them. So don't forget to check out these useful websites when researching ideas for feature articles.

3.6.2   Checking the establishment time of the website

People all over the world are setting up new websites every minute. Though it is not fair to say that these newly-born websites are not to be trusted, like everything else in life, it takes time to build credibility. In the hurried hunt for information, websites that have been around for a while are more trust-worthy. Of course, the credibility should be measured in combination with that of the runner of the website.

On the other hand, it is also advisable to check out the last updated date of the website. Some websites may have been set up a long time ago but also abandoned for a while. On most occasions, for a journalist hunting for the latest information a zombie website may not be the ideal place to go.

3.6.3   Seeking out websites with expertise and beware of "self media"

Just as a journalist often looks for expert opinion to provide a kind of scientific pivot to her story, when gauging the reliability of a website, one should look for sites with specialist knowledge, i.e. sites that specialize in the kind of information that corresponds to a particular research purpose. For example, if the story is on the novel coronavirus, such websites as run by World Health Organization or National Health Committee are more likely to provide useful and accurate information because of the expertise and professionalism of those running them.

"Self-media" is the collective name given to the many social media accounts that generate the kaleidoscope of content that fills the web and has become a huge source of information. The vast majority of daily news is first reported by "self-published" accounts concentrated on social media applications such as

Weibo，WeChat and Douyin. It has become a regular practice for mainstream media，which have been scrambling to set up camp on social media platforms themselves，mining the contents created by users for possible coverage. However，most social media accounts survive on click-throughs and pageviews. As a result，popular tastes are shamelessly pandered to and sensationalism is blatantly promoted；with at best sporadic fact-checking measures in place，"self-media" also produce a huge amount of misinformation and fake news on a daily basis. And these fake news stories spread widely and quickly. A study by researchers at Massachusetts Institute of Technology found that falsehoods spread faster and deeper than the truth online，in all categories of information，by a substantial margin. [1] So，in all likelihood，"self-media" can be a mine of useful information or a minefield of potential problems. With this in mind，when searching for information from the user-generated content，always find the original post and verify the information through other independent sources.

3.6.4　Dealing with anonymity on the Net

Anonymity is a property of the Internet，which，on the upside，contributes greatly to the prosperity of the Net for it offers protection for unpopular speech，allows a person to express his or her views freely，with little fear of repercussions. An individual may treat the internet as a tree hole and say things he or she may not feel comfortable to say in the physical world. Anonymity，on the downside，contributes as greatly to the dark side of the Net. The widespread of rumors and all forms of cyber violence all have anonymity to blame to a degree. And the beneficial and detrimental effects of anonymity have been pondered over and argued about ever since the arrival of the internet. When it comes to researching for feature stories，anonymity poses a special problem：nameless or pseudo-named authors may be a sign for unreliable and unusable information. Articles or studies whose authors are named are often—though not always—more reliable than works with no name attached or an obvious pseudo one. The real byline shows that the author believes in what's in the article and is willing to stand by it. More importantly，it means that someone is willing to take responsibility for the information contained.

---

① Li Shuangyi. How self-media chaos has sparked widespread outrage in China[EB/OL]. CGTN. (2019-03-30) [2020-7-30]. https://news.cgtn.com/news/3d3d674d77457a4e33457a6333566d54/index.html.

3.6.5   Using common sense in judgment

There is a simple solution to finding useful facts in the sea of information on the Net: use common sense. If the piece of information sounds bizarre or a bit too out there, and conventional wisdom tells you that this can't be true, then there is a high probability that the information is fake. Much notorious fake news is improbable on its face. For example, in September 2019, a bizarre piece of "news" went viral after dozens of media outlets reposted it on various social media platforms. The story goes that a woman from Xuzhou, Jiangsu Province got pregnant because the courier was late with her rushed order of a condom. The news, complete with video and photos "borrowed" from the internet, turned out to be fictitious, made-up to attract traffic. It is almost sad that such unbelievable fiction was thoughtlessly picked up and dispersed. If a thread of common sense had been used in judging the authenticity of the "news", it would have been recognized as fabrication at a most superficial glance.

3.6.6   Verification in the digital age

Journalism tradition decrees that information that goes into a story must be confirmed from independent sources. Rarely a single-source story is considered to be acceptable. Accuracy is a fundamental requirement for any journalistic articles. To achieve accuracy, a time-honored way is to verify the information from multiple sources. In fact, journalism is defined by some as a discipline of verification. So for every piece of information turned up from searching online, it must be confirmed by other independent sources to make sure it is fact, not fiction.

Besides, in the digital age, with the rise of mobile Internet and the smart phone getting increasingly smarter, verification of information has become more difficult than ever. Often before truth has the chance to get out the falsehood has already become public and spread far and wide. The authors of "*the Elements of Journalism*" suggest a new formula for verification of unsubstantiated material that is already public[1], including tracking down the

---

[1]   Bill Kovach & Tom Rosenstiel. The Elements of Journalism [M]. 3rd ed. New York: Three Rivers Press, 2014: 126-127.

first publisher of the information to verify it, contextualizing the now public allegation as much as possible, sharing with the public what would need to be established to prove the accusation, and for news organizations to acknowledge their community obligations and professional journalists their responsibilities in verifying the allegations that have already been made open.

3.7 Observation

Observation is a time-honored way to gather information for news and feature stories. No amount of playing armchair reporter can match good solid legwork. Only by being on the scene in person, feeling the ambiance and soaking up the sounds and flavors, a writer can depict it effectively and convincingly later in the story. Observation is also a special form of research. In observation, a reporter is not a casual onlooker, but a witness, using all senses and getting down everything. She may take note of her own reaction to the scene as well, for everything might be potentially useful. Productive observation depends on two things: concentration and analysis. Conscious concentration insists on exerting intellect when recording the scene, analyzing where this item is going and what it means. Observation is not just cataloging reality but revealing it: what does the data gathered signify? What is the essence of the scene?

3.8 Keeping a beat memo

Researching feature story idea means a search that's specific and with a definite purpose. A one-shot effort. However, in reality, many journalists who work in larger print-style newsrooms or niche publications work on specific areas of coverage called beats. Beat reporting refers to thematic specialization and routines (places to go, people to see) in journalism. The term reflects the distinction between general assignment reporters and specialized (beat) reporters covering a specific area (beat) as well as the subject-matter or geographic divisions between areas of reporting by which media organizations seek to structure the social environment they cover.[1] For feature writers who

---

[1] Melanie Magin and Peter Maurer. Beat Journalism and Reporting, Subject: Communication Theory, Journalism Studies, Political Communication Online Publication [EB/OL]. (2019-05) [2020-07-05]. DOI: 10.1093/acrefore/9780190228613.013.905.

work on a specific beat, researching is actually accumulative. Every story researched and written adds to the writer's understanding and growing expertise of the beat. So it seems only practical to keep a beat memo for the materials and contacts amassed over time, through which researching feature article ideas becomes an almost immersive experience. The knowledge acquired will contribute to writing all the stories on the beat.

Exercise

1. My research plan

   So far, do you have a story idea in store? Make a research plan for your story idea. Identify the who, what, when, where, why and how of your research plan. Then do some preliminary research and consider the credibility of the information turned up. Can you verify it from independent sources?

2. Seizing the essence of the scene

   Observe a scene, a corner of your campus, a street, a building, or anything that catches your attention, and write down what you have seen. Start your description with an overarching sentence that sums up the scene.

3. Finding the new angle of an old story

   Every spring, at the beginning of April, the Chinese celebrate the Qingming Festival, or Ching Ming Festival. People go to visit the graves of their beloved family members or friends to pay their respects to their ancestors. Suppose you are assigned to write an English feature story about the Qingming Festival and you are to come up with a new angle for your story to keep it current. Please research your new angle, learn as much as you can about it, and present your findings for discussion.

Chapter 4　Interviewing For Feature Stories

Interviews are a critical part of researching feature story ideas. The material gleaned from interviews can give feature stories an originality and authenticity that are unmatched by anything else. It is no exaggeration to say that without interviews there is no story. And this crucial step is also considered by many professional journalists to be the most difficult part of reporting and writing a feature story. Sometimes it is difficult to find the right person to interview. Sometimes the time to book an interview is fleeting and gone before you can take advantage of it. Sometimes, for various reasons, the right interviewee is unwilling to talk to the media. Sometimes the interviewee simply has trouble articulating his or her story. There seem to be a million ways in which an interview can go wrong or simply fail. However, acknowledging its trickiness, we can always take heart in the fact that interviewing is the kind of skill that can only really be learned through practice. Every successful interview is a rewarding experience, and every failed interview is a valuable lesson. Practice makes perfect. Interviewing is something that one can only get better at.

This chapter will review some established guidelines and proven techniques that will help in conducting a successful interview. First and foremost, make sure you are properly prepared before rushing into an interview.

4.1　Preparing for the interview

4.1.1　Getting the face-to-face interview

When preparing for an interview, the first question to consider is what kind of interview to conduct. Generally speaking, interviews can be conducted in person, in a group, by email, by telephone, or through one of the many instant messaging applications available today. Of all these options, always opt for a face-to-face interview if possible, especially with the main actors in the story.

The advantages of face-to-face interviews are obvious: the interviewer and the interviewee are in close contact and they can see each other during the conversation. This seemingly obvious value should not be underestimated, especially in a digital context where virtual communication has become the norm and people are increasingly interacting online without the need to actually meet in person.

Above all, the personal touch of face-to-face interaction will help overcome the awkwardness that naturally arises when strangers are forced to socialize, and assist journalists in making friends. A relaxed interviewee is more welcome and more effective than one who is guarded. This is difficult to achieve through other forms of interviewing. Trust and a real connection are not built through text messages. Secondly, journalists can pick up on non-verbal cues and adapt accordingly. Facial expressions and body language are important forms of communication. Some might argue that a video conversation would produce the same effect. But for anyone who has been involved in videoconferencing, which became very popular during the enforced quarantine caused by the COVID-19 pandemic, it is clear that the person seen through the small window on the digital device is not themselves. The video conversation was more like an enhanced phone call. People appeared stiff, a rigid image with little detail. Communication felt unnatural and the conversation was both forced and rushed. Thirdly, face-to-face interviews are more effective. It seems easier to communicate via digital apps, and admittedly, meeting up takes time, making appointments, negotiating transport etc. However, actually meeting in person can actually save time by allowing for continuous and uninterrupted conversations, which is vital to the effectiveness of the interview. Fourthly, a face-to-face interview gives the journalist the opportunity to observe the interviewee. Facial expressions, body language, mannerisms, physique, manner of dress — all these details provide clues about the interviewee. Observation helps the journalist to get to know the subject better and ultimately write a better story.

Other forms of interviewing are used when personal interviews are not possible. They should be reserved for secondary characters in the story. The telephone interview has one advantage: it's quick. And it is often used to clarify a vague point after the main in-person interview. Unable to meet the person and establish the rapport that can only come from face-to-face contact, journalists can mitigate this by working on their telephone etiquette and providing verbal reinforcement for the interviewee. Sometimes, a little extra warmth can make up for the lack of physical presence.

Interviews through such instant messaging service as offered by WeChat are primarily conducted for its convenience to access distant sources and to save on airfares. However, the drawbacks are the same as for telephone interviews; although emojis and memes are used to make up for the lack of facial expressions, they are only effective to a certain extent. In addition, though cute and funny, emojis and memes can make people look rather unprofessional and like any other emoticons, they leave much space for misinterpretation.

Panel interviews and interviews conducted via email are alternatives to no interview at all. If possible, these practices should be avoided.

4.1.2　Who to interview

Usually the central idea of your story will tell you who to interview. For any feature writer that is serious about his or her story, the "who" is always in the plural rather than the singular.

Generally speaking, in reporting the feature story, there are three essential criterial by which sources, or potential interviewees, can be judged. First, are the sources accessible; second, are they the best informed and most reliable; and third, are they, when necessary, multiple?

Accessibility of the sources determines whether the story works. If a source is not available or can't be reached within the window that time restrictions allowed, the reporter must come up with an alternative choice. Therefore, when preparing for interviews, always make room for plan B or C. Dig deeper and find more possible candidates for the interviews.

The sources should be **best informed** and most reliable. This criterion seems obvious, but in reality is rather difficult to meet. Generally speaking, sources who are best informed must be directly involved in the core issue somehow. For example, you want to do a story on the condition of nursing homes for old people. You've lined up experts who've written books on aging problems. But these experts are only secondary sources. To give substance to your story, you need eyewitnesses, participators, such people as the managers of nursing homes, nurses and elderly residents at the nursing homes who are the first-hand sources and the best-informed in such a situation. For any given story, it seems that there are plenty of experts and specialists keen to offer their opinions, which, mere digressions as comments on the action, play no role in pulling the story along. On the contrary, what is hard to track down are the people who are right in the middle of things. Best-informed, they are the most valuable sources for it is what they do that push the story forward.

Are sources **multiple**? Rarely will a single-source news story be accepted, not to mention feature stories. Sources work best when they are multiple. First, manifold life stories from multiple sources give the feature story the magnitude it needs. Most issues worth exploring have impact that's wide and far-reaching and usually affect different people in a variety of ways. A single source, even a typical one, can't represent the whole picture. The scope and richness of a proper feature story demands diverse sources. Second, different accounts from multiple sources, especially eyewitnesses, will render the story accurate, or as accurate as a journalistic article can be. It is quite common for a feature story to be based on interviews of dozens of sources. Human memory is notoriously unreliable, especially when it comes to details. Scientists have found that prompting an eyewitness to remember more can generate details that are outright false but that feel just as correct to the witness as actual memories.[1] In view of this inherent drawback of human memory, multiple eyewitnesses need to be interviewed to get the accurate picture. That's also the essence of verification which by definition is fact-checking with independent sources. Different accounts will correct and complement one another. The whole thus obtained is convincing. Third, doing multiple interviews is what responsible reporters do. Relentless digging and diligent legwork are the hallmark of a journalist worth her salt. And no efforts will be wasted. Even when the results obtained from different interviews are all similar, the similarity of the multiple accounts proves the credibility of the content.

4.1.3 Convenient subject

When tracking down interview subjects, a common temptation is to choose convenience over best fit. Instead of looking for the right person to interview, student journalists may choose to interview a friend or relative who is easily accessible to them. However, the person chosen for the interview should be just right for the story, someone who can strongly represent the conflict in the

---

[1] Rachel Barclay. Your memory is unreliable, and science could make it more so. Healthline [EB/OL]. (2013-11-13) [2020-07-30]. https://www.healthline.com/health-news/mental-memory-is-unreliable-and-it-could-be-worse-091313#Now-You-Remember,-Now-You-Dont.

story, or someone who can adequately represent the core issue. Someone who is merely serviceable will not do. Even for secondary sources, not just any experts will do. A perfunctory canned remark thrown in by a know-it-all "specialist" contributes little to the story. Every character, every line, every word in the feature story should be instrumental. Choose carefully the interview subjects and the right subject will prove to be worth the efforts.

4.1.4   Reluctant interviewee

A common problem many journalists face is reluctant interviewee. Often interviewees have real and good reasons for refusing to answer questions. The interview subjects may fear harassment or retribution, or fear stigma and ridicule from private information that they disclose. Or interviewees may have undergone some ordeal that they dread to relive. To persuade a reluctant source to speak requires persistence and tact. Here are some time-tested techniques that may help.

First, it's important to find out what exactly the potential source has problem with. If the problem is something you can correct, correct it, and provide the source as much reassurance as you can in order to conduct an interview. But don't make promise that you can't keep. Honesty is the best policy. If things are out of your control, be prepared to let it go and find an alternative to the original plan. Professional ethic codes dictate that you must obtain informed consent to publish.

Journalism means publicizing, rather than protecting, information. Details of people's intimacies in life, emotional or financial health, or traumatizing experiences, are sought after and valued as information by journalists. But this kind of personal information under normal circumstances should be protected and released only with the utmost care. To mitigate the possible negative impact, informed consent is advised and advocated by the more ethical-minded in the profession, though the practice of which has been followed to various degrees of satisfaction depending on the ethical standards of the news organizations.

Cambridge dictionary online defines informed consent as agreement or permission to do something from someone who has been given full information about the possible effects or results. So asking a source, "Is it OK if we publish what you say?" and getting permission does not count as informed consent. The source must be given full information and made to understand the potential consequences of publication, the risks, and the precautions that can (and cannot) be taken, and agrees to publication fully informed. A source fully informed is a stronger source and will give strength to the story eventually. Also, these candid conversations revolving around informed consent will help cement the reporter's relationship with sources and will engender truthful conversations.

4.1.5　Where and when to conduct the interview

To be fully prepared for the interview means to be in full control of the whole process. Apart from knowing who to interview, a reporter must plan as well when and where to interview key subjects. Telephone or text message your subject beforehand and make an appointment at a time that is convenient at least for your subject. The length of the time is very important. You should plan and ask for as long as suitable for an adequate interview.

As for the locale where the interview should be conducted, the first choice should be your subject's home or workplace. That will render you the opportunity to get a glimpse of your subject's home life or to watch him at work. Both are valuable glimpses that will add to your understanding of subject. If it seems out of question to hold the interview at either the subject's home or his workplace, choose a mutual place, like a coffee shop. But it should be a quiet one, you wouldn't want to shout at each other during the interviews and you want a place where both you and your subject can feel at ease and talk.

4.1.6　Researching the subject

One important step that can't be skipped in preparing for interviews is to research the interviewing subject beforehand. Serious research does not stop at a Baidu or Google search that may or may not turn up much, depending on the notability of the subject. Serious research means a visit to a city or an academic library, or to an electronic/online database. But the library research should be supplemented, if possible, with calls to people who know the interviewee and understand the topic of the intended article. Find out as much as possible about the interviewing subject but do so in a polite and inoffensive way. More often than not the interviewee will be pleased if he/she finds out that the reporter has done her homework and know what she is talking about. The interviewee may become more friendly and forthcoming with his/her story.

4.1.7　The question list

In addition，a reporter should write down or type out the potential questions in advance. The questions should ideally be based on the research that has been done. The question list can serve as a crutch during the interview，something the reporter can fall back on when the talk runs to a stop. But be flexible and prepare to go where the actual interview leads and follow any new line of inquiry emerged. The interview is a two-way conversation that unfolds naturally，not a scripted dialogue. The list of questions prepared should only function as a jumping-off point for the interview.

4.1.8　Be punctual

Last but not least，in preparing for an interview，remember to set off a bit earlier than necessary and be punctual. Is that insultingly obvious advice? But you have to make allowance for bad weather or other accident that may occur on the way. Even if nothing happened，by arriving early you give yourself time to get organized and observe the surroundings and get familiar with the locale. Composed and ready，you will start your interview with confidence and a sense of being in control.

Exercise

Pick a topic of your interest，and identify the potential interviewing subjects involved. For the purpose of this exercise，let's assume the subjects are all accessible，and you only need to consider the other two criteria: are the sources best informed? Are the sources multiple? Research the subjects and craft a list of interviewing questions (no less than ten) based on the research you've done.

4.2　Conducting the personal interview

4.2.1　Where to sit

Just before you actually start the interview, you may be faced with the seemingly innocuous question of where to sit during the interview. As many interviews may be conducted around a conference table, the obvious answer may be to sit opposite your interviewee. However, sitting directly across the table can mean confrontation, especially with the camera also pointing at the interviewee. The interviewee may feel that he/she is facing an intruder or in a job interview and become defensive without meaning to. In this case, the journalist may also start to act more formally than necessary. It is difficult to engage in small talk across the table. A journalist who asks questions in an overly serious manner will only be met with equally serious platitudes. It is therefore strongly recommended that the journalist sits diagonally opposite or next to the interviewee. Such a sitting arrangement is non-confrontational and, if executed well, can even feel intimate. After all, people are more likely to share "secrets" with a friend who is sitting with them, and more likely to ward off intruders through platitudes and empty answers.

4.2.2　Making friends

A journalist's job is twofold: to gather and disseminate information. One essential ability that a journalist must cultivate is the interpersonal communication skills, which are put to test during an interview. As discussed above, a good interview is not a one-way interrogation, but a two-way conversation, the success of which depends as much on the interviewer as on the interviewee. That's why the first piece of veteran advice for conducting a personal interview is to make friends. At the beginning of the interview, don't go into the key questions bluntly. Take a moment to chat casually and break the ice. This small talk can take any direction, as long as it accomplishes the purpose: putting the interviewing subject at ease. It is also advisable that the reporter tells the subject about herself a bit. It's hard to trust a complete stranger, not to mention spilling the beans. If the plan is to use a recording device to ensure completeness and accuracy, ask the interviewing subject for permission of recording the conversation. However, don't forget the main purpose of the interview, and get back to the key questions once the interviewee appears to be sufficiently relaxed and ready for the real questions.

Remember that even when the interview enters the stage of real questions, it's unwise for the reporter to get suddenly all serious. Often the most valuable information is gleaned from a natural casual talk where the interviewee is off guard and willing to share.

4.2.3   Keeping in sight the purpose for the interview

The goal of all interviews is to get information. A reporter should keep this purpose in sight throughout the interview. This may seem obvious, but is easily said than done. As discussed above, a reporter is advised to make friends at the beginning of the interview. However, sometimes the newly acquainted friends get so carried away that the purpose of the interview is forgotten. When the interview is over, the reporter may find that there is little useful information that can be gathered from the lively talk. Sometimes, the reporter may even forget she is there to listen, to get information from others, not to show off her own. She may become so involved in the excitement of the talk that she starts to argue with the subject, while she is not supposed to interrupt even if the answer is not going the way as planned. To avoid such missteps, the key is to keep the goal for the interview in mind and keep a delicate control of the conversation. When the subject is in the mood to talk, stay quiet and listen. When the subject becomes quiet, pick up the conversation tactfully, fall back on the prepared question list if necessary. The goal is information and never let it out of your sight.

In addition, always be certain of the information obtained from the interview. Verify spellings and meanings of technical terms. Ask a second time if necessary. Follow up the responses with questions designed to clarify, such as "why?" Don't be afraid to look stupid. Although writers must become "temporary experts" on the wide array of subjects they are called upon to cover, few of them have more than a couple of areas of real expertise. Be honest with your ignorance so you can gain knowledge for the readers. The best time to ask for clarification is while the interview is ongoing and the interviewing subject is still in the mood to talk. Don't hesitate to say, "I don't understand," or "What does that mean?" or "Put it in layman's language, please." On the one hand, answers to these questions fulfill the ultimate purpose of the interview: to get accurate information. On the other hand, such questions may prompt the interviewing subject not just to shed light on an obscure point, but also to give illustrative examples in their explanation that may come in handy in the writing of the story.

4.2.4   Don't fill in the silence

A reporter is supposed to put the interviewee at ease and keep the conversation going. However, when the subject falters and fumbles for words, don't help him by filling in the silence. First, you don't want to put words in the subject's mouth, finishing his/her sentence. That's worse than asking leading questions. Second, you might lose the chance to get some great quotes. The halting indicates the subject is thinking, trying to come up with the right words. When the subject finds his words, what he/she reveals may be out of your expectation, stuff for great quotes.

4.2.5   Judging the usefulness of the answers

The information gathered from interviews will constitute the major part of the final story. So it might be wise to judge the usefulness of the answers given by the interviewing subject during the interview. That is to mentally edit the words of the interviewee into parts of the eventual article while talking still continues. The mental editing is trying to see where this or that piece of information could go in the final story. If you find that it goes nowhere, then maybe you should stop the line of questioning and turn to something more productive.

For example, as a precaution to curb the expansion of the COVID-19 pandemic, many people chose not to go back to their hometown but to stay where they had been working over the Spring Festival Holiday of 2021. Suppose you were doing a story on that. You noticed that many shops that used to close during the lunar new year festival chose to open this year to cash in on the sudden rise of foot traffic. You visited a few shops and interviewed several owners and some employees. They were all eager talking to you, enumerating their various promotion campaigns expecting the holiday customers. On hearing them talk, it gradually occurred to you that you'd interviewed enough shop owners and staff members and you needed to stop and talk to someone else. What they had been talking about on end amounted to one or two brief quotes most in the story and these quotes would play a supplementary role in the final story at best. Moreover, the information they provided sounded all very self-serving and must be severely sifted for the facts that would be useful to the readers. After this timely mental editing, you realized that what you really needed was to talk to people who chose to stay put. Their individual stories would play a central role in the final story.

With this real-time mental editing, you can avoid wasting time amassing insignificant trivialities. Moreover, this pondering over the possible draft in the back of mind will tell you whether and how the information is of service to the story. For example, suppose you were interviewing for a story on how a community dealt with its aging problem. You learned from your interviewee that the community got a yearly government grant designated for elderly care. The number which indicates the size of the grant was obviously meaningful. You might feel satisfied with this piece of information at first. However, if you had tried to see how this information would do in the final story, you would have soon realized that this number alone was far from enough. The scale of the government funded project could only be truly reflected by presenting the per capital funding for the community old. To calculate that, you needed to ask for the number of the elderly population of the community as well, which might be easily obtained while the interview was still ongoing.

Both of the above examples are to make the same point: reporting and writing are never two separate acts despite they appear to be different processes. Quite the opposite, they are one indivisible act. Only by truly understanding this can a reporter effectively tailor the interview to the needs of the story.

4.2.6　Taking notes

Various recording devices become increasingly popular for recording the interviews in place of the traditional notetaking. The advantage is obvious, the recording will guarantee complete accuracy of the interview and will allow the reporter to use the actual words said, cutting the risks of misrepresentation and libel. But a traditional notepad has its own advantage: the notetaking is a simultaneous editing process. In note-taking, a reporter usually would not take down every word of the subject. Usually what the reporter gets down is what has caught her attention, the important part after mentally filtering out the trivial. The interviewee's words become clear on paper, so do the gap in conversation and the confusing points. Spotting them, the reporter can ask for clarification in time. In addition, the interviewee's mannerism, physical appearance, reactions, and clothing can all be taken down. Compared with leaving everything to a recorder, the reporter who takes notes is kept on alert throughout the interview, analyzing while listening; sometimes the logic of the story will emerge from this conscious selecting process and the story takes shape from points taken down. Of course, not all interviews take place in a setting that allows the notetaking and sometimes a recording device might be the only choice. But remember for a set-piece interview using a recording device may prolong the interview into a long relaxed conversation and the transcription afterwards can take three times as long as the interview. You may wish you hadn't taped the interview, when faced with the task of transcribing it.

4.2.7 Asking the right questions

You should carefully structure your questions. In most cases, you may want to ask open-ended questions, that is, questions that cannot be answered with a simple "yes" or "no," or with a specific piece of information. Open-ended questions give the interviewing subject scope to give the information that seems to them to be appropriate. For example, you want to do a story on a new privacy law, the reception of which is rather mixed. In your interviews, instead of "Do you agree with the new privacy law?" try "What is your view of the criticism that the new privacy law lacks specific legal remedy for breaches of personal information?" That should get a discussion going easily. However, when you get a lengthy answer, stop and think about whether the readers will get it. Perhaps there's something unclear that needs to be clarified. In such a case, ask a closed-ended question, which will incur a brief answer and is used frequently for clarification.

Avoid "leading" questions if possible. Leading questions are those that prompt the answer you want, whether the prompting is in the words, the phrasing or the tone of voice. For example, questions like "Do you support garbage sorting, which will save the earth?" or "How do you view college students moonlighting which hurts their grades?" might not get you a real answer. You've already embedded your opinions in the questions. Sometimes, out of misguided politeness or for the sake of convenience, the interviewee may just agree with you without giving serious consideration. Rephrase the questions and keep clear of any preconceived notions. Ask instead, "Do you support garbage sorting, why?" "How do you view college students moonlighting?" As a journalist, you really shouldn't put words in people's mouth.

Loaded question, an informal fallacy or logical fallacy, should also be avoided. The logical fallacy is committed when someone asks a question that presupposes something that has not been proven or accepted by all the people involved. This fallacy is often used rhetorically, so that the question limits direct replies to be those that serve the questioner's agenda. For example, a famous loaded question runs: have you stopped beaten your wife? It's impossible to answer the question without being forced to admit the presupposition in the question — "you beat your wife". Treat your subject fairly and respectfully, don't trick him/her with loaded questions.

Intrusive questions. Sometimes the interview gets into sensitive territories and you may want to get from the subject a piece of privacy which you believe to be essential to the story. You may have to ask some intrusive questions. However, you will be surprised that there are not many intrusive questions in the work of top reporters. Intrusive questions often give rise to ethical concerns. It's best to avoid these. Try to stand in the shoes of your subject before you make your decision. And if you still conclude that the answers are indispensable, you need to get the subject's consent to talk about the more private issues before the interview starts.

4.2.8 Empathy, not sympathy

Empathy, simply put, is the capacity to put oneself in another's shoes. When conducting the personal interviews, the proper attitude for the reporter is empathy, not sympathy, especially when the interviewee has gone through some trauma or the interviewing topic is somehow sensitive. Comments such as: "Oh, how dreadful. You poor thing!" should be avoided. Never say "I understand what you have gone through" because you don't, not truly. Provide a safe space for an interviewee to share his or her story. Assume a neutral, open listening style and give regular, encouraging feedback. Give time for the person to gather their thoughts or master their emotions, if needed. Stop taking notes if the note-taking becomes oppressive for the interviewee and just listen. Let your human instincts guide you. Treat the interviewee as you would like to be treated.

In short， show respect and make sure that your questions are not insensitive. Yet at the same time be rigorous and not afraid to ask difficult questions. Also never be a sycophant to the interviewing subject，either. The goal of the interview is to gather information，and you are not there to impress or be impressed.

Exercise

1. The following story[①] from *Shanghai Daily* is about a national debate on "what it means to be a man in today's China." As the headline of the story suggests，the article presents multiple perspectives on the aesthetics of masculinity. Read the story carefully and underline all the quotes（direct or indirect）from all sources. Consider each source and think about why the source is chosen. Can you divide the sources into different categories? What are they? What roles does each category of sources play in the story? What are their relationships? Explain how each source contributes to the theme of the story respectively. Do you think there is/are a voice/voices missing? If so，what are they? Why?

Redefining what it means to be a man in today's China

Yao Minji

"Man up!" A Shanghai resident surnamed Chen，now in his 60s，knows all about that term.

As a boy with a "soprano" voice and a diminutive stature，he was ruthlessly ridiculed as a sissy by his middle school classmates in the 1960s. Last year，at a class reunion，he was still the butt of jokes about his effeminate qualities.

"The 'little girl' is now a man，" one of his former classmates said，explaining that he thought it would cheer Chen up.

Chen，offended，remained silent.

Now a grandfather，Chen often tells his 5-year-old grandson to "man

---

① Yao Minji. Redefining what it means to be a man in today's China [N/OL]. Shanghai Daily. (2021-02-09) [2021-08-16]. https://www.shine.cn/news/in-focus/2102094574/.

up" to avoid bullying.

"I don't think I was sissy in my adolescence," Chen told *Shanghai Daily*. "It was just the pitch of my voice. But I do think that some boys today are effeminate. They were brought up as single children and coddled. They need to man up."

Chen said he was surprised recently to see renewed national debate on masculinity and sissies, or niangniangqiang in Chinese.

Indeed, one online "influencer" has been publishing articles stating that he's the so-called niangniangqiang people criticize — denouncing the term and outdated gender stereotypes, and defending the right "not to be like a man."

The fierce debate online followed a proposal by Si Zefu, a member of the Chinese People's Consultative Conference. He issued a call to "prevent the feminization of young males" and said lily-livered teenage boys were a "threat to the development and survival of the nation."

The Ministry of Education responded by pledging to recruit more and better physical education teachers to whip young boys into shape.

Though many people agreed that children — of both sexes — needed more regular exercise, the words "feminization of male youth" stuck in the craw of many.

Many asked why "feminine" had suddenly become such a bad word.

Others agreed that some of today's boys lack masculinity.

One hashtag on the issue drew more than 1 billion views on Weibo.

The masculinity issue — in Chinese called yanggang zhi qi, or "spirit of yang" — clearly divides people.

One survey done by ifeng.com of about 2 million participants showed that more than half oppose the idea that "boys ought to have the spirit of yang." Another survey of over 120,000 showed that about half of people consider it necessary to cultivate that spirit as long as it is not framed in wording related to "feminization." A fourth of poll participants said Si's concerns were valid.

Then the debate became how to define "the spirit of yang."

State broadcaster China Central Television weighed in on Weibo, stating that "it is a beauty for men to show 'the spirit of yang' in presence, spirit and physique, but it shouldn't be simplified to mean 'muscular behavior'."

It added: "Education is not about cultivating 'men' or 'women,' but more about teaching kids to be proactive and responsible, civilized in spirit and strong in physique. The key is the healthy development of both physical and mental wellness."

Shen Yifei, an associated professor in sociology at Fudan University, wrote in a recent column on the topic.

"Many people think of effeminate men as weak with small statures," she commented. "But it's not their fault. It's in the genes. What's bad about that?"

She went on to write that it's important for men to be able to express their emotions, even to cry.

"What's so bad about getting men to forsake their fists and become more peaceful?" she asked "What's so bad about having men more considerate, compassionate and caring?"

Shen said many contemporary concepts about men stem from their Stone Age role as hunters and muscle-bound protectors — attributes somewhat outdated in modern life.

At the same time, today's women no longer need to adhere to the gender stereotype of caretakers and keepers of the hearth.

This isn't the first time that gender norms have bubbled to the surface of national debate.

In 2018, the term xiaoxianrou, or "little fresh meat" — generally referring to good-looking entertainers — drew criticism from media, academics, netizens, actors and directors.

" Little fresh meat " entertainers were often derided as niangniangqiang, for their heavy makeup, pierced ears and trendy hairstyles.

People's Daily, CCTV and various local TV stations criticized the popularity of the term "little fresh meat" and its toxic impact on teenage fans. But China Women's News, took a different stance.

In an article entitled "Respect for Diversified Aesthetics, Build Sunshine Spirit," the publication said diversified aesthetics are the side product of a safe, stable and prosperous society. It argued that well-to-do society should cultivate a civilization based on understanding, respect and inclusiveness. Instead of calling for masculinity, it called for an upbeat and healthy "sunshine spirit" for all genders.

Even earlier debates on the subject can be traced back to the 1970s and 80s, when Japanese superstar Ken Takakura became a national idol in

China for his brooding style and stoic presence. He became the symbol of manliness.

For a time, Chinese actors tried to emulate those traits. Handsome Chinese actor Tang Guoqiang, later best known for playing Chairman Mao in various TV and films, had suffered criticism as a "creamy boy" — a term similar to today's "little fresh meat."

Aesthetics changed as audiences became more inclusive and diversified.

In the 1990s, such "creamy boys" started to fill movie screens, though they fell short of Generation Z's "little fresh meat."

In the first decade of the 2000s, audiences again embraced "manly" actors like Zhang Hanyu and Wu Jing — tanned men with well-built muscles who played fighters or soldiers.

"Many people just naturally equate masculinity with the male hormone, but I don't agree," said 25-year-old Yang Jia, a native of Shanghai who works in the makeup industry, which is often considered a "feminine" job.

He works with photography studios, helping people project the image they want in photos. Male customers often ask Yang to use makeup and shadow effects to fake or highlight muscles. Others want to look "civilized and metrosexual."

"Shanghai men are often considered by others in China to be less masculine," Yang said. "We cook at home and we are often deferential to girlfriends or wives. I check all the boxes on that list, and I'm proud of it."

Yang has four ear piercings, shapes his eyebrows, polishes his nails and still considers himself masculine. Some friends, both men and women, tease him about being a sissy. Others consider him "metrosexual," a term coined in 1994 to describe men who are meticulous about grooming and appearance.

"It's not in the appearance or behavior," Yang argued. "We are more inclusive and diverse, compared with older generations. There are traditional gender norms, but there is also traditional Chinese culture that advocates a balance of yin and yang. I interpret that to mean you are a better man with some female characteristics."

Referring to China's legendary woman warrior, he added, "Think of Mulan. We all love her, don't we?"

Source: SHINE　Editor: Liu Qi

2. Nostalgic accuracy

Interview four to five people in their 40s or 50s and ask for what the year 2000 was like in their memories. Write a short passage (500 words) in third person reconstructing the year 2000 based on the interview results. And bring your passage to class for discussion.

4.3　After the interview

When the interview is over and you have seen the interviewee off, it's time for you to deal with the information gathered.

4.3.1　Organizing the notes

If you have taken notes, fill in the blanks and complete the incomplete sentences while the talk is still fresh in your memory. It is advisable that you type out the notes on a computer as soon as you've got the chance, for the notes on the notepad might be illegible or become so with the time lapse. Try to finish the task within the same day. As you are editing the notes, make sure you understand them completely. If not, call your interviewing subject to clarify.

If you have used a recording device, you are faced with the transcribing. However well-controlled an interview is, talk is more rambling and repetitive than printed material. This is something more conspicuous to the eye than to the ear. So when you deal with the transcription, squeeze out all the "water". But be careful, when doing so, not to distort. Recap the watery part you want to remove in a few sentences if they are needed for context. Check over the phone with your subject if you think there may be any danger of misrepresentation in the editing.

It is advisable to identify and space out quoted pieces, indirect speech pieces, background pieces in a satisfactory pattern. This division will help you think clearly about both the quotes and the story. The quoted pieces are the most colorful, selected for the punch packed in the words. The indirect speech pieces are chosen for their explanatory values. They describe and interpret what happened for the readers. The background pieces may serve as contextual information combined with results from further digging.

4.3.2 Faithful translation

Don't hype or sensationalize what the subject said. It's unethical and borders on fabrication. Treat the subject's words with respect and keep them as original as possible. There is a problem unique to reporting China in English: most of the interviews are done in Chinese, sometimes even in local dialect. Proper translation from Chinese to English is needed when writing the story. Proper translation means, first and foremost, faithful translation. The source "stays in character" when his/her words are translated from the mother tongue to the foreign language. How to do that? Use simple and direct language in translation. Avoid big words and flowery language. The goal is accuracy, not attractiveness of the speech. In translation, it is so much the better if you can preserve the original flavor of the speech. But that demands a higher level of language skills. Most times, preserving the original meanings of the sources' words will do. Incidentally, experienced writers also suggest two similar standards in playing the quotes: Brevity and fair play. Brevity means you should clean up the language in translation as the best you can. Fair play means you must not distort the meaning of the original words in translation or take them out of their context.

4.3.3 A selecting process

One common beginner's mistake is to put quotes in successive paragraphs. The novice journalist doesn't want to waste a single bit of effort spent and puts everything gathered from interviews into the final story. The result is not a real story, but a piling of materials in the form of quotes. What lacks is the logic underlying any readable story, which is formed in a selecting process. When studying the words from the sources and selecting and deciding which go where, you are actually organizing the story in your head. The conscious decision of which quote to be kept and which to be discarded is based on logic, the seemingly intangible string of choices and judgments that tie the story together. So you need to hit a balance between your narration and the quotes in a story. Quotes are essential and breath life into the story, but only the punchy ones can do that. You may find that much of what the subject has said is boring, irrelevant and repetitive. Get rid of the dreary part and only save the most important and colorful.

4.3.4   Hesitant and broken speech

Not every interviewing subject is an eloquent speaker. In fact, most people confronted with a reporter and the accompanying camera tend to get nervous and stumble. The resulting speech may be hesitant, broken, and disorganized. When transcribing and editing the notes, the reporter needs to provide the missing parts and string the words together into a coherent sentence. But do this with caution. Keep the original meaning intact. Add only what's absolutely necessary.

The interviewing subject may have an accent or speak in a local dialect. When this happens, it is advisable to indicate a person's accent or the dialect at the start if it helps to build the character. However, the quotes should be as clear as possible. Clarity prevails over any other concerns.

Exercise

"Man on the street" interview

"Man on the street" interviews are conducted to get fresh, unscripted reactions from the public on a certain topic. The idea is to generate a representative sample of public opinion on the topic under investigation. Sometimes these interviews are conducted live for a television news program; sometimes these interviews are conducted for gathering information for a newspaper story. It is hard to interview random people on the street. People are naturally suspicious of approaching strangers. They may feel harassed and unwilling to talk. So approach the potential interviewees in a respectful manner. Ethical conduct means you should identify yourself and tell them about your story and ask them politely if they would like to participate. If they refuse, thank them and move on. If they agree, then begin, but with easy questions. You may scare them away by starting with pointed questions right away. In addition, you need to make it clear to the interviewee that they're entering the public record, and address any concerns they may have. Once the interview begins, be patient and give your subject time to respond. If they stray too far, try redirect. In addition, it is important to note that man-on-the-street interviews are designed to get a diverse representative sample of public opinion.

Avoid places where opinions may be homogeneous. Pick a venue used by a lot of different people，such as a public park or a shopping mall. You should never let preconceived notions or personal biases affect your random sampling. Be generous and willing to talk with anyone who wants to talk. At the same time，if you realize you've only interviewed a certain demographic，such as middle-aged women who do square dance，make an effort to talk to people of a different age，gender and even ethnicity. Interview the most diverse sample of people you can.

Now give yourself 30 minutes and go out and interview as many people on the street as you can on the topic：what you learned from attending kindergarten. You must identify yourself as a student reporter and don't misrepresent yourself. And it is advisable to get the name，age，occupation and contact information of the interviewee at the end of the interview. After the 30 minutes of street interviews，organize your notes and see whether any common theme can be discerned from the notes? For example，what did they learn from life at kindergarten? Are what they learned values or knowledge? Moreover，single out at least three quotes that you believe to be important and explain your choice.

Chapter 5   Writing The Feature Lead

Generally speaking, lead is the first sentence or paragraph. It "tells the story." A lead often stands on its own, that is, it gives a complete account of the event that is accurate in every way, without need for further clarification. The account is not only complete but also concise, summing up a story in one sentence or two. The obvious example is a summary lead for a news story, which tells the story, the who, what, where, when and why, in a clear and brief paragraph.

In comparison, the lead of a feature story more often than not deviates from the 5W formula. Instead of summing up the story at the very beginning, a feature lead **sets up** the story. This is usually done by carefully describing a scene, using an illustrative anecdote, focusing on a specific item, showing a contrast, or presenting some strange fact. There are a million ways to open a feature story. Regardless of which method is used, the function of the feature story lead is similar. The opening paragraphs are meant to set the tone of the story, capture and encapsulate the mood of the story, and promise what's to come. This usually requires more space than just a single sentence or a succinct paragraph. This is not to say that single-paragraph leads are rare in feature writing, just that many feature leads can have several paragraphs, building suspense and unfolding slowly, as the feature writer is allowed more creative space.

It goes without saying that lead is crucially important. There ought to be at least some minor fireworks going off at the outset of a story. A good story won't get read unless it manages to capture the reader's imagination immediately. It is based on the lead that the reader makes the decision whether to continue reading the story. All serious writers work hard to fashion the lead first. The efforts are well spent. A well-crafted lead helps the writer to focus the story. Once the right lead is in place, the rest of the story will follow.

5.1   Opening with an example

Many feature stories open with an example of what is to follow. It could be an actual anecdote that illustrates the main point, a piece of description that sums up the mood the story, or even a quotation or question that conveys the main message. Whatever the specific shape, the lead should be able to illustrate the main section of the story.

5.1.1　An illustrative anecdote

For example, the following lead, taken from the Sixth Tone story — How Wuhan Cared for Pandemic's 'Temporary Orphans[①]', contains a mini-story where social worker Li Ren left her own son and went to care for Yiyi, a small girl left alone because her parents were ill with COVID-19 and her grandmother died of the contagious disease. The lead runs several paragraphs but is self-contained as the anecdote recounted is complete.

> HUBEI, Central China — When social worker Li Ren told her son she'd be going on a monthlong business trip, it was the biggest **lie** she'd ever told him.
>
> In **truth**, Li was volunteering to enter a quarantine center in Wuhan, the city in Hubei province where China's COVID-19 outbreak began, so she could accompany a 4-year-old daughter of hospitalized coronavirus patients. "Her grandmother died of the disease, and both of her parents were ill," Li tells Sixth Tone. "Nobody in the family was able to look after her."
>
> On Feb. 19, Li received a call from a local government officer asking her to help out. The girl's mother, who hadn't immediately been admitted to the hospital because she only had mild symptoms, received word that a bed had become available. And so Li, after convincing her husband this was the right thing to do, set out into the cold and quiet night to pick up the girl, Yiyi — a pseudonym to protect her privacy.
>
> When Li met Yiyi, she was timid, with her hair in a ponytail and her eyes red from crying. It was close to dawn when the two arrived at a hotel-turned-quarantine center and were given a room on the seventh floor, which housed six more children — ages 4 to 17 — who were all in the same situation as Yiyi.

---

① Yuan Ye and Wang Lianzhang. How Wuhan Cared for Pandemic's 'Temporary Orphans'[EB/OL]. The Sixth Tone.（2020-04-27）[2021-08-04]. http://www.sixthtone.com/news/1005559/how-wuhan-cared-for-pandemics-temporary-orphans.

The lead begins by a clever play of a pair of contrasting words: lie and truth, and thus smoothly connects the life of the volunteer with that of "the temporary orphan." The story of the social worker and the small girl succinctly told in the lead foretells what is to come: volunteers helping thousands of moms and dads sick or quarantined in the stricken city. Take note of the fourth paragraph where we understand that the small girl named Yiyi is not the only child temporarily orphaned by the terrible disease. This is a crucial linking paragraph that helps make the transition from the lead to the rest of the story. Thus, the anecdote in the lead is like a close-up shot giving the readers a vivid image in details. Then, by zooming out, the story allows the readers to see the big picture: there were more children involved in the same situation. Later, in the body, as the story goes on, more information, details, and context are provided.

Anecdotal leads such as the one above are probably the most common in feature writing. The success of this type of lead depends on the anecdote itself. It must be compact, able to stand alone. It ought to be interesting, drawing the readers in. It needs to be illustrative, a harbinger of what is to follow. The following lead meets all three requirements. It is condensed, introducing the heroine (of the lead) and narrating her story all in 95 words. It is funny, depicting a young intern making an innocent yet hilarious mistake. It is representative, the harmless stumble speaking volume of the theme of the story: if journalism is something that can only get better by doing, why attend school for it? Later, the story[1] by Teresa Méndez introduces more examples, facts, and opinions to give a current panorama of the eternal debate on the necessity of the journalism school.

Heather Saucier learned the lesson of the "nut graf" the hard way. (In journalism jargon, the "nut graf" is a paragraph near the top of a story that concisely lays out its thesis.)

Ms. Saucier was still in college, working as an intern for the now-defunct Houston Post. She filed a piece on the city's troublesome squirrel population. The story was fine, her editor said, "But you're missing a nut graf."

She'd already written about squirrels chewing through telephone wires

---

① Teresa Méndez. Journalism students ask: Why am I here? [N/OL] Christian Science Monitor. (2004-10-26) [2019-03-01]. http://www.csmonitor.com/2004/1026/p12s01-legn.html.

and gnawing on wood, so she dashed off a short paragraph about their diet: nuts.

Example lead is so popular that sometimes when a real anecdote is nowhere to be found, a hypothetical one is used. Like the following one.

We all know that guy, let's call him David, whose smartphone battery is always perilously on the brink of being dead. He'll ask you to hold on for 20 minutes while he charges and later bug the waiter to see if there's an outlet behind the bar. He just needs a little juice before heading to the next spot. "That cool?" he asks as the table collectively rolls their eyes.

This lead containing the hypothetical anecdote is from a story[1] on new charging technology by Joshua Fruhlinger. Battery problem is a universal problem for smartphone users and it is the commonality of the problem that makes a hypothetical situation like the above one reasonable. The "David" in the lead could be anyone.

One more advantage of anecdotal lead is that by placing such a mini story (even a hypothetical one) at the very beginning of the feature story, the reader is shown, not told, what the story is going to be. This is in perfect sync with the golden rule of feature writing: "Show, don't tell." The "temporary orphan" Yiyi in the Sixth Tone story is not just a stick figure symbol, but a frightened little girl "with her hair in a ponytail and her eyes red from crying." Learning by doing is a trite conception, and nut graf is a journalese jargon, both of which were made interestingly accessible by the narration of the young intern's slip in the J-school story. The phone battery headache is common, but rendered freshly concrete by the description of finding a charging outlet familiar to all smartphone users.

5.1.2　An opening scene

Apart from anecdotes, a piece of description is often used at the beginning of a story to put the story in the right mood. Journalist Susan Faludi opens her

---

[1]　Joshua Fruhlinger. You may never have to plug in your smartphone again[J]. Wall Street Journal. (2018-05-31) [2021-08-18]. https://www. wsj. com/articles/you-may-never-have-to-plug-in-your-smartphone-again-1527776901.

highly critical story[1] on Facebook's Sheryl Sandberg and the Lean-in movement she champions by a detailed description of a scene from one of the movement's conventions. The scene described in the lead is enveloped in a fervid ambience: the speaker, Facebook's Sheryl Sandberg, was sketched as sleek, successful, energetic, and demagogic while the followers of the movement fanned, feverish, agitated and brainwashed. In setting up the scene, an analogy is drawn between a meeting in a university auditorium and a religious service held in a church. Words such as congregation, prophet and hymn are used to refer to the audience, the speaker and the speaker's new book on the Lean-in movement. With more religiously charged terms such as "tent revival" and "pearly gates", the metaphors running through the three-part introduction reproduced the cult-like fervor in the audience, a symptom of this particular, corporatized thinking about feminism.

> The congregation swooned as she bounded on stage, the prophet sealskin sleek in her black skinny ankle pants and black ballet flats, a lavalier microphone clipped to the V-neck of her black button-down sweater. "All right!! Let's go!!" she exclaimed, throwing out her arms and pacing the platform before inspirational graphics of glossy young businesswomen in managerial action poses. "Super excited to have all of you here!!"
>
> "Whoo!!" the young women in the audience replied. The camera, which was livestreaming the event in the Menlo Park, California, auditorium to college campuses worldwide, panned the rows of well-heeled Stanford University econ majors and MBA candidates. Some clutched copies of the day's hymnal: the speaker's new book, which promised to dismantle "internal obstacles" preventing them from "acquiring power." The atmosphere was TED-Talk-cum-tent-revival-cum-Mary-Kay-cosmetics-convention.   The salvation these adherents sought on this April day in 2013 was admittance to the pearly gates of the corporate corner office.

The key to recreate a scene in the lead lies in the demonstrativeness of the scene. For example, the following opening paragraph from a business feature[2]

---

[1]   Susan Faludi. Facebook Feminism, Like It or Not [EB/OL]. The Baffler. (2013-08-23) [2021-08-18]. https://thebaffler.com/salvos/facebook-feminism-like-it-or-not.

[2]   John Gravois. A toast Story[EB/OL]. Pacific Standard. (2014-01-13) [2021-08-04]. https://longform. org/posts/a-toast-story.

on a piece of artisanal toast focuses on a scene that portends what is to come in the rest of the story. The paragraph goes:

> All the guy doing was slicing inch-thick pieces of bread, putting them in a toaster, and spreading stuff on them. But what made me stare — blinking to attention in the middle of a workday morning as I waited in line at an unfamiliar café — was the way he did it. He had the solemn intensity of a Ping-Pong player who keeps his game very close to the table: knees slightly bent, wrist flicking the butter knife back and forth, eyes suggesting a kind of flow state.

Food that's gone viral online or anything that's gone viral online has become an increasingly run-of-the-mill subject nowadays. However, John Gravois's story about a viral piece of bread takes a fresh approach. It doesn't focus on how the three-dollar-a-piece artisanal toast becomes an overnight sensation. Nor does it denounce the outrageous price by showing how ordinary the toast actually is. Instead, the story starts by showing a person in action, cutting up bread and making toast. From the very beginning, we understand this is a story not about the food, but about humanity.

Here's another feature story that starts with a telling scene. The Sixth Tone story titled "The Latest Front in China's Battle for School Places: Gym Class" by Ni Dandan explores the new change in China's education policy emphasizing PE lessons[1]. The story starts with a swimming scene which is created mainly by a reconstruction of the anxious conversation between a parent and the swimming coach with the coached child splashing away in the pool. The conversation says much about what the impending change means for the young students.

> At a steamy indoor swimming pool in Pudong New Area, Qiu Chenchen checks her stopwatch and frowns.
> "Don't let your legs go floppy, kick them hard!" the coach shouts at the child splashing in the water next to her. "Go faster!"
> The student, Panpan, gamely finishes his length, but Qiu is dissatisfied with the 10-year-old's time of 27 seconds. "You weren't giving your best

---

① Ni Dandan. The Latest Front in China's Battle for School Places: Gym Class[EB/OL]. The Sixth Tone. (2021-02-05) [2021-08-04]. https://www. sixthtone. com/news/1006802/the-latest-front-in-chinas-battle-for-school-places-gym-class.

effort," she says sternly. "Take a break and let's do it one more time."

Panpan's mother, who has been watching the lesson from a nearby bench, approaches with an anxious expression. "How did he do?" she asks. "He isn't concentrating enough, is he?"

"Not good enough for him," Qiu replies. "He should at least complete this distance within 25 seconds." Panpan gazes down at the water sheepishly.

"We'll urge him to practice kicking his legs better at home," the mother assures Qiu.

The coach, however, continues to explain the consequences if Panpan fails to improve his lap times. In four years, the boy is due to take the zhongkao — China's all-important high school enrollment exams.

"This pool is just 20 meters long," says Qiu. "The standard short-distance swimming test in the zhongkao is 25 meters. And to get a full score, you need to finish within 25 seconds."

As the above examples show, feature lead, often descriptive and full of details, strives to give the readers a flavor of the following story. Thus the readers can judge for themselves if they want to continue to read or not. However, such illustrative materials are valuable and hard to come by. So much thought should be given to crafting the lead even at the early stages of reporting. Always keep an eye out for that example that embodies the whole story.

5.2   Providing facts

To grab the reader's attention, lead must dazzle. Feature leads are usually highly descriptive, full of telling details. The idea is to catch the eye busy with everything vying for attention in the information-overloading age. But that is far from enough. A very important but often forgotten rule for lead writing is the lead must contain solid information. After the stunning opening lines, the lead must do some real work as more thought is given to providing information than simply enticing. However, this doesn't mean that being descriptive is at odds with being informative. On the contrary, good description is inherently informative. Good feature leads are usually both attractive and meaty. The information is often provided through descriptive details.

Look at the following lead from Rick Bragg's feature article[①] on an old black woman who donates her lifesavings to a university and see how information is provided through description. In the first paragraph we know the name of the subject, her age and her way of making a living. In the second paragraph, we get to know where the subject came from and her work history and her views on work. In the third paragraph, we get to know the important fact embedded in the news peg. The black washer has lived a frugal life and has amassed a saving amounting to ＄150,000 which we understand from the rest of the story that she donates to a college.

> Oseola McCarty spent a lifetime making other people look nice. Day after day, for most of her 87 years, she took in bundles of dirty clothes and made them clean and neat for parties she never attended, weddings to which she was never invited, graduations she never saw.
>
> She had quit school in the sixth grade to go to work, never married, never had children and never learned to drive because there was never any place in particular she wanted to go. All she ever had was the work, which she saw as a blessing. Too many other black people in rural Mississippi did not have even that.
>
> She spent almost nothing, living in her old family home, cutting the toes out of shoes if they did not fit right and binding her ragged Bible with Scotch tape to keep Corinthians from falling out. Over the decades, her pay — mostly dollar bills and change — grew to more than ＄150,000.

As the above lead shows, good description is as revealing as it is entertaining. Similarly, a competent anecdotal introduction should also provide a wealth of information. There are many such examples. The Sixth Tone story titled "Bilibili vs. Bilibili: The Culture Clash Dividing China's YouTube"[②] delineates the internally-conflicted development of the video platform from a niche anime fan site to a mainstream video site targeting China's Generation Z as a whole. The story starts with a typical anecdotal lead depicting one early

---

① Rick Bragg. All She Has, ＄150,000, Is Going to a University[N/OL]. New York Times. (1995-08-03) [2018-10-09]. https://www.nytimes.com/1995/08/13/us/all-she-has-150000-is-going-to-a-university. html.

② Liu Siqi and Kenrick Davis. Bilibili vs. Bilibili: The Culture Clash Dividing China's YouTube[EB/OL]. The Sixth Tone. (2020-08-07) [2021-08-04]. http://www.sixthtone.com/news/1006027/bilibili-vs.-bilibili-the-culture-clash-dividing-chinas-youtube.

user and her story with the site. Take a look at the following lead, and see how the life example contained is as illustrative as informative.

> When Qin Yuzi was in high school in 2015, her happiest time of the week was when she'd binge-watch anime, gaming videos, and music mashups on video site Bilibili Sunday afternoons.
>
> Despite being alone, Qin felt like she was part of a tight-knit group of friends on the platform. As she watched, witty and endearing comments from other users would glide across the screen — a function called danmu, or "bullet screen comments."
>
> "They were what attracted me to Bilibili the most," the 22-year-old tells Sixth Tone. "Everyone commented using our own lingo and inside jokes."
>
> The niche website — which was then mostly dedicated to Anime, Comic, and Games (ACG) content — became a safe space for Qin. The native of Guangzhou in southern China made friends with 70 other ACG fans through Bilibili, with whom she'd chat and play games.
>
> Today, however, the platform feels almost unrecognizable to her.

This neat story at the beginning of the article tells as much about Bilibili the website as Qin the early user. Through Qin's experience with the site, we understand why the site is a niche one and what the site was like at its budding stage. Such key features of Bilibili as ACG contents, Danmu and the clannish atmosphere of a close-knit user community are all introduced in the first three paragraphs. In addition, the last line, which brings the website to its present-day development, serves as the link between the lead and the body of the story.

5.3 Continuing to build

Good lead is both self-contained and an integral part of the story. A well-written introduction always ends in such a way that the introductory part merges naturally into the rest of the story. Sometimes a green writer makes the mistake of forgetting about this and the result is some form of false advertising with a lead that has little to do with the main story or that has little bearing on the main section of the story. So a feature lead must be highly relevant to the theme of the story. The anecdote chosen, the scene picked to describe, the symbolic specific item, all must illustrate the following story in some way. Thus it is possible for the lead to blend effortlessly into the body of the story. Remember this even in the reporting stage. Sometimes you may run into a funny story or some odd fact that you believe would make a good lead. However, make sure that this story or the fact is pertinent to the theme of the story. If not, however funny or surprising, it has no place in your story.

The fact that lead is an integral part of the story also means that a feature article is a cohesive whole with each paragraph built on the previous one and each paragraph substantiating the prior one by way of explanation, exposition or description. The famous dramatic theory applies here, the so-called "Chekhov's gun", that if you say in the first chapter that there is a rifle hanging on the wall, then in the second or third chapter it absolutely must go off. If it wasn't going to fire, it shouldn't be hanging there. You should therefore be more careful about continuing to build the story after a carefully crafted lead. The promise in the introduction must be fulfilled in the rest of the story. The shots must ring out. In fact, the opening section of a feature story often consists of a lead, a connecting paragraph (sometimes just one line or half a sentence), a nut graf (the theme statement) and the following background paragraph. It is so structured because the logic of the story requires it: the lead draws the reader in, the connecting paragraph acts as a transition, a nut graf tells the reader what the story is about, and then the background paragraph provides the big picture, putting the story in context. Each paragraph gives rise to the next, and each paragraph amplifies the previous one. The writing is therefore continuous, with each paragraph contributing to the whole.

The following opening part is taken from a Sixth Tone story[1] titled "China's Hidden Crisis: A Growing Elder Care Gap", which focuses on the crisis of the needs of elder care not met. The anecdotal lead, consisting of the first four paragraphs, homes in on one family troubled by poor elder care. The last line of the lead, saying the problem is prevalent in Shanghai, connects the lead with the nut graf, the fifth paragraph, which sums up the core issue in a nutshell. Then the sixth and seventh paragraphs put the story in context by providing the background information: with the rising percentage of the elder population in China, the problem the story delves in is real and pressing.

SHANGHAI — Huang Ernan knows the live-in caretaker she hires to

---

[1] Ni Dandan. China's Hidden Crisis: A Growing Elder Care Gap [EB/OL]. The Sixth Tone. (2020-08-18) [2021-08-04]. https://www.sixthtone.com/news/1006061/chinas-hidden-crisis-a-growing-elder-care-gap.

look after her elderly mother isn't really up to the job.

At 73 years old, the woman is only a few years younger than Huang's mother, who is 85. And she often lacks the focus required to provide good care to a patient who has suffered multiple strokes over recent years.

On one occasion, the caretaker left the house without locking the door, allowing Huang's mother to wander off down the street. Other times, she failed to help her client after she'd wet the bed — an issue that became so common, Huang eventually started buying her mother adult diapers.

Huang, however, has no intention of firing the woman. In her home city of Shanghai, finding a replacement would be far from easy.

The eastern metropolis is ground zero for China's elder care crisis, offering a glimpse into the pressures that could impact other cities as the country's population rapidly ages.

By 2050, one-third of China's citizens will be aged 60 or over — a demographic transformation that threatens to create deep social and economic challenges.

But in Shanghai, the future has already arrived: The country's most elderly megacity has 5.2　million residents aged over 60 — over 35% of the registered population.

Of course, not all feature stories open like this, and should not. The key word is relevance as the lead is an organic part of the whole story. Also pay special attention to the ending line of the lead which often serves as the bridge that connects the lead with the rest of the story.

5.4 Keeping it simple

Leonardo da Vinci says, "Simplicity is the ultimate sophistication." "Simple can be harder than complex: You have to work hard to get your thinking clean to make it simple," observes Steve Jobs. These quotations make a lot of sense. Indeed, simple language is difficult to attain. Simplicity in language results from clarity in thinking. Good feature lead is always simple ones. The deceptive simplicity stems from a great amount of chewing upon the issue at hand and much fussing over which details to go where. The reason why feature lead must be simple is twofold.

Firstly, simple writing is the best kind of writing. Writing is as fundamentally a means of communication as a form of expression. The writer is obligated not to burden the reader with obtuse script and excessive sentiments. Simplicity is a necessity rather than a choice of writing style. Needless to say, simple, neither too little nor too much, is not simplistic. It means lean unpretentious language, every word carefully chosen and serving its unique purpose, the syntax and grammar all in place.

Secondly, simple lead is easy to understand and less daunting a task for readers today who seem to suffer universally from the great hurry that is called life and thus are most of the time inconveniently impatient. For that reason, the illustrating example chosen for the lead should be simple itself, something that only takes a few lines to narrate in full. The more complicated examples should be saved for the main body of the story where the thorny issues could be explained at more leisure. Moreover, long convoluted details like long names of places or complex addresses or cumbersome titles should ideally be left out of the lead unless it is absolutely necessary for them to appear at the very beginning of the story.

Though leads strewed with a lot of figures will lose the readers for difficulty in comprehension, this is not a flat rule. Sometimes, especially used in contrast, numbers will make the lead. The following lead contains one number showing the contrast that piques the readers' curiosity.

> A statue of Han Yu, a writer, poet and official who was banished because of his offensive speeches to an emperor of Tang Dynasty, sits side by side with a statue of Guan Yu, a general known for loyalty and righteousness in the late Eastern Han Dynasty and **six centuries** older than Han.

Another example of effective use of numbers showing contrast in lead can be seen from the Sixth Tone story on scarcity of good elder care in Shanghai, which is cited in the previous section. In that lead, two numbers are given, both age indicators: a 73-year-old woman is hired to care for an 85-year-old stroke patient. From these two figures alone, we get immediately the seriousness of the issue at heart of the story.

The following lead is an another example of simplicity in lead writing. The short opening focuses in succinct language on the superfast growing of this Chinese skateboarder at the Tokyo Olympics from a layperson to a professional sportswoman. The brevity of the time she spent in growing into an Olympics athlete is key to illustrate the theme of the story① which discusses the development and training of professional skateboarders for Olympics in China.

> Just four years ago, Zhang Xin was a trainee cheerleader who had never ridden a skateboard. Now, she's preparing to skate for China at the Tokyo Olympics.

As the above examples show, a simple lead is also a focused lead. In observing the "keep it simple" command, irrelevant trivialities are pruned away. The result is a condensed introduction in brief language. In addition, a feature lead is essentially a mini-story itself and like any other well-told stories, it must contain only one point. You can't do everything in the lead. A lead will only put the readers at a loss with a bit of everything thrown in. Readers need to see from the lead where the story is going and a mixture of unsorted information will point to all directions or none. If that happens, in all probability, the reader will give up reading, which means not only the lead but also the story has failed.

5.5 Capturing the reader's attention

5.5.1 Playing a twist on the reader's expectation

A feature lead must grab the reader's attention. But what might be of interest to the reader? What will strike the reader's fancy? Generally speaking, people love surprises in reading, being delighted by the thrill of encountering an unexpected turn of events. If you start off with a twist on the reader's expectation, you will surprise the reader into attention.

Take the following lead from a story② on livestreaming study.

> The video opens with medical student Jamie Lee at her desk, working on a computer and writing in a notebook. In the eighth minute, she pulls her hair

---

① Du Xinyu and Wu Yurui. Team China Aims to Conquer an Unfamiliar New Sport: Skateboarding[EB/OL]. The Sixth Tone. (2021-07-23) [2021-08-05]. https://www.sixthtone.com/news/1008029/team-china-aims-to-conquer-an-unfamiliar-new-sport-skateboarding.

② Hilary Potkewitz. Quiet! I'm Cramming for Finals —By Watching Some Else Study[N/OL]. Wall Street Journal. (2018-06-03) [2021-08-04]. https://www.wsj.com/articles/quiet-im-cramming-for-finalsby-watching-someone-else-study-1528045886.

up into a ponytail. At 11:20, she adjusts her glasses. She says nothing. She doesn't leave her seat. She never looks at the camera. This 53 minutes of footage has been watched almost 500,000 times.

As the school year comes to a close, lots of students are cramming for finals. Some are doing it on camera.

A student cramming for test is commonplace. Doing it on tape? A bit unusual, but still not interesting to an Internet-jaded audience. A reader's expectation may be this is just another campus story of the exam season. But at the end of the leading paragraph, it reveals that the student is being watched half a million times, a figure indicating that she is probably making money from it. That's something unexpected. This twist on the reader's expectation will delight the reader and get his/her attention.

Readers love being surprised. But how to find the surprising details? Sometimes the answer appears to be serendipitous. Take this beginning from a travel story① on road signs.

There I was, cycling slowly up a country road in northern Norway, dazzled by the gorgeous scenery, when I came across a curious sign.

I stopped and stared.

"Farts dampere," it said. There was even a little pictorial graphic to indicate the municipal traffic regulation to which the words obviously referred.

"No damp farts allowed?" I wondered.

I could easily understand that sanitary suggestion, useful virtually anywhere in the world, although not necessarily in the great outdoors. I was wrong, of course. I cycled further up the valley and came across several more of the same signs and it soon became apparent they referred to what we call speed bumps at home.

Nothing to do with noxious or gaseous indiscretions.

This is a light-hearted story on strange road signs, the meaning of which sometimes lost in translation. It starts and captures readers' attention with an odd fact that the writer has discovered when travelling along the road. Oddity, or strangeness, is innately interesting and will pique the reader's curiosity. It is

---

① Michael McCarthy. Not necessarily signs of the times; Laughing Matter; Messages on roadways and businesses don't always mean what the authors intended [N]. the Province. 2015-01-03.

something writers always look out for. Sometimes it is pure luck that a writer stumbles upon something curious. But more often than not, luck favors the observant, the one with the eye for details. Learn to look for your material everywhere, especially the things other people might overlook. If some odd fact or a novel detail surprises or delights you, it might work the same wonder on the reader.

Sometimes even the obvious might be the stunning piece that puts the lead right. Look at the following opening paragraphs from Alice Steinbach's Pulitzer Prize-winning story[1] on a blind boy.

> First, the eyes: They are large and blue, a light, opaque blue, the color of a robin's egg. And if, on a sunny spring day, you look straight into these eyes—eyes that cannot look back at you—the sharp, April light turns them pale, like the thin blue of a high, cloudless sky.
>
> Ten-year-old Calvin Stanley, the owner of these eyes and a boy who has been blind since birth, likes this description and asks to hear it twice. He listens as only he can listen, then: "Orange used to be my favorite color but now it's blue," he announces. Pause. The eyes flutter between the short, thick lashes, "I know there's light blue and there's dark blue, but what does sky-blue look like?" he wants to know. And if you watch his face as he listens to your description, you get a sense of a picture being clicked firmly into place behind the pale eyes.
>
> He is a boy who has a lot of pictures stored in his head, retrievable images which have been fashioned for him by the people who love him—by family and friends and teachers who have painstakingly and patiently gone about creating a special world for Calvin's inner eye to inhabit.
>
> Picture of a rainbow: "It's a lot of beautiful colors, one next to the other. Shaped like a bow. In the sky. Right across."
>
> Picture of lightning, which frightens Calvin: "My mother says lightning looks like a Christmas tree—the way it blinks on and off across the sky," he says, offering a comforting description that would make a poet proud.
>
> "Child," his mother once told him, "one day I won't be here and I won't be around to pick you up when you fall—nobody will be around all the time to pick you up—so you have to try to be something on your own. You have to

---

[1] Alice Steinbach. A boy of unusual vision [N/OL]. Baltimore Sun. (1984-05) [2016-04-25]. https://longform.org/posts/a-boy-of-unusual-vision.

learn how to deal with this. And to do that, you have to learn how to think."

This lead starts with and revolves around the blind boy's sightless eyes, and is very well described throughout. The lead is structured in such way that it only gradually dawns on the reader that the eyes, the blueness of which is heartbrokenly beautiful, actually can't see at all, but merely decorative. This contrast and unexpectedness make the lead intense and strong. In addition, these tightly-written leading paragraphs have a natural flow that reflects the compactness of this highly focused lead.

5.5.2 Action sells

One stunt the feature writer can borrow from fiction writing is the action opening. Also known as a "narrative hook," it places the reader at the center of a dramatic situation. The notion can be traced back to Horace, whose edict suggests starting "in medias res," and going straight "into the middle of things."

Take the following leading paragraphs from a 5842-word story[①] by David Kushner from *Rolling Stone* on the man that started the so-called dark net.

On October 1, 2013, inside the science-fiction section of the Glen Park library in San Francisco, one of the Internet's most-wanted man sat typing quietly on his laptop. He'd allegedly assumed multiple identities and made nearly half a billion dollars in under three years. He was said to be as grandiose as he was cold-blooded, championing freedom while ordering hits on those who crossed him.

None of the geeks milling around the stacks that day, nor even those closest to Ross Ulbricht, suspected that the slightly pale twenty-nine-year-old was, according to prosecutors, the notorious hacker known as Dread Pirate Roberts. He was allegedly the founder of Dark Net, an online illegal-goods bazaar that had been dubbed the eBay of vice. A Texas Native with a master's in materials science and engineering and a mop of brown hair, Ulbricht bore such resemblance to Robert Pattinson that girls stopped him in the street to take their picture with him. The library was near where he had been living

---

① David Kushner. Dead End on Silk Road: Internet Crime Kingpin Ross Ulbricht's Big Fall. Rolling Stone[EB/OL]. (2014-02-04) [2021-08-05]. https://www. rollingstone. com/culture/culture-news/dead-end-on-silk-road-internet-crime-kingpin-ross-ulbrichts-big-fall-122158/.

since moving to the city a year earlier. He liked to come here for the silence and the free wifi.

But at three-fifteen p.m., the quiet was broken when, out of nowhere, a young woman in street clothes **charged** toward Ulbricht **yelling**, "I'm so sick of you!" and **grabbed** his laptop. Ulbricht **leapt** from his seat to **grab** it back, when the half dozen other readers at nearby tables suddenly **lunged** for him, **pushing** him up against a window. Hearing the commotion, the librarian **rushed** over to assist Ulbricht. "Go back to your desk," the woman who had started it all told her. "We are making an arrest."

Stripping off their civilian shirts to reveal FBI vests, the agents told Ulbricht to turn around. He had no expression when the **cuffed** him. As they led him toward the door, the female agent **turned** to the mystified onlookers and said, "Surprise!"

This opening is an action-packed arresting scene (pun intended). The scene is set against the backdrop of a serene library. This sereneness and slow-going at the beginning of the lead sets up the dramatic action scene that follows, providing a stark contrast. The action scene presented in the last two paragraphs is created with strong active verbs, most of which are within four letters. The abruptness and decisiveness connoted by the short and strong verbs give a crispy and snappy feel. The scene is written as cleanly as the subject matter depicted and is over before the reader has a chance to think about them. Such riveting action scene is like a movie trailer, pushing some of the drama — the subject nabbed by the FBI in a library in the above story — to the top and teasing an audience's attention with it. Like a movie trailer, your opening lines are to sell what follows. And action sells.

5.5.3   Starting with specificity

Good lead sometimes paints a riveting imagery that catches the readers' imagination. Often this is achieved by focusing on a specific item, the one microcosm object that embodies the story. The following story[①] from the Sixth

---

① Wang Lianzhang. Bones of Contention: China's Unhappy Cosmetic Surgery Patients[EB/OL]. The Sixth Tone. (2021-07-05) [2021-08-06]. https://www.sixthtone.com/news/1007902/bones-of-contention-chinas-unhappy-cosmetic-surgery-patients.

Tone examines the chaotic cosmetic surgery market and its unhappy patients. The article starts with a specific imagery where the bones removed from a patient's nose are floating inside a jar in the patient's bedroom. The slightly nauseating scene is symbolic of the uncertain craziness of the cosmetic surgery market.

> In her bedroom, Gao keeps a small medicinal jar containing what she hopes will be key evidence for her lawsuit. Inside, submerged in formaldehyde, sit two pieces of cartilage that earlier this year were removed from her surgically resculpted nose. They don't seem to fit the descriptions in her medical files, leading Gao to suspect foul play: was someone else's cartilage inside her nose?

The above lead involves the removed bones of plastic surgery. The following lead[①] contains a specific view that stuns the reader with its unusualness.

> Fifty-seven-year-old Tibetan herdsman Gesang owns a house with the most unique mountain views. On Sunny days, the top of Mount Qomolangma, the world's highest peak, is framed in his doorway like a wooden picture on his wall.

Lead works best if it involves specificity, as the above two examples illustrate. Details are the key and the specificity can take any form. The following lead[②] starts with a specific daily ritual. In the story telling about the hardships of HIV patients in Uganda during the COVID-19 pandemic, the description of the specifics of daily life establishes both the main subject and the story quickly.

> Before Uganda's coronavirus lockdown, HIV-positive Matina had a morning routine. After waking she drank tea, ate something small and took her antiretroviral drugs as doctors instructed.

---

① Wang Qin'ou, Li Jiaxin and Cao Aifeng. The untrained herdsman who beat Everest[N/OL]. Shanghai Daily. (2020-07-25) [2021-08-04]. https://archive. shine. cn/feature/The-untrained-herdsman-who-beat-Everest/shdaily.shtml.

② Sally Hayden. HIV patients suffer as food shortages bite[N/OL]. Shanghai Daily. (2020-05-26) [2021-08-04]. https://archive.shine.cn/feature/HIV-patients-suffer-as-food-shortages-bite/shdaily.shtml.

But since restrictions to stop the spread of COVID-19 were introduced in March, her situation has changed. She has nothing to eat so she avoids her medicine as it makes her feel nauseous and dizzy if taken without food.

The following lead from a story[①] headlined "Diary: Google Invades" by Rebecca Solnit from London Review of Books revolves around a shuttle bus. Here is how it rolls.

> The buses roll up to San Francisco's bus stops in the morning and evening. But they are unmarked, or nearly so, and not for the public. They have no signs or have discreet acronyms on the front windshield, and because they also have no rear doors they ingest and disgorge their passengers slowly, while the brightly it funky orange public buses wait behind him. The luxury-coach passengers ride for free and many take out their laptops and begin their work day on board; there is of course wifi. Most of them are gleaming white, with dark-tinted windows, lie limousines, and some days I think of them as the spaceships on which our alien overlords have landed to rule over us.

The feature story tells a fascinating tale of how the new boom town, the Silicon Valley, is slowly destroying the inclusiveness of the city of San Francisco. The sleek shuttle bus from google is emblematic of the fissures running through this city once friendly to outsiders. Artists, African Americans, Latinos, and immigrants are overrun by a new class of techies who all come from essentially one demographic. These Silicon Valley people who are gradually edging the cultural and ethnic groups out come to and from the city riding the bus.

5.5.4   Last but not least

In this chapter, we have examined feature leads characterized by descriptiveness, delayed to build up the suspense or tension, and involving a human element. But there is no fixed formula in feature lead writing as form is to serve content, not the other way around. If the story demands, even a traditional summary lead should be chosen. Take the following summary lead

---

① Rebecca Solnit. Diary: Google Invades [EB/OL]. London Review of Books. [2021-08-20]. https://www.lrb.co.uk/the-paper/v35/n03/rebecca-solnit/diary.

from a story[1] on the most successful coffee brewer in the world moving towards a pricier market.

> Howard Schultz is stepping down as chief executive of Starbucks Corp. to lead an effort at the company to build high-end coffee shops that will charge as much as $12 a cup, his next attempt to revolutionize the way Americans consume coffee.

Summary lead is concise, newsy, to the point, and particularly effective for a story just breaking. The above story is newsy and the summary lead fits perfectly. There's another advantage of using summary lead: it helps save life examples, which are hard to come by, for the body of the story. The no-nonsense opening gets straight down to business, leaving the illustration for later. Take this lead from a story[2] that takes a lengthy look at the revival signs of the small businesses in America after tourists returned, despite the threat of the more contagious Delta variant of the coronavirus. In the summary lead, the issue is concisely summed up to let the reader know at the very beginning what is going on.

> Small businesses in the US that depend on tourism and vacationers say business is bouncing back, as Americans rebook postponed trips and spend freely on food, entertainment and souvenirs.

Exercise

1. Evaluate feature leads

Instructions: Review the following feature leads and decide for yourself which topics are engaging and which leads are strong. Explain your decisions and try to formulate guidelines of dos and don'ts about lead writing on your own.

1. Judah Huang works deep in the global supply chain at a Chinese company

---

[1] Julie Jargon. Starbucks CEO Turns Focus to Pricier Brew[N]. the Wall Street Journal. (2016-12-02) [2021-08-20]. https://www.wsj.com/articles/howard-schultz-to-step-down-as-starbucks-ceo-1480626061.

[2] Mae Anderson. Small businesses lifted by return of tourists [N/OL]. Shanghai Daily. (2021-08-04) [2021-08-05]. https://archive.shine.cn/feature/Small-businesses-lifted-by-return-of-tourists/shdaily.shtml.

that makes nonstick coatings for cookie sheets, frying pans and grills sold in stores such as Wal-Mart.

Until a few years ago, the pans and griddles were made in China, but most of the materials that went into them were not. Mr. Huang imported most of the resins, pigments and pastes for his coatings from multinational suppliers such as Dow Chemical Co. of the U. S. and Eckart Effect Pigments of Germany.

Now, in a shift that is echoing throughout China's vast manufacturing sector, he is buying more than 70% of those things from local suppliers.

"All these raw materials, now somebody in China makes it," says Mr. Huang, chief technical manager of GMM Non-Stick Coatings, which has a factory in this city near Macau.

2. Everything in the work of Rebecca Horn is intimate, yet nothing is personal. A sculptor who makes fantastic machines, a filmmaker who realizes her wildest dreams, a writer who concocts wry texts to accompany her museum and gallery installations, this German-Swiss artist (with a pure profile worthy of a cameo) never stops telling her secrets — only they are coded, as in dreams. Those secrets are now on display in New York City during a major retrospective at the Guggenheim Museum through September 8; the show fills half the museum.

3. The stock market has continued to reach new highs, troubled only fleetingly by rising interest rates, sluggish corporate earnings and new and uncomfortable political realities.

4. In the evening, when her husband and son are fast asleep and the house is enveloped in silence, Han Shimei goes to a place that is hers alone.
Lying sideways in bed and clutching her phone, the day's mundane affairs come flooding back to her. Han will transform these memories into words, adding a rhyme here and there. She'll spend hours like this in the soft glow of the screen.

5. A four-grade-boy is talking with his teacher through the computer screen. "I also have a secret to tell you, Miss Zhang," he said. "My mom has passed away two years ago. Maybe that's why my father is so strict about my studies".

6. Liu, aged 48, from a poor small village, is now a manager of the company named FUSAN majoring in production and sales of construction machinery.

7. Lin Yongxiang, a 25-year-old ceramist graduated from Jingdezhen Ceramic University, located in China's ceramic capital, came to Yaojing village, southwest of Shanghai last year. He said when he was in Jingdezhen, it was difficult to realize his value — made pottery that he likes and taught other people to make it — so he came here.

8. It was now the delightful season of the Yaojing Village, Maogang Town in Songjiang District of Shanghai: the heat of summer faded, the tempered sunbeam of September fell, and the vast green paddy field extends wide and soft—soon it would embrace the second round of an excellent harvest.

9. A face mask, a white vest, an ID card and a khaki bag crammed with folders and papers——this is basic kit for Zhang Yanjun, a 70-year-old woman who volunteers as a census taker in Shanghai.

10. At Shanghai International Studies University, the students mark one of Songjiang's cultural heritage by planting their cotton. Songjiang's international reputation of cotton textiles goes back to the 18th century; it used to be the nation's cotton textile industry center.

Huang Daopo innovated cotton textile tools which enabled the people of Songjiang to master weaving skills. Handwoven Songjiang cotton cloths are rich in texture and high in quality. It earned its reputation not only due to global trade but remained an intangible cultural heritage.

2. The Human element: News-gathering field trip and writing exercise

One effective approach for feature writing is to employ a certain human element to thread the story together. You may start your story with a person who is closely related to the issue at heart, then use a link paragraph that connects the anecdote in the lead to the theme paragraph. During the discussion of the issue in the body of the story, you may go back to this person to give the issue a human touch, then finish off by revisiting the person. Not all feature stories are written in this way, but the approach is effective because it contains the human element that gives an otherwise dry issue a human face.

Instructions:

Go to the downtown of your city and

➤ You are to talk to people and get their stories on working/studying/living in the city.

➤ Take detailed notes when interviewing and get the names and contact information of your interviewee in case you need to get back to clarify certain points of your original interview. Also take down the physical appearance and mannerism of your interviewee.

➢ Try to interview more than one person in case the story of your primary subject turns out to be uninteresting.

➢ You are to write a six-paragraph beginning part of your story based on the information gathered from the interview and bring it to class for discussion. These six paragraphs will consist of the lead, the link, the nut graf (theme paragraph), and the context paragraph.

➢ Be safe and have fun.

Chapter 6　Organizing The Feature Story

The construction of feature articles enjoys more freedom in design. There's no fixed formula like the inverted pyramid structure that the hard news writers concern themselves with. Within the broad rule of starting well and holding the readers' attention until the finish, anything goes. Over time, a great variety of leads and organizational plans are suggested and put into practice. Whatever the exact organization, most feature stories are roughly composed of four parts: the lead, the nut graf, the body, and the ending. Each part fulfils a distinctive role in the article.

The lead, which we discussed at length last chapter, is where you cajole the reader and give him/her a reason for reading on. However, at this stage, the reader, mildly interested, is yet to be committed to the story. After the carefully-crafted introduction, you need to tell the reader what the story is really about, which brings the story to the next stage: the nut graf. Nut graf is journalistic jargon that means the single paragraph where the gist of the story is stated in a nut shell. As the name suggested, nut graf is characteristically brief and to the point, the theme of the story tersely stated with few details. The bluntly-put thesis requires context to render understanding. Thus the nut graf is often followed by one or two contextual paragraphs putting the story in proportion for the readers. This/these amplifying paragraph/s also serves as the transition from the introduction to the main body of the story, bridging the two parts seamlessly by continuing to build. The third stage, the body of the story, contains the real substance of the story. This is where you have to prove with clear logic and convincing evidence what you've promised in the lead and what you've announced in the nut graf. This part takes careful plan and organization for this is where the real work is done and where all the questions should be answered. Then at last, comes the ending of the story. Like the ending of all articles, the finish of a feature story is supposed to be natural and forceful, a couple of concluding sentences that help the readers remember the story.

6.1　Sorting out the materials

Writing a feature story is a lot like cooking a meal. Before the actual cooking, you must go out to get the ingredients and then prepare them for the dish, cleaning, sorting, and deciding which go where. Similarly, before sitting down to write, you must first gather materials through researching and interviewing, and then sort out the materials by studying them and deciding which go where.

Sorting out the materials means identifying the information gathered. You may have in your possession interview transcripts or notes, news story clippings, bits and pieces of information from digging online, and a general understanding of the topic. What you need to do now is to read your materials and to pigeonhole each piece. An efficient way to do this is to tag the materials. The labels can be quotes, indirect quotes, anecdotes (life examples), statistics, descriptive details, reference sources such as policy announcement or survey results, contextual information, or general background information that may not go into the story but gives you a grasp. This careful tagging or cataloguing of the materials helps you analyze the available materials. Having to name each one, you'll see straight away which is missing and which you have enough. For example, you may have gathered lots of data and expert opinions but few anecdotes. This is not good because such a combination is likely to result in a lopsided story with heavy abstract theorizing but little real life. Or after a careful study of quotes you may find most of them to be commonplace, repetitive, or downright boring. It dawns on you that it might be necessary to redo the interviews if you want to avoid a story padded with dreary quotes. Or worse, you may find you have enough (actually too many) secondary sources but few first-hand ones. You may be forced to quote in plenty from other published stories, a practice frowned upon by serious journalists. There are many ways a story could go wrong. Taking an intelligent inventory of your materials before writing will help you detect them in time. A good story is rooted in adequate reporting. This inventory will give you an idea whether the reporting you've done is adequate.

In addition to tagging, sorting out the materials also means selecting. It is irresponsible to put every bit of materials gathered into the final story. It borders on foolishness and the resulting piece will be unduly inflated and a burden to the reader. What's more, the piling of the materials shows that the writer hasn't bothered to establish the logic for the story or has failed to discern the central point of the story. So it is clear that the selection of collected materials is a necessary step that can't be skipped. And the single criterion for selection is relevance. Every piece of information that goes into the story must contribute to the theme in some way. Otherwise it stays out no matter how much effort is spent in obtaining the piece. This sometimes painful selection process is crucial to giving real shape to the story. Be severe in picking the materials and keep the theme of the story in sight all through the selection. Ideally the ratio of what goes in and what stays out is often one third or even less.

Last but not least，sorting out the materials leads to a possible outline. What materials are there that might fit for the lead? Is there a quote that has such a finality sound to it that it will conclude the piece? What is the theme of the story and what evidences there are to bear it out? Which piece of information go where? Is there a sequence to arrange them that makes sense? By scrutinizing every piece of information you may have answers to the above questions. What underlies the structure of a story is the story logic which will only become clear in the study of the relationship between the information. Sometimes，subtopics will also emerge by grouping pertinent materials together. You may see clearly which will make the central point of the story and which will make the minor ones.

6.2　Writing the headline

Though it is the editor's job to finalize the headline/title of the story，you are encouraged to formulate one on your own. The headline is the story condensed in a few words，the distilled essence. So crafting the headline helps the writer to sharpen the focal point of the story and to remain focused during the whole writing process. Another function of the headline is to capture the readers' attention. This requires your headline to be simple yet attractive. Your headline must be simple，something to be understood at a hurried glance. Complexness at the stage of the headline will lose the readers in no time. Your headline also needs to be enticing，exquisitely put together in a way that charms and intrigues the readers. The rule for writing the feature headlines is the same as that of news：use present tense and keep it short. A beginner writer should study the headlines of the English-language publications for guide. However，beware of the "clickbait" headlines that promise more than the story delivers. These hollow headlines，product of the sensationalism and the click culture in the digital age，will discredit the story as well as the writer after the five seconds during which time the reader clicks the story and gets disappointed.

Here are a few examples of well-written headlines from Chinese English-language media.

The following headlines have one thing in common: They are all simple summation of the story. They are like an even briefer version of the summary lead. Seeing the title, the reader will get immediately what the story is about.

　◇　Online resources help minds, bodies stay fit amid confinement[①]

　◇　Food frugality: empty plates, no leftovers[②]

　◇　For China's Middle-Aged Women, Depression Is an "Invisible Killer"[③]

The following headline, by using chirping and croaks, employs alliteration, a common ploy in the headline.

　◇　When the chirping stops, a market croaks[④]

Here's another example of alliteration.

　◇　Surgical or homemade, face masks mark a major shift in thinking[⑤]

The following headline involves a pun by using the word "Grounded!". On the one hand, the international students may feel some certainty (grounded) about their future after the US policy change. On the other hand, many of them still can't fly (grounded) to their destination for study.

　◇　Grounded! International students face hard choices after US policy change[⑥]

More headlines with pun intended. The first two are rather self-evident. The third is the headline of a story about the first orchestra with a live audience since the pandemic, hence "face the music." The fourth one is the headline for a story on an artisan using straws to make her crafts. Hence there's no last straw

①　Yao Minji. Online resources help minds, bodies stay fit amid confinement [N/OL]. Shanghai Daily. (2020-04-28) [2021-08-21]. https://www.shine.cn/feature/wellness/2004287179/.

②　Hu Min and Ding Yining. Food frugality: empty plates, no leftovers [N/OL]. Shanghai Daily. (2020-08-19) [2021-08-21]. https://archive. shine. cn/metro/Food-frugality-empty-plates-no-leftovers/shdaily.shtml.

③　Fan Yiying and Zhang Shiyu. For China's Middle-Aged Women, Depression Is an 'Invisible Killer' [EB/OL]. the Sixth Tone. (2021-05-20) [2021-08-21]. https://www.sixthtone.com/news/1006992/for-chinas-middle-aged-women%2C-depression-is-an-invisible-killer.

④　Zhuying. When the chirping stops, a market croaks [N/OL]. Shanghai Daily. (2020-07-11) [2021-08-21]. https://archive.shine.cn/feature/When-the-chirping-stops-a-market-croaks/shdaily.shtml.

⑤　Samuel Petrequin. Surgical or homemade, face masks mark a major shift in thinking [N/OL]. Shanghai Daily. (2020-07-14) [2021-08-21]. https://archive. shine. cn/feature/Surgical-or-homemade-face-masks-mark-a-major-shift-in-thinking/shdaily.shtml.

⑥　Yao Minji and Maggie Xu. Grounded! International students face hard choices after US policy change [N/OL]. Shanghai Daily. (2020-07-12) [2021-08-21]. https://www. shine. cn/news/in-focus/2007121990/.

for the innovative traditional artisan.

◇ Fitness industry bent into new shape[①]

◇ Fallen leaves turn over a new leaf in creative artworks[②]

◇ Audiences face the music again at concert celebrating hope[③]

◇ The last straw? Never for these traditional artisans[④]

The following headline of the book review contains irony that gives it more resonance.

◇ Jim Carry gets real with satirical fictional memoir[⑤]

Using antonyms in headline writing is an old trick that brings a sense of symmetrical satisfaction.

◇ The struggle to keep a dying Syrian craft alive[⑥]

◇ The Man Shepherding China's Best Zoo Through Its Worst Year[⑦]

The following use of onomatopoeia grabs the readers' attention as an action comic will do.

◇ Ugh! The city is suffering from an infestation of termites[⑧]

◇ Lip-smackin' good! Where crayfish lovers turn up at night[⑨]

---

① Xu Qing. Fitness industry bent into new shape [N/OL]. Shanghai Daily. (2020-07-15) [2021-08-21]. https://archive.shine.cn/metro/Fitness-industry-bent-into-new-shape/shdaily.shtml.

② Zhu Ying. Fallen leaves turn over a new leaf in creative artworks [N/OL]. Shanghai Daily. (2020-08-08) [2021-08-21]. https://archive. shine. cn/feature/Fallen-leaves-turn-over-a-new-leaf-in-creative-artworks/shdaily.shtml.

③ Yao Minji. Audiences face the music again at concert celebrating hope [N/OL]. Shanghai Daily. (2020-07-20) [2021-08-21]. https://archive. shine. cn/feature/art-and-culture/Audiences-face-the-music-again-at-concert-celebrating-hope/shdaily.shtml.

④ Zhu Ying. The last straw? Never for these traditional artisans [N/OL]. Shanghai Daily. (2021-07-23) [2021-08-21]. https://www.shine.cn/feature/art-culture/2107232474/.

⑤ Jake Coyle. Jim Carry gets real with satirical fictional memoir [N/OL]. Shanghai Daily. (2020-07-08) [2021-08-21]. https://archive. shine. cn/sunday/book/Jim-Carry-gets-real-with-satirical-fictional-memoir/shdaily.shtml.

⑥ Maher al-Mounes. The struggle to keep a dying Syrian craft alive [N/OL]. Shanghai Daily. (2020-07-08) [2021-08-21]. https://archive. shine. cn/sunday/The-struggle-to-keep-a-dying-Syrian-craft-alive/shdaily.shtml.

⑦ Su Jing and Xing Yifan. The Man Shepherding China's Best Zoo Through Its Worst Year [EB/OL]. the Sixth Tone. (2020-02-13) [2021-08-21]. https://www. sixthtone. com/news/1006844/the-man-shepherding-chinas-best-zoo-through-its-worst-year.

⑧ Hu Min and Song Yiyang. Ugh! The city is suffering from an infestation of termites [N/OL]. Shanghai Daily. (2020-07-12) [2021-08-21]. https://archive.shine.cn/metro/Ugh-The-city-is-suffering-from-an-infestation-of-termites/shdaily.shtml.

⑨ Lu Feiran. Lip-smackin' good! Where crayfish lovers turn up at night [N/OL]. Shanghai Daily. (2020-07-24) [2021-08-21]. https://archive. shine. cn/feature/Lipsmackin-good-Where-crayfish-lovers-turn-up-at-night/shdaily.shtml.

The following headlines rhyme, which is always a delight to ear.

◇   Farm-to-table dining takes on new meaning①

◇   Softly, softly, an all-female patrol keeps the east riverbank orderly②

◇   Grand Theft Auto: 90-year-old games her way to fame③

◇   Looms to heirlooms: Artisans weave silk into premium carpets④

Contrast is also a common device in headline writing. The following headline puts home and tourism, two contrasting conceptions, in one line and it works.

◇   There's no place like home in rural tourism⑤

Homophone is fun. The following story has a penetrating look into the one year after the implementing of garbage sorting in Shanghai.

◇   One year on: we've bin there, done that⑥

The play of lexically-related words puts the spark in the headlines. Examples are plenty.

◇   Airlines in the doghouse over bringing pets back to China⑦

◇   Champagne losing its fizz as pandemic puts a cork on consumption⑧

①   Lisa Rathke and Patrick Whittle. Farm-to-table dining takes on new meaning [N/OL]. Shanghai Daily. (2020-07-11) [2021-08-21]. https://archive. shine. cn/feature/Farmtotable-dining-takes-on-new-meaning/shdaily.shtml.

②   Hu Min. Softly, softly, an all-female patrol keeps the east riverbank orderly. Shanghai Daily [N/OL]. (2020-07-14) [2021-08-21]. https://www.shine.cn/news/in-focus/2007142086/.

③   Shingo Ito. Grand Theft Auto: 90-year-old games her way to fame [N/OL]. Shanghai Daily. (2020-06-14) [2021-08-21]. https://archive. shine. cn/feature/Grand-Theft-Auto-90yearold-games-her-way-to-fame/shdaily.shtml.

④   Zhuying. Looms to heirlooms: Artisans weave silk into premium carpets [N/OL]. Shanghai Daily. (2021-08-06) [2021-08-21]. https://www.shine.cn/feature/art-culture/2108063221/.

⑤   Yang Wenjie. There's no place like home in rural tourism [N/OL]. Shanghai Daily. (2020-06-23) [2021-08-21]. https://archive.shine.cn/district/minhang/Theres-no-place-like-home-in-rural-tourism/shdaily.shtml.

⑥   Hu Min and Song Yiyang. One year on: We've bin there, done that! [N/OL] Shanghai Daily. (2020-07-01) [2021-08-21]. https://archive.shine.cn/metro/One-year-on-Weve-bin-there-done-that/shdaily.shtml.

⑦   Tian Shengjie and Li Anlan. Airlines in the doghouse over bringing pets back to China [N/OL]. Shanghai Daily. (2020-08-02) [2021-08-21]. https://archive. shine. cn/sunday/Airlines-in-the-doghouse-over-bringing-pets-back-to-China/shdaily.shtml.

⑧   Thomas Adamson. Champagne losing its fizz as pandemic puts a cork on consumption [N/OL]. Shanghai Daily. (2020-08-06) [2021-08-21]. https://archive.shine.cn/feature/Champagne-losing-its-fizz-as-pandemic-puts-a-cork-on-consumption/shdaily.shtml.

◇　Nose prints offer the purr-fect way to ID your pets[①]

A Six Tone feature explores the story of a boy from the countryside falling victim to the voyeur mania of the internet celebrity because he looks inexplicably like Jack Ma，the founder of Alibaba. Its headline makes a clever allusion to the classic novel of Milan Kundera.

◇　The Unbearable Likeness of Being：The Story of "Little Jack Ma"[②]

Here's another headline from *Shanghai Daily* alludes to one of the most famous soliloquys of Hamlet.

◇　A wave or not a wave，that is the question …[③]

As the above examples show，good feature headlines are easy to understand. Figures of speech are frequently used to make it more enticing. Thus headline writing feels like a game playing with words. It is fun and rewarding. While honing your language，it allows you to bring your story further into focus. Once you have pinpointed the focus through the headline，you will get a clue for the layout of the whole article.

6.3　The lead-nut graf-context paragraph opening

Nut graf，a journalism slang，is defined as a paragraph or paragraphs in which the main points of a story are summarized. Nut grafs are often used in conjunction with delayed leads in feature stories. Leads tease readers with a stunning example of what is to come，while nut grafs concisely tell the readers what is really going on. It boasts other fitting names such as billboard paragraph，summary paragraph，and main theme statement paragraph. Succinctly stating the theme or thesis，nut graf often falls neatly into one paragraph，but that's not always the case. There are many stories where the nut graf runs for several paragraphs. Nut graf writing demands the ability to summarize and condense which in turn requires a clear understanding of what the story is really about on the reporter's part.

---

① Lu Feiran. Nose prints offer the purr-fect way to ID your pets [N/OL]. Shanghai Daily. (2020-08-08) [2021-08-21]. https://archive. shine. cn/feature/Nose-prints-offer-the-purrfect-way-to-ID-your-pets/shdaily.shtml.

② Ming Que. The Unbearable Likeness of Being：The Story of 'Little Jack Ma'[EB/OL]. The Sixth Tone. （2021-03-18）［2021-08-21］. https://www. sixthtone. com/news/1006988/the-unbearable-likeness-of-being-the-story-of-little-jack-ma.

③ Tan Weiyun. A wave or not a wave，that is the question [N/OL]. Shanghai Daily. (2021-07-30) [2021-08-21]. https://www.shine.cn/feature/art-culture/2107302896/.

The nut graf often comes right after the lead is established, or played out, as it informs the readers of the central point as soon as the lead is out of the way. Since a nut graf, as the name suggested, is usually short and to the point, and it needs to be amplified or explained further. That's why it is often followed by one or two supporting or amplifying paragraphs which will further clarify the theme statement or provide necessary context. Sometimes, this explanation is in the form of a quotation from the primary character or an authoritative source. Thus, rather than the lead alone serving as the entire introduction, the opening part of a feature story is actually composed of the lead, the nut graf and the amplifying paragraphs. This narrative combination, and its sequence in perfect agreement with the story logic, can be found in many feature articles.

The following opening paragraphs are from a story[1] of Sixth Tone on Chinese college students stuck in fake majors. This 2000-word story starts with an anecdotal lead that contains the first eight paragraphs. The lead tells the story of a single student who was cheated by her college and wasted years in a major that doesn't even exist. The microcosm tale contained in the lead is an engaging one, but the reader still has no definite idea as to what this feature article is really about. That's the job of the nut graf, the ninth paragraph in this story, where Zhao's experience is tied to similar ones around the country and the reader is also let on the reason: the private vocational schools cheat to recruit. Next, comes the amplifying paragraph containing an indirect quotation from an expert to give validity of the theme statement.

Lead

JIANGSU, East China — Zhao Yangyang thought she was on the fast track to a bright future. She was three years into a program to become a high-speed rail attendant — a secure job that would allow the then-18-year-old to travel across the country. But last August, those plans suddenly derailed.

Zhao knew something was wrong when she arrived to pay the tuition fees for her final year at Mingda Polytechnic Institute, a private vocational school on the outskirts of her hometown Sheyang, in eastern China's Jiangsu province. Instead of allowing her to register like usual, the receptionists told Zhao that the school wanted her to transfer her program from high-speed rail attendant to tourism management.

---

[1]　Yuan Ye. The Chinese Students Stuck in Fake Majors[EB/OL]. The Sixth Tone. (2019-08-270) [2021-08-04]. https://www.sixthtone.com/news/1004486/The#.

A young girl and her family seek justice after she spent three years in a high-speed rail attendant program that didn't exist in Sheyang, Jiangsu province.

Zhao was confused. She had no interest in tourism. In a few weeks, she was supposed to be starting an internship as an attendant. Her new uniform was already hanging in her closet. She asked why the school wanted her to switch programs on such short notice.

That's when Zhao received the bizarre, yet life-altering news. "They said that the (high-speed rail attendant) program did not exist, and that she would have to transfer to the tourism program," Yang Ling, Zhao's mother, tells Sixth Tone.

All around her, Zhao's classmates were having similar exchanges with Mingda staff, and things began to get heated. Eventually, the school agreed to set up a meeting between the students and the school's executives.

The meeting took place three days later. The families of nearly all 35 students in the high-speed rail attendant program squeezed into a conference room on the Mingda campus. The school's vice dean, Zhou Kaimeng, said a few words, announcing that the school did not have a government license for the program, and so it was impossible for the students to graduate. He urged the students to transfer to tourism management. Zhao burst into tears.

"I'd spent years working on this, and now someone was telling me that it was all for nothing," she says.

Nug graf

Many other students across China have been caught up in fake major scandals as the country's private vocational schools struggle to recruit new pupils. In May, students at a vocational school in the eastern city of Nanjing disputed with staff after they discovered they would not receive qualifications for nursing, as they had been promised, but in home economics.

Supporting paragraph

According to Zhang Run, a lecturer at the People's Public Security University of China, there are many similar cases that go unreported because the students' families reach a settlement with the school.

By Shi Yangkun/Sixth Tone

Take another story, the lead of which we cited earlier in the book, that opens in the similar way. The anecdotal lead tells an incident where one reporter learned the lesson of the 'nut graf' the hard way, showing to the reader the conundrum that an aspiring journalist faces: Whether to get a formal journalism education or not? The lead is followed closely by the nut graf, from which we understand that the story is about the eternal debate on J school's necessity as illustrated by Ms Saucier and her amusing learning-on-the-job experience. Then the ensuing paragraph amplifies the nut graf by presenting the reply of the journalism schools to the debate. This amplifying paragraph also serves as the news peg. The curriculum reform launched by Columbia University brings new attention to the old debate.

Lead

Heather Saucier learned the lesson of the "nut graf" the hard way. (In journalism jargon, the "nut graf" is a paragraph near the top of a story that concisely lays out its thesis.)

Ms. Saucier was still in college, working as an intern for the now-defunct Houston Post. She filed a piece on the city's troublesome squirrel population. The story was fine, her editor said, "But you're missing a nut graf."

She'd already written about squirrels chewing through telephone wires and gnawing on wood, so she dashed off a short paragraph about their diet: nuts.

Some would argue that Saucier learned this essential of the journalistic craft in the best possible fashion — on the job. Others, however, might point to Saucier's story as an example of one of the oddities of journalism: So many enter the field with so little formal instruction.

Whatever the answer, Saucier stayed her course. But as time went on, she considered returning to school. After five years as a features writer, her stories regularly took third place in competitions. She wanted "to be a first-place writer," though, and thought "there has to be something I don't know that I can learn."

In journalism graduate school, she says, content was held in higher esteem than style. And she discovered what had been missing from her work - substance.

Nut graf

It's one of the most circular and enduring debates in journalism: whether to bother with a graduate degree that certainly doesn't guarantee a job, and, unlike law or medicine, has never been required.

Amplifying paragraph (news peg)

Nearly a century after the first journalism school opened in 1908, schools are in flux — Columbia University's vaunted program, where Saucier earned her degree, is in the final stages of an overhaul.

As mentioned above, nut graf often works in conjunction with delayed lead on feature stories. Since not all feature stories start with delayed lead, not all feature stories follow the formula of lead-nut graf-amplifying paragraph opening. Especially when a news feature (issue-based feature) employs the summary lead, the lead itself tells the reader what the story is about, making the nut graf redundant. Take the following opening of a *Shanghai Daily* story[①] reporting on the standoff between China's largest smart locker company keen on cashing in and consumers demanding the company to continue its free service. The story starts with a straightforward summary lead which recapitulates the story in one neat sentence. After that, the story continues to build, each following paragraph putting the issue in context by giving more information about the currently largest locker company in China where the delivery business is huge.

Summary lead

Hive Box, China's largest smart locker company, is facing a consumer boycott in neighborhoods across the country after ending the free services that propelled the firm to popularity.

Continue to build

Under the new policy, non-member customers can leave e-commerce deliveries in a Hive Box locker free of charge for the first 12 hours. After that, a fee of 0.5 yuan (7 US cents) will be charged for every 12 hours thereafter, up to a maximum 3 yuan. Alternatively, users can pay 5 yuan a month to become a Hive Box member.

Hive Box's change of policy came after the company acquired its largest competitor, pushing its market share to nearly 70 percent.

Locker services are considered the "last mile of delivery" in the world's largest e-commerce market. Every day, deliverymen put millions of parcels ordered online in lockers supplied by Hive Box or other similar services.

---

① Yao Minji. Consumers smart over new smart locker fees [N/OL]. Shanghai Daily. (2020-08-14) [2021-08-04]. https://archive.shine.cn/feature/news-feature/Consumers-smart-over-new-smart-locker-fees/shdaily.shtml.

6.4 Story structures

Story structure, or story line, is the plot of a story, the way a story develops. We understand from previous discussions that feature writers are less concerned with formula writing than their hard news counterparts. They rarely resort to inverted pyramids in putting together a story. Feature articles are usually organized according to the contents of the story. The contents decide the form, not the other way around. Even the lead-nut graf-supporting graph structure can be varied. The point is the chosen structure can deliver the story effectively. However, despite the tendency to freestyle, there are some time-tested structural approaches at the disposal of a feature writer. To get a better grasp of these options, let's outline a few stories and see from the dissecting how a story is organized.

6.4.1　The multiple-profile approach

The following story[①] appearing on the lifestyle section of *Shanghai Daily* takes a lingering look at the bird and flower markets in Shanghai that are on countdown to close.

When the chirping stops, a market croaks

Zhu Ying

(1) Shanghai's bird and flower markets are withering away.

(2) Just half a year ago, we bade farewell to the Qinqing flower market in Xuhui District. Now, another popular venue called Wanshang in Huangpu District will be shuttered at the end of this month.

(3) Such markets are fast becoming memories in Shanghai as authorities cite fire risk and other public health and safety factors for their closures.

(4) Started more than 20 years ago, Wanshang is probably the most bustling of the once prolific flower and bird markets in Shanghai. Located on Xizang Road S., the market was perhaps most famous for "exotic" pets, like Chinese crickets, cicadas and grasshoppers. Its air is filled with the cacophony

---

① Zhu Ying. When the chirping stops, a market croaks [N/OL]. Shanghai Daily. (2020-07-11) [2021-08-04]. https://archive.shine.cn/feature/When-the-chirping-stops-a-market-croaks/shdaily.shtml

of chirping insects.

(5) Singing insects and fighting crickets have deep cultural roots in China. The originally aristocratic hobby can be traced back to the Tang Dynasty (AD 618-907). Though not as popular as it once was, the custom still enjoys considerable popularity among those nostalgic about the past.

(6) "For many elderly people, keeping insects as pets became habit," says Bai Zixiao, a stallholder selling insect-related paraphernalia.

(7) "I once encountered an old man who had hearing loss but still came here to buy singing insects. He was endowed with memories of the past."

(8) Born in 1990, Bai is the youngest insect-gear retailer in the market. Influenced by his father, a Shanghai zhiqing, or young intellectual, who was sent to aid the development of Heilongjiang Province, Bai has had a passion for insects since his childhood.

(9) Although Bai didn't operate his stall in Wanshang market until 2018, his connection with the market goes back much further. He recalls childhood visits to Wanshang market with his father every summer just to buy a singing insect. At the time, the family lived in the Heilongjiang city of Daqing. He often took insects to his school to show his classmates.

(10) "I thought it was very cool," says Bai. "However, the hobby made it difficult for me to make girlfriends."

(11) Taking out two boxes from his backpack, Bai shows me two singing insects — a huangling, or yellow cricket, and a zhuling, or tree cricket. One of them is placed in a round, acrylic container called a wanti because of its similarity to Shanghai Stadium, which is called wanti guan for short in Chinese. Another insect lives in a little house made of bamboo.

(12) "The equipment that I sell is high-end," says Bai. "The prices range from 2,000 yuan (US $ 285) to 30,000 yuan."

(13) The costly insect containers are displayed in an ordinary glass cabinet, which is the sum total of Bai's stall on the side of an aisle.

(14) "I think it is closer to visitors," says Bai. "People can inquire about the works more freely."

(15) Bai graduated with a bachelor's degree in business administration from an Australian university. Most of his friends who went on to start their own companies are puzzled by Bai's choice of work.

(16) "In 2016, I had an accident while riding my motorcycle," says Bai. "Two bones in my thoracic vertebra fractured. During a one-year recovery,

singing insects kept me company and cheered me up."

(17) Indeed, many enthusiasts of singing insects can't live without them. They are lulled to sleep by the melody of their chirping. They talk to them and even give them decent burials.

(18) For serious insect lovers, it's often not easy to find the one that captivates them most.

(19) Holding a flashlight, a middle-aged man at the market carefully peruses groups of guoguo, or long-horn grasshoppers, which are enclosed in green plastic cages. He inclines his ear to them to listen carefully. He wanders from one stall to another for an hour, persistently looking for the one insect that catches his fancy.

(20) "Some customers spend a whole day in the market in order to find a satisfactory insect as a pet," says Zheng Haixian, 36, an insect-stall owner. "The use of flashlights and magnifying glasses helps buyers to examine the insects' limbs."

(21) Zheng is a native of Huangshan in Anhui Province, home to the huangling. She has known the insect since her childhood. During summer vacations, she and other children helped traders catch huangling in the woods as a way to earn pin money.

(22) In 2007, Zheng herself became a trader of singing insects. She set up a temporary stall at Wanshang market in the autumn, when the insects hit their peak. In 2009, she had her own store at the market and settled down in the city.

(23) More than 20 kinds of singing insects are available at Zheng's store, along with pet insect paraphernalia.

(24) "Ordinary insects live in 'apartments' while the rare ones live in 'villas,'" says Zheng. "The price of the insects ranges from 5 yuan to thousands of yuan."

(25) An "apartment" is a paper box or plastic cage. "Villas" are containers made of bamboo. According to Zheng, the exquisite containers create better sound effects.

(26) Zheng has operated her insect stall from 9am to 5pm every day, except during Spring Festival.

(27) "I need to feed insects every day," says Zheng. "They are living souls like human beings. For the huangling, I cook millet congee and prepare apples to feed them twice a day. Guoguo eat edamame (immature soybeans), which must be fresh and plump."

(28) During our conversation, a guoguo escapes from its cage. Zheng grabs hold of the fugitive immediately.

(29) "I spent my golden days in this market," she says. "Its closure makes me very sad."

(30) However, Zheng has found a new home for the insects. She gives me a newly printed business card that says she is moving to a flower and bird market called Lanling in Putuo District.

(31) Many other stallholders in the market are going there, too, including vendors selling accessories like walnut shell bracelets and amber necklaces.

(32) Fu Zhulin, 35, has been operating an accessory shop in the market since 2014. However, her first visit to the market was as early as in 2006.

(33) "My husband, who likes keeping insects, brought me to the market," says Fu. "It was crowded with people. The hustle and bustle felt like a glimpse of Old Shanghai."

(34) Rubbing rudraksha beads ceaselessly, Fu says the years in the market were valuable in taming her temper.

(35) "The walnut shells and rudraksha beads are living things," says Fu. "They can change by rubbing and touching them for a certain time. While I am rubbing them, I ignore everything else and calm myself down."

(36) Thriving in 2015 and 2016, Fu was so busy that she often skipped meals, which resulted in the stomach trouble. The illness taught her a valuable lesson: Health is more important than wealth.

(37) Since then, she cites the greatest "wealth" as the friendship of customers and other vendors. Knowing the market is closing soon, many customers have come to express their solidarity with her loss.

(38) "City life is stressful and fast-paced," says Fu. "Flower and bird markets are oases of calm, especially for elderly people."

(39) While young people can socialize in shopping malls, elderly people prefer going to traditional markets not too far from their homes. The crush of urbanization seems to be choking off their little joys of life.

(40) According to Fu, insect retailers from across the country had set up temporary stalls in Wanshang, attracting crowds of people, including foreign visitors who were fascinated by bugs kept as pets. Some curious foreigners even bought tickets for cricket fighting competitions or bamboo cages as souvenirs.

(41) The lively scene of the market was subdued during the coronavirus outbreak. Soon even that will be snuffed out.

(42) "I will miss the market," says Bai. "In flower and bird markets, you can capture the beauty of the seasons. You can even tell the month just by seeing what plants are blooming."

An outline of the above story

Lead

Para. 1

Direct one-line lead: The market is going.

News peg

Para. 2

Wanshan market is to be closed at the end of this month.

Thesis restated

Para. 3

The theme made clear again with the direct reason given.

Body

Para. 4

Anecdote: Back to Wanshan market focusing on the popularity of the singing insects.

Para. 5

Background info putting in historical and cultural context the anecdote in para. 4.

Para. 6

Quote from a vendor offering further explanation to illustrate the cultural preference of Chinese people.

Para. 7

Anecdote delivered in quote to further illustrate the love of singing insects.

Paras. 8-16

Anecdote: Life example of Bai, the vendor quoted in the above section who sells singing insects in the market.

Para. 17

Transition: The story zooming out from Bai's individual experience with the singing insects to the group shot of many enthusiasts of similar love.

Para. 18

This paragraph connecting the insect lovers back to the market.

Para. 19

Anecdote: A persistent buyer in action.

Para. 20

Quote from another vendor, Zheng, explaining that the previous buyer is not an incidental case.

Paras. 21-30

Anecdote: Another mini profile of the market vendor given with a focus on the insects this time. Para. 30, transition indicating the vendor is moving to a new venue as the market is shutting down.

Para. 31

Again, the story turning from the one individual to the group of stall holders who are forced to move, including those selling accessories.

Paras. 32-38

Anecdote: The third mini-profile of this story on the stall holder who sells accessories, with a focus on the warm aspect of the market, which provides a respite from the fast-paced and stressful city life.

Para. 39

The story turning to one group of regular customers: the elderly, trying to explain why they prefer to frequent the market.

Para. 40

Another particular group of the patrons, the foreigners, introduced through an indirect quote from Zheng.

Para. 41

Back to the theme of the story by telling in general terms that the market is withering with the coronavirus outbreak and the eventual termination.

The ending

Para. 42

A quote from vendor Bai, the subject of the first mini-profile of the story, nostalgic of the soon-to-disappear vitality of the market.

As made clear by the editor's note, the flower-and-bird-market story is part of a series feature articles that explores the heart and the soul of the city of Shanghai through depicting the local activities and social circles of similar interests that make the sprawling metropolis throbbing with humanity and vitality. This particular "grassroots" story attempts to present the city and its people from a specific angle by painting a detailed portrait of one bird and flower market that's about to be closed. The story is obviously heavy on human interest, and the best form to present such stories is the multiple-profile approach where the story is told through multiple life examples.

The multiple-profile approach is common, especially in stories involving a strong human element. Simply put, under this construction, the body of the story is organized around several (usually three) life examples of carefully-chosen individuals. As in the above story, the tale of the flower and bird market is told through three mini profiles of stall holders in the market. It is understood that the market is not the real story, but the people involved are. The success of this structure depends on the profile subjects chosen to illustrate the story. Not anyone will do. The multiple subjects must all represent the story, but not repetitively; each ideally should make its unique contribution to the demonstration of the central point. Each of the three profile subjects in the above story, though all vendors in the same market, plays a distinctive role. The first vendor, boasting a bachelor degree from an Australian college, appears to be an unlikely presence in the market. His bond with the market originates from his childhood visits and the comfort he got from the singing insects when he was confined to bed by fractured bones. This comfort resonates with other enthusiasts and the story flows naturally from one person's obsession to the common interest showed by the circle of fans of the singing insects. The second vendor, different from the first one, is all serious about the business of trading the singing insects. From her story, the reader gets a glimpse of the commercial raising and keeping of the insects and gets a grasp of the business side of the market. At the end of Zheng's story, the reader understands that she and many other vendors are moving to a new market; this piece of information answers the question the reader may have all along when reading a story on a closing market. The last vendor is different from the first two in that she sells accessories instead of singing insects. Reading about her, the reader gets to know the range of the market and the unique function of the market as a place where people came for friendship and escape from the rushing city life.

Going over the outline, we can see the frequent appearance of anecdotes and quotes. The story moves from anecdote to anecdote, linked by summaries that work as transitions. The central point of the story is not preached but illustrated vividly by these mini stories. The story appeals to the emotion of the readers and the underlying tone is nostalgic and slightly melancholy, fitting for a story about a disappearing market that the locals love dearly. The last but two paragraph mentioned the foreign patrons of the market, an effort to make the story directly relevant to the foreign audience.

6.4.2 The problem-solution approach

The following story appearing on the In Focus section of *Shanghai Daily* is a news feature that explores the latest reactions to the national call for food frugality. A news feature, also known as issue-based article, takes an in-depth look behind the central news event and usually takes the problem-solution approach.

Food frugality: empty plates, no leftovers[1]

By Hu Min and Ding Yining

1) SHANGHAI resident Yao Gang, 35, carefully packs a "doggie bag" of leftover fish, chicken and rice after finishing lunch with his mother at a restaurant.

2) "We don't want to waste anything, especially after the central government's call not to waste food," said Yao, surveying the now empty dishes on the table. "The weather is hot, so these leftovers will save us the trouble of cooking to-night's dinner."

3) Wang Xiaping, manager of catering at Xing Hua Lou, the 169-year-old Shanghai restaurant where Yao had lunch, said the venerated eatery has made some adjustments since President Xi Jinping last week urged people to curb food waste in the country.

4) "The amount of soup we served in a big tureen in the past could be shared by four to five diners," she said. "Now we serve in individual bowls, because leftover soup is hard to pack up and take home. We are serving dim sum based on the number of diners as well."

5) The restaurant is also undertaking waste-free practices in the kitchen.

6) "Many people don't like fish tails, so we make them into fish balls to prevent their being thrown away," said Wang. "We have also trained our staff to re-mind diners to order only what they think they can reasonably eat."

7) Signs on all tables remind diners to end food waste.

8) "The majority of diners — families and friends — voluntarily pack up leftovers," said Wang. "Waste is more common at business banquets where

---

① Hu Min and Ding Yining. Food frugality: empty plates, no leftovers [N/OL]. Shanghai Daily. (2020-08-19) [2021-08-04]. https://archive. shine. cn/metro/Food-frugality-empty-plates-no-leftovers/shdaily.shtml.

diners don't take food home. We now divide dishes onto diners' plates, which they will usually finish."

9) Sunya Cantonese Restaurant on Nan-jing Road Pedestrian Mall, which began operating in 1926, has similar waste-warning signs on tables.

10) "We began an 'empty plate' campaign years ago," said executive chef Huang Renkang. "We remind diners not to order too much. Most people are very cooperative."

11) Qin Meifang, 63, who dined at the restaurant with friends, agrees with President Xi's directive.

12) "We absolutely echo his sentiment that stopping food waste is a matter of traditional merit," she said. "We ordered five dishes for the three of us because that's what we thought we could eat."

13) Jin Peihua, deputy secretary-general of the Shanghai Restaurants Association, said his group is encouraging members to present menus that realistically re-flect what people can eat.

14) But it's a slow road to depart from the old Chinese tradition that leaving uneaten food is a compliment to the bountiful generosity of the host of a dinner.

15) At the Shanghai Classical Restaurant, about 5 percent of food is still left uneaten.

16) "For Chinese, mianzi (face) is important," said a diner surnamed Li. "I don't want to lose face, so I order several dishes more than needed because those at the table are my clients. Packing up uneaten food would be embarrassing."

17) At an outlet of Food Republic chain in Putuo District, a cleaner said white-collar workers tend to be less wasteful than families when it comes to food.

18) "On workdays, little is left on the table, while on weekends, some families visiting us order great numbers of dishes — more than everyone can eat," said the cleaner surnamed Huang.

19) Food delivery platforms are also encouraging thriftier portions of takeaways.

20) The China General Chamber of Commerce, the China Cuisine Association, the China Hotel Association, the China Chain Store and Franchise Association and takeaway platform Meituan issued a joint statement calling on all food caterers to support the cause against food waste.

21) Meituan said delivery services are responding. Some have optimized digital menus with clear guidelines on the type and amount of food suitable for takeaways.

22) For menu items, restaurants are spelling out ingredients, tastes, portions and other information about dishes to help customers make wiser choices and avoid food waste. Others are keeping records and collecting user feedback to decide on the right portions to put in lunch bento boxes.

23) Zhang Lijun, deputy director of the China General Chamber of Commerce, said traditional dining customs and the catering industry's often careless use of raw materials have played a major part in the food waste.

24) Han Shuo, head of Meituan's catering business platform, said: "It's important to combine the demand for catering services with consumers' preferences in order to make a more sustainable effort to curb food waste."

25) Allowing restaurants to showcase set menus through digital platforms like Meituan gives consumers the opportunity to make better choices, raise operational efficiency and help avoid waste.

26) Since early August, Meituan's delivery orders for smaller portions of lunches, dinners or desserts have risen 30 percent from a month earlier.

27) At Alibaba's flagship grocery retailer Freshippo, fresh vegetables are being packed in 200-250 grams instead of the normal 500g packaging to help shoppers avoid waste at home.

28) Its latest offerings include set menus for lunch or dinner, and a quarter of roast duck so there won't be any leftovers.

29) On online food service Ele.me, some 600,000 canteens are offering smaller servings of food takeaways.

30) Cities with the most orders of smaller servings include Shanghai, Beijing, Hangzhou, Chengdu and Suzhou.

31) Since early this year, Ele.me has been promoting a campaign to encourage customers to order a half serving "to save food and support children in poorer rural areas."

32) For its merchants, the online site is also offering clear guidelines for them to note where a half or a quarter serving is available for takeaway.

33) Shanghai-based Dingdong Maicai is offering home-cooking customers two-vegetable packs suitable for one meal at a time.

34) The vegetable combo packages, at 600 grams and 400 grams each, are bestselling items, with 5,000 sold on a single day in Shanghai. Smaller offerings

of cooking ingredients such as garlic, spring onions, scallions and chili peppers are also available.

35) Zhao Wentao, head of merchandising at Dingdong, said the company is also planning to offer small combo packages of meat and vegetable as well as small fruit boxes.

36) The tourism industry is also joining the "stop food waste" campaign.

37) "Waste is common in group meals of tourists, and we are reducing meal volumes," said Zhou Weihong, deputy general manager of Shanghai Spring Tour. "We have asked restaurants to provide food based on the number of tourists, and our tour guides will keep reminding tourists to avoid waste when having breakfast buffets."

38) Online travel operator Tongcheng said it is changing its dining model for group tours and reminding travelers to treasure cuisine and not to waste food.

An outline of the above story

Lead

Paras. 1-2

Anecdote: A customer packs a "doggie bag" to avoid food waste.

Body

Para. 3

Summary statement in the form of indirect quote: A Shanghai-based restaurant made various adjustments to reduce food waste.

Para. 4

Adjustment in serving: serving in smaller portion.

Paras. 5-6

Adjustment in the kitchen: making use of all food.

Paras. 7-8

Adjustment in dining process: installing signs that remind diners and dividing dishes onto diner's plates.

Para. 9

Summary statement: another famous restaurant also takes similar measures.

Para. 10

Direct quote providing the previous summary statement with validity.

Paras. 11-12

Anecdote: A customer orders just enough food.

Para. 13

Indirect quote from an industry authority.

Para. 14-16

The cultural reason explaining the waste of food.

Paras. 17-18

Anecdote illustrating the above tradition.

Para. 19

Summary statement: Food delivery platforms take measures to reduce food waste, too.

Para. 20

Joint call for food frugality from various catering industry authorities.

Paras. 21-22

One delivery platform optimizing the menus in collaboration with various restaurants to avoid food waste.

Para. 23

Authoritative source offering another reason for food waste.

Paras. 24-26

Back to the delivery platform: The optimization of menus pays off.

Paras. 27-28

A giant grocery retailer offering food in smaller portions.

Paras. 29-32

Another big online food service taking measures to reduce food waste.

Paras. 33-35

A Shanghai-based online grocery store offering smaller packages.

Para. 36

Summary statement: The tourism industry is joining the food-saving bandwagon.

Papa. 37

A Shanghai travel agency taking measures targeting package tours.

The ending

Para. 38

A big online travel operator doing its bit.

The above outline reads like a laundry list, with invisible headings and subheadings. It fits a structural approach called the problem-and-solution structure. Under this construction, the writer first of all cites the problem. He then divides the major issue into sub-issues, provides the answers to the sub-issues and moves on to the big answer to the problem. This approach is particularly effective in dealing with a story boasting a wide reporting range. The main question of the above story is how the whole catering industry responds to the call for saving food. The writer divides it into three smaller questions and provides answers one by one. The feature article starts with a simple anecdotal lead, then goes right into the main problem by exploring respectively solutions from restaurants, online food services, and tourism industry, all key players within the catering industry. The readers are offered a bird's eye view. The advantage of this structure is self-evident: the story contains real substance. By taking a sweeping look at fast pace, the story gives the impression that the whole industry, not just a few actors, is taking prompt proactive actions. However, the downside of this structure is also obvious. The story, with the lead illustrating the central issue, and the body taking the various aspects of the issue one by one, reads almost like a laundry list. The links, frequently using words like "also," have an inevitability about them. Sometimes this inevitability may come across as dull. One way to make up for this structure-induced dullness is to provide a variety of evidences to give the story diversity. In the above story, we see quotes from authoritative figures who make policies as well as a cleaning lady who cleans the table and sweeps the floor after the meals are finished. We also see anecdotes, quotes, statistics, descriptions, explanations, and other types of materials, all working together to bring out the theme of the story and render the story more interesting.

6.4.3   A combined approach

The following story[①] appears on the deep tone (feature) section of the Sixth Tone, the Shanghai-based English news website. The 2000-word story is accompanied by a four-minute video showing the story of the main character who talks in a calm, almost melancholy voice throughout. The accented voiceover was made intelligible by an English subtitle. More than a dozen photos and graphs are also posted alongside the story. As a result, the story comes alive both in words and in images.

---

① Wu Haiyun. Temples for the masses[EB/OL]. The Sixth Tone. [2021-08-04]. https://interaction.sixthtone.com/feature/2020/Temples-for-the-masses/.

Temples for the masses

In northern China, overstretched local authorities are asking ordinary residents to restore historic monuments. But things don't always go according to plan.

1) Feng Cai opens the doors to Longquan Temple, the centuries-old monument near his home in northern China, and walks slowly to the back of the room.

2) Without saying a word, he grabs a chunk of wallpaper and starts tearing it from the temple walls, reams of paper piling up on the dusty floor.

3) As the 67-year-old continues pulling, a hidden alcove slowly materializes: a brick ledge lining the entire chamber, on which dozens of clay Buddha statues solemnly sit.

4) Feng stares at the figures for a beat, then mutters: "When I see them, my heart feels conflicted. Look at these Buddhas."

5) Compared with the rest of the building, the statues are in a pitiful state: chipped, discolored, and dirt-stained. It's a contrast that clearly pains Feng.

6) A short, round-faced man with sleepy, mournful eyes, Feng has dedicated years of his life and millions of yuan to restoring the ancient temple, which sits near the entrance to his home village of Nanlinjiao in the northern Shanxi province. But he's never been allowed to complete the project.

7) Halfway through the work, Feng was told repairing religious icons was banned in China. The Buddhas have remained trapped in their paper purgatory for over five years.

8) The standoff over the statues is just one example of the tensions that have arisen since Shanxi province launched a campaign encouraging local people to "adopt" regional heritage sites a few years ago.

9) One of China's most historic regions, Shanxi is overrun with ancient artifacts. Local authorities have identified over 53,000 "immovable cultural relics" — more than any other Chinese province — but the government has only been able to put one-fifth of them under official protection.

10) The adoption scheme — launched first at the county level, then rolled out province-wide in 2017 — aims to fix this problem. It calls on entrepreneurs and local communities to take over responsibility for unprotected monuments, funding the restoration of the relics themselves.

11) Shanxi authorities have already signed deals with 88 civil partners, many of them ordinary villagers who have long wanted to repair local ancestral

shrines and other spiritual sites. The government says another 290 projects are in the pipeline.

12) But the adoption deals are also generating controversy. Experts have labeled repairs "destructive." Disputes have emerged over spiraling costs. And policy restrictions have prevented some temples from being fully restored.

13) Like many involved in the scheme, Feng's desire to renovate Longquan Temple long predated his 2010 agreement with the local authorities. For years, he'd dreamed not only of patching up the damaged building, but also of making it a thriving place of worship once more.

14) A mainly wooden structure built in the traditional northern Chinese courtyard style, the temple was established in around the 14th century and had served as the center of spiritual life in Nanlinjiao for centuries.

15) But over recent decades, the temple had fallen into disrepair. During the 1960s, when anti-religious sentiment was at its height in China, villagers converted the building into a flour storehouse and vandalized its stone steles — the scratch marks covering the inscriptions still visible today.

16) For Feng, restoring Longquan to its former glory would allow the village to reconnect with its past. Like many locals in Shanxi, he's fiercely proud of the region's heritage. Over 2,500 years ago, the area where Feng now lives lay at the center of the state of Jin, one of China's most powerful kingdoms during the turbulent era known as the Spring and Autumn period.

17) "My whole family works as farmers. ... I have feelings for our village," says Feng.

18) The adoption program appeared to offer Feng the chance to realize his vision. For decades, the government had directly undertaken historic preservation projects, but a few forward-thinking officials in Shanxi were beginning to question this approach.

19) Sun Yonghe, who served as the head of the cultural relics bureau in Quwo County — the area where Nanlinjiao is located — from 1995 to 2013, was one of those advocating a more flexible policy.

20) "The country has taken care of all the maintenance of these ancient buildings, but in fact it's not strong enough," Sun, now retired, tells Sixth Tone. "There are many things the country has to do. If children are going to school in dilapidated buildings, how can you prioritize refurbishing ancient monuments?"

21) In 2002, Sun had turned to local entrepreneurs to help fund the

restoration of Sipailou, a 400-year-old tower in Quwo. He'd first tried asking local cadres for donations, but had only managed to raise 165,000 yuan (then $ 20,000).

22) Feng Cai, who was running a successful iron and steel company at the time, chipped in 6,000 yuan. The generous sum impressed Sun, who realized the business community could become a powerful driver of the county's conservation efforts.

23) "I found that entrepreneurs have money in their hands, and they're keen to contribute to the welfare of their local area," says Sun. "They're not just profit-seeking businesspeople."

24) Sun and his colleagues repeated the fundraising trick in 2006, during the renovation of another local monument. Then, in 2010, they went further by drafting a policy that would allow entrepreneurs to directly take responsibility for protecting certain relics in Quwo.

25) Feng was one of the first to sign up. He signed a deal with the cultural relics bureau to adopt Longquan Temple for the next 30 years.

26) The officials, however, inserted several conditions into the contract. Quwo County would retain the right to closely oversee any restoration work. Feng could only use government-approved contractors, and the plans would need to be cleared in advance. The bureau would also conduct regular inspections of the temple.

27) According to Sun, the controls were designed to avoid poor-quality repair jobs. Over previous years, Chinese media had uncovered many examples of botched restorations of priceless monuments, including several famous sections of the Great Wall.

28) "It's about using the original craftmanship, the original materials, and the original standards," says Sun. "Repairing it like it was originally."

29) But the approach had a side-effect Feng hadn't anticipated: It sent the project's budget skyrocketing. The former steel boss estimates he's spent 4 million yuan restoring Longquan.

30) "My eldest son got sick and required two kidney transplants," says Feng. "He fell ill after I started repairing the temple, so my heart is quite bitter ... He can't work, but I haven't paid him a penny."

31) Other projects have also become mired in budget issues as the adoption scheme has expanded.

32) In Beiniuchi, a village around 100 kilometers southwest of Nanlinjiao,

local residents have adopted Xie's Family Temple — an ancestral shrine dedicated to members of the Xie clan.

33) According to Xie Tianjun, head of Beiniuchi Village, the temple is the "heart and soul" of the community, and the villagers had wanted to renovate it for years. For many locals, the completion of the project in 2018 was an emotional moment, he says.

34) "This is our ancestral shrine, but it's also deemed a cultural relic and so we dared not repair it without authorization," the 38-year-old tells Sixth Tone. "Every village head had promised to repair it, but none of them had done it."

35) The project appears to be genuinely popular in the village. On a warm July day, groups of elderly residents sit chatting in the shade outside the temple. Several tell *Sixth Tone* they've donated money to fund the repairs and are happy with the works.

36) Yet the construction has also plunged the village into a financial quagmire. Local people raised 310,000 yuan through donations, but this only covered around half the total costs. The project was halted four times over payment issues, forcing Xie to scramble to raise more money.

37) "The project was originally expected to cost 400,000 yuan, but it wasn't like that during the restoration process," says Xie. "Once the repair work starts, you must do it well ... We still owe the contractor hundreds of thousands of yuan."

38) The village had little control over the budget. The design plan was created by Shanxi's provincial ancient architecture research institute, which set high standards regarding materials and craftsmanship, Xie says.

39) Shanxi has won praise for this focus on authenticity, with the government ordering planners to adopt a principle of minimal intervention and banning contractors from demolishing and rebuilding monuments. Experts, however, have questioned the value of some projects.

40) After photos emerged of two colorfully restored temples in northern Shanxi, critics labeled the repairs "destructive," as the buildings looked "entirely different." Some argued the government should focus on simply protecting historic monuments from damage, rather than actively renovating them.

41) But provincial officials insist the criticisms miss the point. From their perspective, local temples aren't simply ancient relics: They're part of a living tradition.

42）"These temples have been built and rebuilt continuously over generations," says Zhao Shuguang, deputy director of the Shanxi Provincial Cultural Relics Bureau. "In archaeological terms, every repair is like a different level of an excavation site. Each layer is valuable."

43）For the government, the adoption scheme is part of China's wider push for "national rejuvenation" — a strategy that aims to restore pride in the country's traditional culture and promote a stronger sense of national identity.

44）"These cultural relics are like elderly family members," says Zhao. "As the old saying goes: 'An old relative is more valuable than treasure.' This is the cultural heritage of our Chinese nation."

45）In many ways, the local adopters Sixth Tone meets share a similar attitude: Their goal is to revive local traditions and reconnect with their region's cultural heritage. Feng says he longs to see Longquan Temple host Buddhist monks and ceremonies once more, as it did for most of the past 1,500 years.

46）In the current policy climate, however, fully renovating the temple has proved impossible. While the work at Longquan was still underway, a family living nearby objected to Feng's project, citing a 1984 national guideline banning the restoration of damaged religious icons.

47）Unable to touch the statues, Feng was forced to halt the project. Now, the temple looks clean, but half-abandoned. Wild grass can be seen growing from the incense holder at the front gate.

48）Feng says he has no regrets, but confesses he rarely visits the temple, as the place tends to make him feel melancholy.

49）"Right in the thick of it, the country just left the matter unsolved," he says. "How could it not feel bad? You can't retreat; you can't move forward. You can only leave it here."

50）It's unclear whether Feng will ever be allowed to repair the statues. Under China's political system, culture and religion are deemed to be entirely distinct phenomena and are handled by two separate bureaucracies: Religion falls under the purview of the United Front Work Department, a branch of the Communist Party of China, while cultural relics are managed by the Ministry of Culture and Tourism, part of the state bureaucracy.

51）Zhao, the provincial official, says he's eager to see restored temples reprise their former roles as important community centers. At the same time, he says not all the temples' traditional functions can be retained.

52) "We have to make a conceptual cut with the past," says Zhao. "Of course, they (village temples) are still related to the past, but they need to be repositioned — no longer a religious place, but a cultural relic."

53) Feng, however, hasn't given up hope. For now, he plans to leave the Buddhas uncovered, while he waits for the day he's finally allowed to restore them.

54) "I've always wanted to protect what I can during my lifetime and leave something for future generations," he says. "This is my belief and ideal."

An outline for the above story

Lead

Paras. 1-7

Significant scene: Feng, the major actor in the story, pulls off the wall paper revealing the clay Buddha statues behind.

➤ A direct quote from Feng showing his sentiment.

➤ Physical description of Feng that puts a face on the voice.

➤ The incident that lands Feng at the scene.

Body

Para. 8

Nut graf/theme statement: Tensions as illustrated by the scene in the lead arise since the local government asked the local people to adopt regional heritage sites for restoration in Shanxi.

Para. 9

Context: Shanxi boasts more relics than can be restored properly by the government.

Paras. 10-11

More elaboration on the theme: details concerning the adoption scheme.

Para. 12

Theme restated: There are three different manifestations of the tensions arising from the adopting deal between the government and the local people.

Paras. 13-17

Back to the main example of the story, Feng's experience adopting his village temple, which illustrates the theme of the story.

➤ Explanation of how the deal came about.

➤ The history and original state of the temple.

➤ Feng's motivations.

Para. 18

Transition paragraph: story moving from the perspective of the local people, represented by Feng, to that of the local officials, exemplified by Sun, an official that had helped to push the adoption project forward.

Paras. 19-28

The official side of the story, told through Sun.

➢ The financial reasons behind the project.

➢ The early anecdotes of fundraising.

➢ The birth of the policy.

➢ More details of the policy and the official rational behind it.

Paras. 29-38

One manifestation of the side effects of the adoption project mentioned in the theme statement.

➢ Zheng's personal finance drained by the restoration work.

➢ Another example illustrating the money problem: a village was plunged into "a financial quagmire" for adopting an ancestral shrine.

Paras. 39-40

Another manifestation of the side effects of the adoption project mentioned in the theme statement: some restoration work criticized as "destructive".

Paras. 41-42

The official response to the criticism cited in the previous paragraphs.

Paras. 43-46

Context: putting the adoption project against the national drive of rejuvenation in traditional culture and national identity.

➢ Both the official and the local people echo the sentiments of the national drive.

Paras. 47-54

The third manifestation of the side effects of the adoption deal mentioned in the theme: the policy restrictions.

➢ The story returning to Feng's predicament as demonstrated in the lead.

➢ Policy restrictions explained.

➢ The halted state of the temple.

➢ The official view of the new cultural role of the traditional village temple.

➢ Feng's determination to see the restoration completed.

The ending

Para. 55

Ending with a quote from the main character of the story restating his motivation and goal of adopting the local temple.

The Sixth Tone story on adopting cultural relics sites takes the most popular organization approach: a combination of the profile approach and the problem-solution structure. Such a combined approach combines the strengths of both constructions. The main character, Feng, acts as the thread that knits the story together. At the opening of the story, we are immediately drawn by an emotionally-charged scene with Feng at the center. Next from the nut graf we understand the story is about Feng and people like Feng who struggle in their spontaneous heritage conservation initiatives. After that, the story goes back to Feng's experience, illustrating the theme with further details. Then at the end of the story, we see Feng again, in the quandary where he "can't retreat, can't move forward." The story finishes with Feng's words, stating his belief and ideal, underlying the psychological reason, often the most powerful one, for adopting the cultural relics at home. We meet other characters in the story, too, with their stories taking less but important space and providing diversity with different experiences and perspectives. At the same time, we can also see a clear problem-solution structure in place. In paragraph 12, the story's theme is restated identifying three different aspects of the central issue (there sub-issues). Then the story moves on to explore the three sub-issues one by one until the finish of the story. Thus we are offered a comprehensive picture delineating the cultural preservation of the whole province, rather than a single frame depicting the story of Feng. Remember, a typical problem-solution story might be tedious to read as the structure suggests an inevitability making the development of the story predictable. But this one with a combined approach is far from tedious. Various anecdotes, statistics, quotes, descriptions, striking facts are given to render the story a riveting heart-felt piece of narrative.

Besides, the success of the story is also due in a large part to the fact that it finds a most suitable protagonist. The Sixth Tone, the news outlet where the story is published, is known for its human-centric approach and its predilection to "highlight the nuances and complexities of today's China" through subjects embroiled in conflict. Feng, the major character in the above story, is caught between a rock and a hard place. In his own words, he "can't retreat, and can't move forward," yet he is not giving up because he wants to leave something for future generations. This conflict and, more important, the deep emotion detected in his words makes the reading experience intense and provocative.

6.4.4 The hour glass approach

The following story[①] published on the Sixth Tone is about one peculiar storeowner collecting stories on a street in Shanghai. The feature article weaves together depictions of the storeowner, the street and the stories collected into a tapestry showing the pathos and vitality of the city life. An hour glass structure can be found in the story.

The Bard of Yuyuan Road

Kenrick Davis

Each night, **Shanghainese musician** Tang Jiamin turns the personal stories of local residents into songs, revealing the human lives in a fast-changing Chinese city.

1) SHANGHAI — On an old, tree-lined street in central Shanghai, past upmarket cafés, manors, and artsy boutiques built over the ruins of former drug dens, there's a squat little store.

2) Coins, cards, and mobile payment codes are useless here. The **manager** — a large-framed, dreadlocked figure named Tang Jiamin — trades in an entirely different form of currency: **stories**.

3) "Money means nothing here," Tang tells Sixth Tone with a grin. "As long as you give stories, you can have everything."

4) Each weekday evening, **the 32-year-old** sits at the Story Store's open window, strumming a guitar as he waits for passersby to stop and share personal **memories** with him over a glass of beer, wine, or whisky.

5) Tang will then write his guest **a song** based on the tale they've shared, perform it back to them, and hand over **the handwritten lyrics** in a wax-sealed envelope.

6) "After I sing what's on this piece of paper, it's like it contains your pain and sorrow," he says. "I then fold it up, put it in the envelope, and stamp it, sealing your pain inside."

7) For the **musician**, the Story Store is a personal passion project, a way of digging under the polished veneer of modern Shanghai to find beautiful human

① Kenrick Davis. The Bard of Yuyuan Road[EB/OL]. The Sixth Tone. (2020-07-03) [2021-08-04]. https://www.sixthtone.com/news/1006002/the-bard-of-yuyuan-road.

stories that capture the reality of life in the city.

8) Through the project, Tang provides an emotional outlet for the local community on Yuyuan Road, a historic neighborhood that has been radically transformed over the past few years.

9) Since the space opened in June, **the young troubadour** says he's collected stories from over 100 strangers, ranging from mundane **tales** to harrowing **memories** of personal trauma.

10) Passersby have opened up about **experiences of childhood abuse, severe bouts of depression, and attempts on their lives by jealous lovers.**

11) Tang plans to publish the most moving tales as **an online series.** He's also writing **a rock album** about the people and places of Yuyuan Road, he says.

12) "There are many different people in our lives, each with unique and amazing tales," says Tang. "After I write the songs, more people will know Yuyuan Road and understand what real life is like."

13) But the Story Store also plays a complex role in the street's life. Though the project aims to act as a salve for the rapid gentrification transforming the area, it's ultimately part of it.

14) Built between 1860 and 1918, Yuyuan Road was formerly known as a historically significant, but sleepy part of the central Changning District. Its red brick terraces previously housed famous figures from the writer Eileen Chang, to Qian Xuesen, the scientist who helped build China's first nuclear bomb.

15) Since 2014, however, the road has undergone a dramatic makeover as part of Shanghai's citywide chengshi gengxin — or "urban renewal" — drive.

16) Local authorities handed over the job of rejuvenating Yuyuan Road to a private urban redevelopment firm named Creater, which christened the project with the motto, "Living art; arting life." The road, it was decided, would be transformed into an artistic hub that would help attract a younger crowd of professionals and consumers to the area.

17) Over the next few years, Creater set about doing just that, beautifying storefronts, converting a parking lot into a plush lawn, and bringing in all manner of trendy businesses, including a glass workshop, flower arrangement specialist, and design-your-own T-shirt store.

18) It was this wave of urban renewal that brought Tang to Yuyuan Road and eventually led to him becoming its resident **bard.**

19) Like many young Shanghainese, Tang's life has been a journey from country to contemporary — his red-tinted dreadlocks, lens-less glasses, and

tattoos belying his rural roots.

20) He grew up in the '90s in an agricultural part of eastern Shanghai known for growing watermelons. As a teenager, he picked up music and carpentry from his relatives, later learning how to make guitars from a master luthier in the eastern Shandong province.

21) In 2013, this niche skillset helped Tang get a job at X-Music, a music store where he still teaches clients how to play and make guitars as a day job. X-Music is such an important part of his life, he has the store's name inked on his forearm next to the emblem of his favorite soccer team, Shanghai Shenhua.

22) Soon after Tang joined X-Music, however, the store's original location on Changning Road was earmarked for demolition. This prompted X-Music to turn to Creater, and after some negotiating the music firm secured permission to set up a new outlet on Yuyuan Road.

23) Over the following years, Tang built a relationship with Creater, helping the developer organize live music gigs and even writing **a rap-rock song** about the road for one event.

24) The idea for a "story store" first came from Xu Yinlan, the general manager of Creater. She tells Sixth Tone that in 2018, she started to realize Yuyuan Road's revamp had left many local residents feeling alienated.

25) "Most stores on the street had been occupied, but we suddenly found ourselves out of touch with our own lives," says Xu. "We'd renewed the road so much, our old lives had been renewed out of existence."

26) Creater abruptly changed tack and launched a series of projects catering to the tastes of the local community. In 2019, the firm established a "community bazaar" filled with old-time businesses that had been displaced due to the urban renewal campaign, such as tailors, locksmiths, and umbrella repair stalls, as well as restaurants selling cheap and well-loved Shanghai dishes.

27) As part of this effort — and to coincide with Yuyuan Road's 101st anniversary — Xu created a pop-up space where locals could make their **voices** heard and pen their memories of Yuyuan Road.

28) "I wanted to hear a sound that came from Yuyuan Road, no matter if it was residents or visitors, good voices or bad," says Xu. "However they saw Yuyuan Road, I wanted to know what they thought of some of the changes that had happened there."

29) It was **a bold idea: a cool, artistic project** designed to deal with **local complaints** that the road had become too cool and artistic. But the pop-up proved

a hit when it opened last August, attracting attention from both local residents and the media.

30) To get the whole community involved, Creater invited Yuyuan Road locals and storeowners to take turns managing the new space — with Tang taking the first shift. By the time **the pop-up** closed in October, it had received over 2,000 written memories, told by people aged from 7 to 95.

31) In many of the **testimonies**, elderly residents fondly **recalled the sights, smells, and sounds of Old Yuyuan Road**. One writer who went by "Old Yang" **reminisced about** a market bazaar being set up on the street in the 1960s, with palm readers, magicians, and hawkers selling toy trinkets.

32) In those days, local stores sold rice, yellow fish, and gingko, while one vendor would occasionally lead a white mare down the street, prompting residents to rush over with cups to buy freshly squeezed milk, Old Yang wrote.

33) Another resident **described** taking part in a parade celebrating the 10th anniversary of the founding of the People's Republic of China in 1959, when he and other local children followed a float carrying a giant revolutionary coat of arms down the crowded street.

34) But many contributors — especially younger Shanghainese — **expressed** sadness at how the road had changed. "This road has become posh and fancy as familiar things have slowly but surely vanished," lamented one 30-year-old writer, who said he used to come to the street for drawing lessons in the early 2000s.

35) After the Story Store's first season ended, it briefly became a nail salon, before shutting down completely as the coronavirus pandemic took hold in China earlier this year.

36) By this time, X-Music had been informed their store on Yuyuan Road was scheduled — once again — for demolition. So, in April, Tang approached Xu, the head of Creater, with a proposal to reopen the Story Store, but this time as a music-story project. During the day, Tang would use the space as a music classroom and guitar-making workshop.

37) Xu agreed, and the second iteration of the project began in June.

38) Tang began his Story Store experiment with great gusto, transforming multiple stories into songs each night. But he soon had to cut down to one song a day, as the **emotionally charged tales** he'd hear every evening started to overwhelm him.

39) "There used to be so many people every day, but then I'd have way,

way, way too many **emotions**," says Tang. "Many nights, people's emotions aren't very good at all. They have a lot of pain, a lot of unhappiness. They tell it all to me, and I write it down. Then, I'll feel their emotions ⋯ I think I need a therapist."

40) The Story Store may have started as an effort to preserve the spirit of Old Yuyuan Road, but Tang says he's philosophical about the rapid changes taking place in Shanghai.

41) "I definitely miss it (Old Shanghai) to some extent, but this is just the passing of an era," he tells Sixth Tone. "All bad things will become good in the end."

42) For Tang, the destruction of the old is part of building something new. Two of X-Music's stores have disappeared, but the company has still expanded and is working to set up practice rooms for promising bands at another location on Yuyuan Road, he says.

43) The musician prefers to describe his role on the road as a **"life artist."** What motivates him to continue the project, he says, is simply the beauty of uncovering astonishing human stories — good or bad — from ordinary people on the street.

44) Xu, meanwhile, says the Story Store has taught her that what many people want more than anything is to have a listening ear.

45) "Many stories, (people) keep to themselves," says Xu. "They don't want those close to them to know them. But they can accept the warmth of **a stranger**."

46) The only sadness for Tang is that Creater will likely take back the space at some point next month: The Story Store was always meant to be a three-month project. Without the space, he worries he'll lack the legitimacy to carry on collecting stories.

47) Like many things in fast-changing Shanghai, the Story Store and its **guitar-wielding bard** will soon become just another story.

An outline of the above story

(**The upper cone of the hourglass**)

Lead

Paras. 1-3

Unusual fact: A street shop trades in stories.

➤   Descriptions of the street

➤   Physical description of the shop manager

➤ A quote from the manager giving validity to the odd fact.

Body

Central event developed in details

Paras. 4-6

Central point of the story in details: The story store manager writes down the stories shared by strangers as songs.

Paras. 7-8

The significance of the story store.

Paras. 9-10

Details bringing out the width and depth of the central event.

➤ Over 100 strangers share their stories.

➤ The heart-rending stories are deeply personal.

Paras. 11-12

What the bard will do with the stories.

(**The narrow connection at the middle of the hourglass**)

Para. 13

Transition paragraph linking the story store with the street it is on.

(**The lower cone of the hourglass**)

Chronology of the street

Para. 14

The origin and history of Yuyuan Road.

Paras. 15-16

The dramatic makeover of the road in 2014.

➤ The makeover is part of the city renewal drive.

➤ A private firm is charged with turning the road to an artistic hub that would help attract a younger crowd.

Paras. 17-18

The makeover continued over the next few years.

➤ Details of the makeover.

➤ The arrival of Tang who later became the resident bard.

Paras. 19-23

Family and work history of Tang that lands him on Yuyuan Road.

Paras. 24-28

How the idea came about in 2018 and was realized in 2019.

Paras. 29-30

The success of the idea and the shop.

Paras. 31-34

Anecdotes: the contents of the stories collected.

➤   Reminiscences of the lost life of the past.

➤   Lamentations on the vanishing of familiar life as the street becomes trendy and hip.

Paras. 35-37

The store closed after "the first season" and reopened this June at the proposal of the bard.

Paras. 38-39

The bard was overwhelmed by the emotionally-charged stories of the second season.

Paras. 40-42

The subject's attitude towards the new quickly replacing the old.

Para. 43

The bard's view of his own role in the story sharing.

Paras. 44-45

An observer's view of the bard's role in the story sharing.

The ending

Paras. 46-47

Looking forward: The store is to be closed again and becomes another story in the fast-changing city.

The hour glass structure is a hybrid of narrative and inverted pyramid. You begin by telling the news, the central issue your story is about, then after the central point is sold you break the pyramid by starting from the beginning in time: the story turns into a chronology retelling the central event in details following the natural time line. The "heavy" introduction (the upper cone of the hourglass) allows you enough space to give the reader an adequate idea of what the story is about. The narrative followed (the lower cone of the hourglass) offers you the opportunity to start slow and build to a climax.

From paragraph one to paragraph 12, or in the upper cone of the hourglass, the above article concentrates on the present situation of the story store and paints a present street scene. Paragraph 13 works as a transition joining the upper cone and lower cone of the hourglass. From paragraph 14, the story turns to the street itself, starting with the birth of it and continuing the narrative following the time sequence. We can see clear time markers throughout this major part of the body of the story. Following the narrative, we gradually find out that most collected stories also tell about how the street has weathered as time goes by. Most of the stories are pregnant with the pathos and poignancies of the time passed, ballades about the fast disappearing of familiar life in the ever changing metropolis. The hourglass seems the perfect choice of structure here. It feels natural to tell a story that's essentially about the change of time following the time line.

So far, we've discussed four kinds of organizational plans: the multiple profile approach, the problem-solution approach, the combined approach, and the hourglass approach. The multiple profile approach is more suitable when your story takes a strong human element and you have access to people who can represent the same class but have diversified and interesting stories. Feature articles organized this way are lively and readable. However, even if the profile subjects are carefully chosen to represent the core issue, the approach is basically writing about the whole through depicting the individuals, and sometimes there is an unavoidable tendency to overgeneralization. One swallow doesn't make a summer. Sometimes neither three or more. So it is better to supplement the mini-profiles with other key information on the issue to give the reader a full and true picture of the story. The problem-solution approach is more appropriate for an information rich story, often a news feature. The feature story thus structured is written in the style of a news article. It deals with a subject in painstaking detail and requires a large number of facts to support the story. The problem-solution structure has a clear internal logic in terms of organizing large amounts of information in an effective way, although sometimes this rather predictable organizational plan can lead to repetition and dullness if not executed well. The combined approach is the strategical combination of illustrating profiles and the cataloguing of sub-issues and their solutions. This approach is also the most commonly seen in feature writing. The last approach discussed above is the hour glass approach, which is essentially a chronology preceded with an introductory section. This approach enjoys priority when you have a real story in the traditional sense to tell, for it follows the natural sequence of time and builds to climax towards the ending. This approach also has more breathing space in the story: You are allowed to take time to introduce the various characters going onto the stage and paint the landscape along the way in greater details.

Last but not least, apart from the four basic structures discussed above, there are many more organizational plans at a feature writer's disposal. You can practically organize your story in any fashion that comes natural to you, as long as the readers' attention is retained along the way and the story point is made eventually.

6.5　Essential ingredients

The anatomy of the stories above reveals similar key components that work in tandem to bring the story to life.

6.5.1　Meaningful figures

Figures and statistics are frequently used in feature articles. The data, in a straightforward way, helps to put the story in proportion, to bring out the intensity of the issue or to reflect the enormity of the problem to be discussed. To be effective, the figures used shouldn't be just any statistics collected. Use only the relevant and striking ones. Take the following paragraph from the Sixth Tone story "Temple for the masses" and make note of how the two figures embedded in the short paragraph alone reveal the seriousness of the daunting task the local officials face.

> One of China's most historic regions, Shanxi is overrun with ancient artifacts. Local authorities have identified over **53,000** "immovable cultural relics" — more than any other Chinese province — but the government has only been able to put **one-fifth** of them under official protection.

As the above example shows, numbers are very useful, but there are many pitfalls involving numbers. Firstly, a healthy skepticism should be always maintained towards the numbers themselves, as one expert observes "The idealized perception of where numbers come from is that someone measures something, the figure's accurate and goes straight in the database. That is about as far from the truth as it's possible to get."[1] Secondly, even the numbers are accepted as accurate, they themselves should be put in context. In his book,

---

[1]　Michael Blastland, Andrew Dilnot. The Tiger That Isn't: Seeing Through a World of Numbers[M]. 2nd ed. London: Profile Books LTD, 2008: 131.

Michael Blastland suggests[①] that reporters should be on guard of the following five potential pitfalls, all of which are induced by failing to see and use the data in context.

1. Make sure the "big" number is a really big one.

2. Look at runs of data to decide whether the presented data is a new change or tends to follow an old pattern.

3. When making comparisons, make sure the two items you compare are really comparable.

4. Take the wider view as "A 100 per cent increase in risk can be a change in one in a million to two in a million."

5. Ask about where and how the data is obtained in the first place.

These are valuable advice and following them one will produce better stories. Take the following numbers appearing in a story on the aging issue of a Shanghai neighborhood community. The first number indicating the sum of the funding appears to be big. But is it really so? The second figure indicating the number of people benefited from the funding gives the answer by putting the former in context.

> Gu Haiying, the secretary of Jiuyang Community, said that the Shanghai government provides 200,000 yuan (about 30,000 dollars) every year for their community-based elderly care. The community has a population of 763 above 60 years old, which means about 40 dollars per person. "With financial support from the government and assistance from the property management department, the senior citizens in our community volunteer to organize recreational activities," she said. In China, the community-level department to which the proprietors entrust their estate is bound to offer services to improve quality of life.

Another problem in presenting China to the world is that China and other countries have different methods of measurement. Naturally, there is a need to convert between units of measurement of different systems. For example, when it comes to figures that represent monetary values, it is common practice to convert Renminbi into dollars so that foreign readers can understand them immediately. Various conversion tables can be easily found online or in related

---

① MICHAEL BLASTLAND, ANDREW DILNOT. The Tiger That Isn't: Seeing Through a World of Numbers[M]. 2nd ed. London: profile books LTD, 2008.

reference books, and all you need to do is to hit a few buttons on a calculator. This translation between different systems may seem easy, but mistakes do arise. Care should be exercised in conversion. Both the conversion calculation and the measuring units must be right.

6.5.2 Anecdote

An anecdote is a short narrative of an interesting or amusing event, usually to illustrate or support a point in an article, essay or book. It is widely used in feature writing. The main point of the article is explained in a lively way by quoting a true story from life. This is the most important function of anecdotes in feature articles. While the events involved should have some entertainment value, what is really important is that the short story can illustrate certain points in the story. Take, for example, the following anecdote at the beginning of a story about food frugality. The incident described may seem ordinary and banal; a diner packing a doggy bag after a meal may not generally be found interesting by the reader. However, it is appropriate to cast it as the beginning of this particular story about saving food because it illustrates the problem in a simple way.

> SHANGHAI resident Yao Gang, 35, carefully packs a "doggie bag" of leftover fish, chicken and rice after finishing lunch with his mother at a restaurant.
> "We don't want to waste anything, especially after the central government's call not to waste food," said Yao, surveying the now empty dishes on the table. "The weather is hot, so these leftovers will save us the trouble of cooking to-night's dinner."

Anecdotes can be long or short in length, but incidents contained should be simple. The following two-sentence paragraph is taken from the story on the disappearing bird and flower market. The simple anecdote manages to convey the point of the story fully and beautifully in one line.

> "I once encountered an old man who had hearing loss but still came here to buy singing insects. He was endowed with memories of the past."

Anecdotes are essentially serendipitous. It's hard to come by because it takes both work and luck. That's why a good story is often considered to be precious ingredient not to be wasted. On the other hand, it is important to note that an anecdote in a feature article, like everything else that goes into the story, must be real in every way. You can't fabricate a tale if none turns up in your interview or research. It is also considered highly unethical to embellish or "improve" the reality to serve your point.

6.5.3   Quotes

When asked how she decides whether to use a quotation or whether to paraphrase, prize-winning reporter Julie Sullivan answers, "I know as soon as I hear it. The things that make me laugh or that really make the individual stand out are the quotations that I use."[1] Sullivan sums it up well. Direct quotes ideally should be informative, colorful, and punchy. Like nothing else, an incisive quote lends originality and authenticity to your story. As William Zinsser, the author of *On Writing Well*, observed: "His own will always be better than your words, even if you are the most elegant stylist in the land. ... This is a person talking to the reader directly, not through the filter of a writer. As soon as a writer steps in, everyone else's experience becomes secondhand."[2] Therefore, a quote should indicate something more than a mere fact, which can be and is better given in indirect speech. For example, the following quote involved a simile in which the speaker's opinion is embedded. In the quote, we are not told any further information about what's going on. Instead, we are shown how Zhao feels about the cultural relics.

"These cultural relics are like elderly family members," says Zhao. "As the old saying goes: 'An old relative is more valuable than treasure.' This is the cultural heritage of our Chinese nation."

In the same article, this quote from the main subject is brimming with emotions. The fact is simple and has already been stated clearly in the story, i.e. the project halted for policy reason. But this powerful quote goes beyond the fact and gives the reader a glimpse into the man who is thwarted temporarily in his dream to build and leave something to his children.

---

[1]   Best Newspaper Writing 1991[M]. St. Petersburg: The Poynter Institute for Media Studies, 1991:109.
[2]   William Zinsser. On Writing Well [M]. 5th ed. New York: Harper Perennial, 1994: 63.

"Right in the thick of it, the country just left the matter unsolved," he says. "How could it not feel bad? You can't retreat; you can't move forward. You can only leave it here."

Sometimes the almost unintended humor in a quote will add interest to the article. Take the following words from the singing-insect seller in the bird and flower market.

"I thought it (taking insects to school) was very cool," says Bai. "However, the hobby made it difficult for me to make girlfriends."

Don't write a run of quotes. Three or four paragraphs of successive quotes are excessive and annoying to the readers, unless the quoted materials are really good. The proper way is to break the run of quotes by summarizing or paraphrasing. Take the following example: the consecutive quotes are broken in the middle by paraphrasing. Also take note of the fact that both speakers are identified at the earliest opportunity.

" For Chinese, mianzi (face) is important," said a diner surnamed Li. "I don't want to lose face, so I order several dishes more than needed because those at the table are my clients. Packing up uneaten food would be embarrassing."

At an outlet of Food Republic chain in Putuo District, a cleaner said white-collar workers tend to be less wasteful than families when it comes to food.

"On workdays, little is left on the table, while on weekends, some families visiting us order great numbers of dishes — more than everyone can eat," said the cleaner surnamed Huang.

Don't go out of your way to find other words to replace the verb "says". In most cases, "says" is the perfect word to use for its simplicity and exactness. In all probability, readers barely take note of it, as what is being said is what counts. Also it is advisable to avoid using "smiles" and "laughs" in place of "says." No one can smile a word or laugh a word. People say their words.

The past tense of the saying verb is the rule, especially if there are multiple speakers in the story, and each is introduced in a different situation. However, many feature writers like to use the present tense of the saying verb throughout the story as an historic present to provide immediacy, to give the reader the impression of being present as things unfold. However, when doing so, be consistent throughout in the story. Three of the four stories cited above use the present tense of the saying verb. Only one story, the one on food frugality from *Shanghai Daily*, followed the tradition of using the past tense of the saying verb. The present tense is also used to signify unchanging belief, as the following example illustrates. The verb "agrees" is in the present tense, though the whole sentence is in the past.

Qin Meifang, 63, who dined at the restaurant with friends, agrees with President Xi's directive.

6.5.4   Description

One important characteristic of feature articles is that they are often descriptive. Hence the golden rule: show, don't tell. A writer who does much telling and little showing is asking the readers to trust his conclusion without providing the necessary evidence. The resulting article, grounded in interpretation rather than observation, tells more about the author than the subject which is the true reason for reading. Besides, the rule requires a higher level of language that is marked by precision and concreteness. By showing and not telling, the interest level of the story is raised because detailed description is not only enjoyable to read but also surprisingly informative. So instead of telling the reader that the main subject is old, show by describing a bit the grayed hair, the wrinkled face and the hobble in his walk.

Of course, not every feature article is heavy on description. News features, the category that concentrates on exploring a current issue, are often not. Detailed description of each actor appearing in the story is rather a luxury that the reporter can't afford. Most of the time, one short line or a couple of spot-on adjectives will do. In the story on cultural relics, the main character is portrayed as "a short, round-faced man with sleepy, mournful eyes." In the street bard story, the story collector is described as "a large-framed, dreadlocked figure." The value of the succinct physical description is immense. Without them, all the faceless characters will make a rather vague story. The readers hear the man, but can't really see who is talking. The physical description completes the character by giving a face to the voice and makes them real on paper. Physical description also serves to build the character. Later in the street bard story, the bard is further depicted: "Like many young Shanghainese, Tang's life has been a journey from country to contemporary — his red-tinted dreadlocks, lens-less glasses, and tattoos belying his rural roots." From the several details, all revealing his country origin, we get to know the bard a little bit fully: he came to the metropolis in search of change and a better life so it's small wonder that for him, "the destruction of the old is part of building something new."

In addition, description creates mood or atmosphere for the story. "On an old, tree-lined street in central Shanghai, past upmarket cafés, manors, and artsy boutiques built over the ruins of former drug dens, there's a squat little store." So begins the street bard story. This short piece of description manages to set up a scene rich with icons of both the contemporary and the old Shanghai. The tree-lined street, the upmarket cafes, manors, and artsy boutiques all speak of a trendy metropolis we are familiar with. The ruins of former drug dens tell of a Shanghai that's decadent and remote in time. The story on adopting cultural relics also starts with careful description of a scene which is described with more verbs than adjectives or adverbs. Such series of verbs as "open" "walk" "grab" "tear" "pull" "stare" and "mutter" bring out the action of the key character. This action opens the story strongly for the scene thus depicted is significant and symbolic of the conflict at the center of the story: So far, pulling off the wall paper and revealing the Buddha statues are the only thing Tang, the key character, can do. Apart from the verbs, there are some adjectives used in the description: "the statues are in a pitiful state: chipped, discolored, and dirt-stained." Take note that the adjectives used here, "chipped, discolored, dirt-stained," all to depict factual observations; no opinion is involved. The only word that expresses opinion is the adjective "pitiful." But this comment seems fair and is justified promptly by the description followed.

Good description creates image and a sense of place that help to anchor the story and assist the readers in "seeing" and "feeling" the story as well as reading it. Without such anchoring, the actors and what they do (which is supposed to matter somehow) would seem to exist and take place in an abstract world that's faceless, vague, and distant from real life. Good description gives texture to the ambiance of a story. A good feature writer takes advantage of all five senses, offering a full range of sensory information. Take this short piece of description from the bird-and-flower-market story involving a sound element: "Located on Xizang Road S., the market was perhaps most famous for "exotic" pets, like Chinese crickets, cicadas and grasshoppers. Its air is filled with the cacophony of chirping insects."

Good description requires an ingenuous use of telling details. A widely-recognized standard for good writing of any kind is precision in writing. This means providing the right details in the right place. Not all details will do. Some details are so commonplace that they will put the reader to sleep rather than hold his/her attention. On the other hand, telling details will snap the reader out of drowsiness and keep him/her emotionally engaged. By definition, telling details also means these details illustrate certain aspects of the story. For instance, in the following paragraph from the bird-and-flower-market story, "the flashlights and magnifying glasses" speak volume of the gusto of the insect lovers.

> "Some customers spend a whole day in the market in order to find a satisfactory insect as a pet," says Zheng Haixian, 36, an insect-stall owner. "The use of flashlights and magnifying glasses helps buyers to examine the insects' limbs."

6.5.5　Action

Action is a story element that pervades the entire story. Sometimes, the natural unfolding of an event is the main action of the story. For such stories, the central event described often has an inherent dramatic quality. Sometimes, the story follows the actions of the main subject. As in the Sixth Tone article on the adoption of heritage, the main part of the story traces the main subject's struggle to build and leave something behind for future generations. Sometimes, of course, we get a story in which people talk, analyze, argue and generally remain sedentary. Such talky articles, which turn off readers because of their lack of action, usually stem from the lack of real subjects, i.e. people who are directly involved or deeply affected by what is happening. It is therefore important at the reporting stage to find people who are interesting and relevant to the story, rather than just offering an opinion.

Besides finding the right subject, a good command of verbs is essential in delivering the action that entertains as well as informs. Feature writing, like news reporting, favors short, strong, active verbs, instead of long, passive, tedious ones. For an action scene, it is helpful if you keep description of things other than the action itself to the minimum. Also, a use of short, choppy sentences will add to the pace and momentum of the scene. The following paragraphs depict with short strong verbs a hurricane in action[①].

> First the air yanks, then slips its fingers into the tiny gap between door and door frame, then strains at the heavy steel structure until the door actually bends.
>
> Then the awful clutching silence, and the wind returns, up another impossible gear.
>
> By midnight, as the worst of the fury roars nightmarishly over Charleston, the very walls tremble and quake.

6.5.6　Extensive background information

Background information is a key ingredient in journalism writing. Given the space available, extensive background information can be provided at leisure in a feature article. For English feature stories on China, the background information often focuses on explaining traditions, customs, policies that are China specific and that can be dense to a foreign reader. However, it is unadvisable to concentrate background information in one big chunk. It is better to disperse it wherever necessary. The resulting story will breathe more easily and thus more readable. Also, a writer needs to remember that the current issue is the story, not the contextual materials. Therefore, get back to the main theme quickly after whatever point in need of explanation has been clarified.

The following paragraphs are taken from a story on the restoration of a historic residence. The building belonged to a famous newspaper owner in the Republic of China period. This English story[②] is trans-edited from a Chinese

---

① Don Fry and Karen Brown. Best Newspaper Writing 1990 [M]. St. Petersburg: The Poynter Institute for Media Studies, 1990: 56.

② Zhu Yinghong, Qin Yiling. Restoration of newspaper magnate's former residence almost finished[EB/OL]. Shanghai Songjiang APP. (2021-04-07) [2021-08-21]. https://app.sjmedia.net/App/content/detailshare.html? contentId ＝ 5444308&appId ＝ 110139&projectId ＝ 12&shareAppId ＝ 110139&channelType＝4.

story. The original Chinese story[①] doesn't take the trouble to explain who the newspaper owner is. But the English story adds one background paragraph after the lead, introducing the house's renowned owner and putting the restoration in context. After the one-paragraph digression, the story immediately goes back to the restoration which is the main theme of the article.

> "The restoration and renovation of Shi Liangcai's former residence is a major project. We have now finished most of the work. Around April 9, the five-month work period will officially come to an end," said Zhang Chao, the manager in charge of the project. He said that beams and columns, tiles, the wooden structure, the walls, the flower-patterned glazed windows and the wooden windows were the key points in the restoration work.
>
> Shi Liangcai (1880-1934), a businessman, educator and newspaper owner, was one of the most outstanding newspaper operators in China at the beginning of the last century. He is remembered for his famous saying: "The country has its own dignity, newspapers have their own standards, and people have their own personality."
>
> The restoration of Shi Liangcai's former residence has aimed at preserving authenticity as much as possible. The goal is restoration rather than renovation. The restorers have sought to respecting the original architectural style, and have extended the life of the building with ingenuity.

6.5.7   The ending

Compared with news stories, feature articles are more complete in terms of organization. In a sense, a news story doesn't have a real ending. Structured as the inverted pyramid, it tells the story from the most important to the least so that an editor can cut off the end if there's not enough space. Though for news on the web, space is no longer the true concern, attention is, this tradition is retained. On the other hand, feature stories have no fixed structure. It is often written as a piece of narrative, with an opening, a middle, and an end. And much thought is given to how to end the story in a natural yet powerful way.

---

① 朱颖宏.匠心修复延长建筑"生命",史量才故居修缮基本完工[EB/OL].松江融媒体中心.(2021-03-27) [2021-08-21]. https://app.sjmedia.net/App/content/detailshare.html? contentId=5388510&appId=110139&projectId=12&shareAppId=110139&channelType=4.

When to end a story? The answer is simple: end when you are ready to end. A feature story answers certain questions around the issue it explores. When you have examined all necessary aspects and answered all the questions, conclude the story without delay. For instance, the *Shanghai Daily* story on food frugality ends with the food saving measure promised by online travel operator Tongcheng, the last item on the laundry list that the reporter set to enumerate in the story. No further summation or concluding comment is given at the end. The ending may feel abrupt, but on reflection it is appropriate for the story has run its course and said all it has to say. Further summation or conclusion of all the measures taken is redundant and borders on editorializing.

What to end the story? You can basically end your story with anything that seems fit. More often than not, a quote is used. Two of the four stories discussed in this section end with quotes from the main subjects.

How to end the story? A great finish is powerful, provocative, and fulfilling. Above all, it should feel natural: an end grows out of the innate development of the story, not an appendage tacked on at the last minute. In this sense, a writer starts with the finish in sight because the whole article is a coherent whole. Evidence is presented throughout by which readers can come to their own conclusions as the story naturally flows to its ending.

Here are several ways to end a feature story effectively.

Restate the thesis. This is the most common type of ending. At the end of the story, a summary of the story is offered, echoing the theme of the story stated at the beginning. For example, the story on relics adoption ends with Feng, the main subject we meet in the lead of the story. He was placed with his crumbling Buddha statues, the restoration of which being the snag Feng ran into at the start. The ending brings the story full circle to its conflicting opening, achieving a satisfying symmetry. Another Sixth Tone story[1], the opening part of which we cited earlier in this chapter, also ends the same way. The story on Chinese students stuck in fake major begins with telling the misfortune of one such student and ends with the same person. By quoting the subject, the finish reiterates the fact that she was stuck, going nowhere, for lack of a genuine diploma. Here is the last paragraph of the story.

---

[1] Yuan Ye. The Chinese Students Stuck in Fake Majors[EB/OL]. The Sixth Tone. (2019-08-270) [2021-08-04]. https://www.sixthtone.com/news/1004486/The#.

Zhao hopes to start her studies again one day, but she is struggling to move on. The first high-speed train left Sheyang's new station in January. She was not there to see it. "I'm a waste of space at home," she says. "I'm almost 20 now. I tried to find a (decent) job, but without a diploma, I couldn't do anything."

Look to the future. The story on the street bard ends by looking at future prospects of the story store and we understand that the second round of story collection is over and whether the store will be open again is uncertain: "Like many things in fast-changing Shanghai, the Story Store and its guitar-wielding bard will soon become just another story." Future, an essential story element, falls naturally at the end of the story. After all the important questions have been answered, it is only logical to look at the future possibilities. Thanks to its uncertain nature, future involves an element of suspense, which makes for interesting ending. The *Shanghai Daily* story titled "Chinese medicine: defenders and doubters", the one cited in chapter two, ends with a sense of suspense. There's no cure for COVID-19 right now. However, "clinical trials of existing drugs are undergoing around the world, including one traditional Chinese medicine approved of the clinical trial by Chinese medical authorities in late March." This ending leaves things unsolved; this very uncertainty as to what the future might bring accurately mirrors the mood of the time that the story is set in. However, beware of editorializing when looking into the future. You can't offer your own opinion. Ask the interviewing subject to forecast for you, or search for a creditable survey or report that predicts on tomorrows. The following ending is taken from a *Shanghai Daily* story trying to decipher a Chinese bit-part actor's sudden popularity on international social media platforms. At the finish of the story, we see the main subject talk about his own future[1].

The online meme will soon disappear as all pop trends do, leaving Zhang to get on with his life. This year, he said, he will direct a web series with himself in the leading role.

"Acting is a job I love," he said. "I will prove myself."

---

[1] Lu Feiran. Meme's the word: How Eggman struck a chord [N/OL]. Shanghai Daily. (2020-07-10) [2021-08-04]. https://www.shine.cn/feature/lifestyle/2007101900/.

Something new. Yet another effective way of ending is to offer something new at the very end of the story. This piece of new information is intended as food for thought for the readers. Ideally it should involve some new perspective that will start the readers on a new line of thinking. Take special care not to raise a new question at the very end of the feature article that will go unanswered. For example, in a *Shanghai Daily* story titled "Meet a music composer who never sleeps"① and introducing an AI system developed by Microsoft that can compose music "from pop and folk to electronic," the reporter chooses to end the story by a quote arguing for the irreplaceability of human performers. Here's the ending that gives the reader something to chew on.

> But she cautioned that the technological wizardry of today has its limitations.
> "Despite the emergence of AI avatar performers and online concerts, live performances in theatres are irreplaceable," she said.
> "High technology promises accuracy, but live performances promise warmth."

Another story from *Shanghai Daily* titled "If it looks like a duck and quacks like a duck, it may be a pet,"② after describing the exotic experience of raising a call duck as pet, ends with a new aspect of the issue: "A new animal protection law is being drafted and public feedback is being solicited. If enacted, abandoning or abusing animals would be a punishable offense." Clearly, animal abandonment is not the central issue for the story that begins with a pet call duck of a celebrity being stolen and cooked as food. With this ending, the story is bigger than before and the reader is given something new to think about besides the creamy white ducks that can fetch for 6,000 yuan.

6.5.8 Knitting the article together

A well-organized article is coherent. Coherence, the hallmark of good

---

① Ma Yue. Meet a music composer who never sleeps [N/OL]. Shanghai Daily. (2020-09-05) [2021-08-04]. https://archive.shine.cn/feature/Meet-a-music-composer-who-never-sleeps/shdaily.shtml.

② Lu Feiran. If it looks like a duck and quacks like a duck, it may be a pet [N/OL]. Shanghai. Daily. (2020-07-15) [2021-08-04]. https://www.shine.cn/feature/lifestyle/2007152225/.

writing, means all story parts or elements "hang together," well-connected and all heading in the same direction. However, on what exactly do the disparate and diverse story elements hang? What truly pulls the miscellaneous pieces together in the story? The answer lies in that invisible yet crucial string of decisions and judgments that give the story its structure — the story logic. It is logic that truly shapes a story. That's why good stories come above all from good thinking. Failing that, the resulting article, a jumble of bits and pieces of disorganized materials thrown in at the last minute, is unintelligible for lack of coherence.

At the technical level, story coherence is achieved through effective use of transitional devices. A sound structure based on strong logic makes natural transitions possible, which is also the best kind of transitions. Many professional writers advise against writing tortured artificial transitional paragraphs, the sole purpose of which is to make transition. But, more often than not, writers need to be skilled in transitional techniques to achieve flow. Here are a few linking techniques.

Repetition. Coherence can be created between paragraphs through repetition. Repetition of words across sentences helps to reiterate the same ideas between sentences. One way of using repetition to create coherence is to repeat the same word or phrase at the end of one sentence and the beginning of the next sentence to show how the ideas connect. Look at the following three paragraphs[①] and see how repetition of ideas (Ed looked for Katherine) and words (look for, café and shop) are used to link these paragraphs together.

> For more than 50 years, Ed **looked for** Katherine wherever he went.
>
> His heart danced in his chest when he passed a woman with dark, auburn air. He **looked for** her in their favorite **restaurants**. Once, he browsed through her favorite **dress shop** on the pretense of shopping for his mother.
>
> Over the years, the **cafes** were torn down and **the dress shop** closed. She was a true love lost.

Connectives. Repetition is the most common transitional device at a writer's proposal. But it is not the only one. There are assorted connectives, mood changers as identified by William Zinsser, that assist in the logical flow of ideas

---

① Don Fry and Karen Brown. Best Newspaper Writing 1990 [M]. St. Petersburg: The Poynter Institute for Media Studies, 1990: 92.

when used properly. Zinsser advises that a writer must alert the reader as soon as possible in a sentence to any change in mood from the previous sentence[①]. The miscellaneous connectives, the conjunctions, prepositions or adverbs, can serve exactly that purpose. Connectives connect and relate sentences and paragraphs. They help making effective transitions as they signal the relationship between sentences and paragraphs. In a feature article, the material is supported and conditioned not only by the ordering of the material but by connectives which herald order, relationship and movement.

These connectives can express relationships with what has gone before, such as addition of ideas (and, also, besides, further, furthermore, too, moreover, in addition, then, of equal importance, equally important, another); results (as a result, hence, so, accordingly, as a consequence, consequently, thus, since, therefore, for this reason, because of this); example (for example, to illustrate, for instance, to be specific, such as, moreover, furthermore, just as important, similarly, in the same way); purpose (to this end, for this purpose, with this in mind, for this reason(s)); contrast (but, in contrast, conversely, however, still, nevertheless, nonetheless, yet, and yet, on the other hand, on the contrary, or, in spite of this, actually, in fact); and summarizing (in summary, to sum up, to repeat, briefly, in short, finally, on the whole, therefore, as I have said, in conclusion, as you can see).

And the list goes on. Take time to learn these useful connectives and take care when applying them in your story. Make the most of these connectives that develop, relate, connect, and move ideas.

Pronouns and demonstratives. Words like "he" "she" "they" "it" "this" "these""that" "those" are pronouns and demonstratives. They assist in making effective transitions by referring to words or statements further back in the article. Definite article "the" and comparative words like "equal" "similar" "such" "bigger" "smaller" "the former" "the latter" function in a similar way in connecting the story seamlessly.

Synonyms and near-synonyms. These are widely used in feature writing mainly to create variety in language. Additionally, these synonyms and near synonyms function to link the sentences and passages together in an unobtrusive way. For instance, in the second and third paragraph of the street bard story

---

① William Zinsser. On Writing Well [M]. 5th ed. New York: Harper Perennial, 1994:117.

cited in this chapter, such equivalent words and synonymous phrases as "coins" "cards" "mobile payment codes" "currency" and "money" are used in three different places to mean the same thing. Throughout the story, the main subject is referred to as "Shanghainese musician" "the manager" "the 32-year-old" "the young troubadour" "its resident bard" "guitar-wielding bard" "a life artist", and "stranger" who lends an understanding ear. Similarly, the story and the story store appear under different names and in synonymous descriptive terms. The story store is referred to as "a pop-up place" "a bold idea" "a cool artistic project" respectively. The stories collected are intimated in different places as "personal memories" "a song" "handwritten lyrics" "mundane tales" "harrowing memories" "experiences of childhood abuse" "severe bouts of depression" "attempts on their lives by jealous lovers" "an online series" "a rock album" "testimonies" "emotions (that) aren't good at all" "local complaints" "voices," and "emotionally-charged tales." People don't just tell their stories to the bard of Yuyuan Road, they "described" "expressed" "share personal memories with him over a glass of beer, wine, or whisky" "opened up about (personal) experiences" "recalled the sights, smells, and sounds of Old Yuyuan Road," and "reminisced about a market bazaar back in the 1960s." The use of all these synonyms or the near-synonyms contributes greatly in a subtle manner to maintaining the internal coherence of the feature article.

Exercise

Draw an outline of the following story[①] on a couple of special pig-raisers on pig farms in Songjiang and examine how the story is put together. Can you discern a structure? What is it? Is it a proper structure for this particular story? Why?

A Pig Raising Rehab Story
By Li Cathy, Ding Yijie

Stories of addicts may sound like retribution, liability, and the unspoken. Nevertheless, Yao Cuilin escaped the treacherous grip of substance abuse,

① Li Cathy, Ding Yijie. A pig raising rehab story [EB/OL]. Shanghai Songjiang APP. (2021-06-25) [2021-0822]. https://app.sjmedia.net/App/content/detailshare.html? contentId=5749423&appId=110139&projectId=12&shareAppId=110139&channelType=4.

with his sister pulling him out of the dark pit he once sank in and earning his freedom and confidence from raising pigs.

Yao Cuilian wakes up to a life she never imagined herself to have, waking daily at 5 am to check up on the pigs on the farm. Four years ago, Yao Cuilian, in her early 40s, abandoned her office job with decent pay, returning to the suburban town of Shanghai to start a pig farm. Almost everyone around her questioned her decision, but she had faith in herself to help her brother recover from substance abuse and build a future together.

The siblings are only one year apart, the older sister Yao Cuilian had heard that the town they live in was planning to build new pig farms and to hire people raise the pigs, and she thought this was an excellent opportunity, and her brother Lin also agreed to take the chance. Pig farm is unlike most startup businesses; not much money is required, but labor. Yao Cuilin was also under the pressure of over $50 thousand of debt, and the pig farm became the hope to start his life over.

However, many villagers who knew Yao Cuilin were in doubts. "Can he raise the pigs well? What if the pigs escape or get stolen?" a managing director of the pig farm said.

It turns out the pigs are fine after more than three years, all plump and happy. So are the hog-raisers, working hard and living a steady life. A life Yao Cuilin has thought that he may never have the chance to live again.

Eighteen years ago, Yao Cuilin came into contact with drugs, much like many people do, through a fatal curiosity. At that time, he was hanging around with the wrong crowd, leading him to an unhealthy and detrimental lifestyle.

"He was always outside, he never came home and did not have a job," said Yao Cuilian.

Over the years, Yao Cuilin saw the addiction drive away his parents and wife and leave him with nothing but a huge debt. His wife divorced him in 2006 and raised their daughter on her own. Yao and his wife kept Yao's habit from their daughter who grew up not knowing.

Fast forward to the year 2017, Yao Cuilin fell accidently and broke a few bones due to bone frailty caused by drug use. Lying on hospital bed, Yao realized he was over 40 years old (his daughter already in college), poorer in health and deeper in debt, and he could not live on like this. He decided to quit the drug and asked for help, though at that time he didn't know his fresh start in his middle age began with a pig farm and the help and support from his big sister.

That same year, upon Yao Cuilian's repeated pleas and constant assurances, the town leaders decided to give the siblings a chance, and allocated two pig farms, one in south, one in north, to them, allowing them to raise the pigs separately.

Having a pig farm is not an easy job; raising pigs requires immense time and care. On top of that, pork prices constantly change, with potential risks of diseases.

Even in recent months, the pig-raising is one of the industries severely suffering the aftermath of the Covid-19 pandemic. In June, China's national pig price has dropped to around 17 yuan per kilogram from 37 yuan per kilogram at the beginning of the year, according to reports of *Global Times*. The fall in pork prices is due to oversupply, pig obesity and lower demands due to financial pressure in households from the pandemic. Farmers fatten up their pigs in anticipation of a recovery in pork prices; however, this has caused a sell-off of these larger-sized pigs, resulting in an explosive price slump.

In China, pig farms are owned by enterprises and companies, in which they hire farmers to raise pigs. The market price adjustments of pig do not directly affect these farmers. Their income depends on the quality of each pig they raised, according to Ms. Yao.

After working on the pig farm for a while, both siblings realized the difficulty of this job. Lack of strength, knowledge, and experience beat these two to the ground, but neither stayed on the ground. Yao Cuilin turned off his phone, left his previous social groups, ignored the negative influences, and worked on the farm day and night.

"He lost 15 kgs in the first year, but he got a lot more muscle, and the job is getting easier on the farm," the sister said proudly. She also lost a couple of pounds with muscles on her arms.

Yao Cuilian gets up at 5:30 am every day and goes into the pig pen at 6 am to check on the pigs. "We need to check out the pigs' stomachs, to see if the pigs are walking on stilts, and find and treat any slight colds or stomach discomfort in time," she said. "We have to clean up the pig manure twice a day, and the temperature of the pig farm should also be controlled and regulated."

It has been especially hard to deal with the pig manure. The pig pen stinks, the ground is slippery, and a lot of feces stuck to the ground is not easy to clean. The determined woman, thin and small, often spent hours bending over in the pig pen and kept waving the shovel.

In the first two years, the older sister raised three batches of meat pigs per year, one batch of about 750 pigs. "Raising pigs is hard work, just like bringing up children," said the woman who lives on the pig farm all year round. "Late at night you have to go see if the pigs are still okay, hot or cold, and when they are sick, they have to be taken care of day and night."

After a couple of years of getting used to waking up at 5 am every day, learning techniques, vaccination, and intensive care for the pigs, their hard work has paid off. Now the annual income is nearly $32,000, and the younger brother, having mostly recovered from the substance abuse, has been gradually paying off his debts with the hard-earned money. In the past few years, he became one of the top farmers in town, earning a good reputation with his skilled pig raising techniques.

His wife, Wang Fenglian, decided to give him another chance as well: the two remarried. Wang said: "I do resent him for his past actions. Despite his mistakes, he still deserves another chance. It is not easy for him to get back on the right track."

Now, Yao Cuilian and Yao Cuilin see a future of combining farming and breeding. "I hope to build my own brand of organic rice and organic vegetables in the future," said the big sister, who has just bought a few more piglets.

Editor: Lin Yan, Shu Zhengyu

Chapter 7　Profiles

Of all the subjects under the sun, people are the most fascinating. People have a natural interest in learning about other people. The personality profile, being about an individual, is a story that caters to that interest and is considered to be one of the staple genres of feature writing. A good personality profile explores a single quality or achievement in the person who is the subject. Since the personality of the subject is often complicated and achievement multifaceted, it is tempting for the reporter to write all about that person. But the resulting story is often a lopsided and dull account with both the focus and the newsworthiness obscured. Thus it is important to identify early that one quality or achievement that forms the storyline to which you should stick. You should pull all other qualities in the subject towards influencing the one key quality you have decided to write about and angle all actions towards affecting the one achievement central to your story. A profile story, markedly different from a biography or a chronology, is about one and only one aspect of the complex character that is the subject. You can always write about the competing quality or achievement in the next story.

Ideally, a personality profile should focus on what the person does, rather than on the person in general. This does not mean that the story is not about the person; it would defeat the purpose of the genre. Rather, the story portrays the person by investigating his or her actions. After all, it is what the person does that draws the reader's attention in the first place. As a result, the profile story is usually organized around a person's recent achievements, challenges or issues, and background information is provided to explain how he or she got to where he or she is now. Personal information and family history will also be provided, but only briefly. These should ideally be telling details that illuminate the central theme of the story.

The right choice of the profile subject is the key to writing a successful profile story. The most common subject for a newspaper profile story is the news-maker, the person brought into the media spotlight by what happened. The news event, the readymade news peg, forms the basis of the profile story. The profile story seeks to give readers a behind-the-scenes look at the person behind a significant news event.

Prominent people sometimes make great profile subjects because of the natural interest that readers may have in the high and mighty. However，not any celebrity will make a good profile subject. Ideally，the celebrity to be profiled should be currently engaged in something that makes them newsworthy. What your readers want to know is what's happening NOW. For example，the middle-aged actresses who made headlines by attending the hit reality show *Sisters Making Waves* in 2020 have enjoyed fame ever since they made their names in the entertainment business. However，the reality show brought the gender issue，among other things，back on the agenda and the attending actresses rekindled the public's imagination. The unexpected popularity of the show provides the occasion for new profile stories of the "sisters."

Moreover，in reporting China to the world，one special kind of profile subject is frequently sought out：an individual that somehow embodies certain social or economic conflict raging in the country，"the common people with an uncommon story"，or "those most intimately involved to highlight the nuances and complexities of today's China"，to quote the Sixth Tone. Sometimes this subject bursts onto the scene as the person behind a breaking news event. More times，the subject gets entangled in a quandary that can serve as a specimen of the challenges China faces today.

Last but not least，an individual may get profiled if he or she is unique and intriguing in some way. By taking a look into such a person's life，the story offers the readers a glimpse of a life experience that's unusual，unexpected or different from the norm people are used to. This kind of inherently interesting individual sometimes makes the most delightful subject for a profile story.

Whoever the subject，the profile story takes a news peg，the present endeavor or angle that serves as the pretext for the journalistic article. Though the writer needs not，and should not，confine his story to the news peg，it must be addressed in the story. The news peg usually comes right after the lead paragraphs which are often descriptive or anecdotal in an attempt to give the readers a sense of what the person is like rather than just who the person is.

7.1   The newsmaker approach

The Sixth Tone story[1] titled "The Lasting Pain of China's Identity Theft Victims" is a typical profile story that explores the person behind a news event. This story was written around the time of the 2020 Gaokao (college entrance exam), when the nation kept its eye on the most important exam of one's life and was outraged by a number of identity theft scandals that had erupted on Weibo. Gou, who claimed to be "victim number 243," was one of the most high-profile of the many victims who faced diminished prospects due to the stolen identity and the better scores. Gou has caused huge controversy on Weibo because she runs a successful business and her story took place in the past. In the eyes of many, Gou was not the "perfect victim" and she was even seen as stealing the limelight from the 2020 Gaokao identity theft victims. This may be why Gou was chosen as the subject of the profile story.

The story begins with a slightly delayed lead, building up suspense the resolving of which naturally leads the story to the central issue that puts Gou in the media spotlight. The central/current issue is then explored for a few paragraphs, presenting a comprehensive picture of what's going on. Then the story goes back to the origin of the Gou's story, giving the woman facing the storm of public opinions the opportunity to state her story. As a typical profile of a newsmaker, the story explores the personality of its subject by reconstructing the news developments that entangled her. The whole story is more about what happened to Gou, and the reader gets to know Gou as a person through the descriptions of her experience. In addition, such details of Gou's family are given in the story. Gou comes from a struggling rural family that makes a living by "harvesting corns and rice" and is only able to send two of the three daughters to high school and is forced to borrow money to allow Gou to retake her exams. Apart from Gou's family life, the story also provides more details about Gou's work. Readers can see Gou at her workplace, where "the building is dark and deserted, with piles of clothes scattered across the floor." The story ends on a positive note, showing a Gou reconciled to her life. After all that has happened, Gou still holds on to her belief in the value of the

---

[1]   Ni Dandan. The Lasting Pain of China's Identity Theft Victims [EB/OL]. The Sixth Tone. (2020-07-13) [2021-08-21]. https://www.sixthtone.com/news/1005911/the-lasting-pain-of-chinas-identity-theft-victims.

Gaokao. The story runs as follows:

The Lasting Pain of China's Identity Theft Victims

Ni Dandan

For nearly 20 years, Gou Jing believed someone had stolen the life she should have led. Now, an investigation has proved she was right.

ZHEJIANG, East China — On July 3, Gou Jing finally found what she'd been seeking for nearly two decades: closure.

Her entire adult life, the 41-year-old had suspected someone else was living the life she should have led. Now, she knows that wasn't paranoia. When she was in high school, someone did steal her future — a woman named Qiu Xiaohui.

In 1997, Gou was the victim of an elaborate hoax, which resulted in Qiu taking her exam results, her name, and her place at a vocational school in Beijing. Gou was misled into thinking she'd flunked her exams and had to repeat her senior year, plunging her family further into poverty.

For a long time, such deceptions were a silent, but persistent phenomenon in parts of China. Some families used their connections to game the gaokao — China's college-entrance exams — allowing their children to steal the scores of brighter, but less privileged children.

But over recent weeks, a reckoning has begun over these long-ignored historical injustices. In June, an investigation uncovered hundreds of cases of stolen gaokao scores that took place in just one region — the eastern province of Shandong — between 1999 and 2006.

The revelations generated an enormous public reaction, which convinced Gou — who grew up in Shandong — that now was the right time to come forward and seek justice. Though she wasn't among the 242 victims identified up to that point, she felt confident a further investigation would prove her right.

"Consider me number 243," she tells Sixth Tone.

A social media storm managed to win Gou the public inquiry she craved. On June 22, she took to China's Twitter-like Weibo and posted a list of her allegations. The account was deliberately emotive, designed to create the maximum possible impact. Most eye-catchingly of all, she said she believed her gaokao results may have been stolen twice — in both 1997 and 1998.

"I was looking to attract the attention of the authorities, hoping they could provide me with answers to what had happened," says Gou.

The tactic worked. Within days, the hashtag "Gou Jing" was trending on Weibo, receiving over 500 million views and tens of thousands of comments. The Shandong government agreed to investigate, publishing its findings just over a week later.

The report's release, however, has been bittersweet for Gou. Though she at last knows the truth about her past, it's come at a heavy price. Public sentiment has been mainly supportive, but there's also been a nasty backlash.

Netizens have accused Gou, who today runs an e-commerce firm selling children's clothing in the eastern Zhejiang province, of exaggerating the impact the theft has had on her life. Others say she simply went public as a way to promote her company.

When Sixth Tone meets Gou July 6, she has been holed up in her company's warehouse in the city of Huzhou — a one-hour drive north of the firm's headquarters in Hangzhou, Zhejiang's provincial capital — for two weeks, trying to keep her head down. The building is dark and deserted, with piles of clothes scattered across the floor.

"The truth has cost me a calm life and a stable business," Gou says. "I don't regret making my voice heard, though."

The accusations clearly rankle Gou. She stresses she never intended to use the scandal to promote her business: "I don't need to."

And although she understands she's not the "perfect victim" some netizens expect, she's baffled at the idea that the crime committed against her somehow didn't matter. From her perspective, the theft damaged her prospects for years afterward and caused her lasting pain.

Growing up in rural Shandong, Gou was a dedicated student. She knew doing well in the gaokao and getting a college education could transform the fortunes of her family, who made their living harvesting corn and rice.

"For kids from the countryside, the gaokao is the only path to change our fates and those of our parents," Gou says.

Gou studied hard for the gaokao and says she consistently scored well in her mock tests. As the exams approached, she recalls feeling confident.

"I had no plan for the future, but there was one clear thing on my mind: to score highly in the gaokao," she says. "The higher you score, the more choices you'll have."

But when it came time for the results, Gou's teacher — Qiu Yinlin, also the father of the imposter Qiu Xiaohui — took her aside. To Gou's horror, he informed her she'd done terribly, failing to get a score high enough to be admitted to any decent colleges.

Qiu Yinlin told Gou her best option was to repeat her senior year and retake the gaokao in 1998. Gou remembers feeling crushed, but accepted her teacher's advice. She never even submitted her college application form.

"I never imagined anything unfair or even illegal could happen in such a sacred exam," says Gou.

The extra year of tuition was a huge burden on Gou's family. Her parents had invested much of their faith and money into Gou succeeding: Of their three daughters, they'd only been able to afford to send two to high school. For Gou to retake her exams, they were forced to borrow money from relatives.

"It wasn't an easy decision for me and my family," Gou says. "But if we'd simply given up, I'd have felt guilty."

Gou sat the gaokao again in 1998, and this time she succeeded in gaining admission to a vocational school in the central Hubei province. After completing her diploma in just over a year, she moved to Zhejiang to look for work.

Without connections or a decent diploma, Gou was forced to take door-to-door sales jobs hawking shampoo and pay phones to make ends meet. But she couldn't bear to return to her home region after what had happened to her, she says.

"I didn't want to go back to Shandong," says Gou. "It was a place of shame I wished to escape."

It wasn't until 2002 that Gou realized her failure in the gaokao might not have been her fault after all. Out of the blue, she received a letter from her old teacher, Qiu Yinlin.

The letter was a confession. Qiu Yinlin revealed he'd used Gou's gaokao score to help his daughter — Qiu Xiaohui — get into vocational school, begging her forgiveness.

At the time, Gou decided against reporting Qiu Yinlin to the authorities. She'd just given birth a few months before and wasn't in a position to get entangled in the issue, she tells Sixth Tone. For the next few years, she concentrated on her family and career, setting up a store on Taobao — an online retail website that was just beginning to take off — in 2006.

Then, a decade later, Gou discovered something that shocked her even more. At a high school reunion, a former classmate told her Qiu Xiaohui had not only gone to the Beijing school using Gou's grades: She'd also been living and working under the name Gou Jing.

Stealing her identity couldn't have been the result of simple opportunism: It would have required advance planning and a wider network of contacts to tamper with the necessary official documents, Gou realized.

"That was more horrifying to me," she says. "I couldn't stop wondering what they had planned before I even sat the gaokao in 1997. It wasn't just a random plan to take away my score."

Again, however, Gou hesitated about going to the police, as she didn't have any hard evidence to back up her claims. But when the reports on historical identity theft went viral in June, she finally sensed an opportunity to secure justice.

The investigation largely confirmed what Gou had suspected for years. In 1997, Gou scored 551 out of 900 in her exams — high enough to attend vocational school. But as she never submitted her application form detailing which schools she wished to attend, her spot was left open.

Instead, Qiu Xiaohui attended the school in Beijing under Gou's name, despite not having taken the gaokao in 1997. After graduating, she also got a job in Shandong using Gou's identity and continued using her name until 2001.

The fraud was made possible by a network of officials — including employees from local education and public security bureaus — who doctored official records and overlooked discrepancies in Qiu Xiaohui's paperwork at her father's request.

Chinese authorities have so far identified 15 people involved in the deception, with most being dismissed from their posts, given warnings, or having their pensions deducted. Qiu Xiaohui has been fired from her job, while investigations into her and her father continue.

According to the report, there was no evidence of foul play related to Gou's second attempt at the gaokao in 1998.

Gou accepts the authorities' conclusions, saying she now considers the case closed. She wants to focus on putting her past behind her and getting on with her life, she says.

"From the very beginning till now, what I've wanted is not compensation or apologies, but the truth," she says. "They've provided me with the answers."

Moving on, however, may prove to be easier said than done.

Details about Gou's company and her clients have been leaked online, leading Gou to close down her Huzhou facility at least temporarily — both to avoid causing her business partners any trouble, and to prove she's not trying to profit from her newfound fame.

The public discussion about her case continues to simmer. Gou says she understands why her critics have targeted her, but points out her success later in life has given her the power to speak up.

"Many thought I should have ended up begging on the streets or laboring on a farm," says Gou. "But if I were in such a situation, I couldn't have made my voice heard to begin with."

The publicity generated by Gou and the other identity theft victims identified so far has pressured the government to take action. In late June, policymakers began discussing legal revisions that would finally make stealing another person's gaokao score an act punishable under China's criminal law.

A central Chinese Communist Party commission has also published a commentary on Gou, underlining that identity theft undermines the very foundations of the gaokao system.

Many thought I should have ended up begging on the streets or laboring on a farm.

—— Gou Jing, identity theft victim

"If even the most basic equity cannot be guaranteed, talking about the fairness of the gaokao from other perspectives is just pie in the sky," the article states.

Fortunately, reforms to China's education system since the late 1990s have made it much harder to falsify students' exam results, according to Xiong Bingqi, deputy director of the 21st Century Education Research Institute, a Beijing-based think tank.

Gaokao scores are now stored digitally in centralized databases, meaning individual teachers and local officials no longer have the ability to tamper with them. "It was impossible (for students) to verify what they scored before," says Xiong.

Even now, Gou says she still wonders what her life might have been like had she been able to attend the school in the Chinese capital all those years ago.

"As a child from an average farming family, it's a source of huge pride to receive your education at a school in Beijing," she says. "I could have had a more stable job. ... I could have avoided the jobs that required more physical labor."

Yet despite everything, Gou still considers the gaokao the fairest way for colleges to select applicants — although she says life has taught her not to judge others by their academic backgrounds.

"When I brought up my daughter, I never let her grades define her," she says. "I told her there's a lot she can learn outside the classroom."

Her daughter, however, has proved to be a stellar student. Last summer, she took the gaokao and — in a moment of poetic justice — won a place at one of China's top universities.

"Everything that's taken away from you in life will be returned to you — in one way or another," says Gou.

Now, Gou hopes to make a return of her own. She's closed down her Weibo account and says she'll soon depart her shuttered warehouse, instead heading back to Hangzhou.

"I'm going home and leaving all this behind," she says. "I need to get back to my life now."

Contributions: Liu Siqi; editor: Dominic Morgan.

Another particularly important point is most profile stories on a news maker result from a lengthy interview. That's why sometimes profile story is also called an interview piece. Once you have chosen a subject with the requisite news peg, you have to arrange a meeting. And the main interview should be supplemented with talks with the friends, colleagues and other relevant people. If time allowed, you should spend more time with the profile subject other than the interview, hang out and observe the subject at work or in action. And it goes without saying that apart from the interviews, extensive background research on the subject is also necessary.

7.2   The microcosm approach

Here is another profile story[1] from Sixth Tone, which focuses on the cancer patients faced with the dire situation of running out of life-saving drugs due to the China-India Travel bans in the COVID-19 pandemic.

---

[1] Ni Dandan. The Silent Victims of China-India Travel Bans: Cancer Patients[EB/OL]. The Sixth Tone. (2020-09-02) [2021-08-04]. https://www.sixthtone.com/news/1006136/the-silent-victims-of-china-india-travel-bans-cancer-patients.

The Silent Victims of China-India Travel Bans: Cancer Patients

Ni Dandan

Thousands of Chinese living with cancer rely on medication produced in India. But this lifeline is now under threat.

When the mail arrived last Thursday, Ying Junjing nearly wept with relief: She was safe — for another few months, at least.

The 43-year-old has been living with chronic leukemia for two decades. To maintain her health, she relies on regular shipments of imatinib — a targeted drug developed by the Swiss pharmaceutical firm Novartis and sold under the brand name Glivec.

But over recent months, the deliveries have become increasingly unreliable. Now, when Ying orders a fresh batch of imatinib, she's unsure when — or whether — the vital medication will be dispatched.

"It used to take a week to 10 days for the drugs to arrive," Ying tells Sixth Tone. "But after the pandemic broke out, things became unpredictable — it could be over a month, or completely unclear."

The problem is that Ying buys the drugs from a company in India, which sells a generic version of imatinib at a fraction of the price charged by Chinese suppliers. For thousands of Chinese cancer patients, importing pills from South Asia is the only way to afford potentially life-saving drugs.

Through 2020, however, travel restrictions between China and India have thrown this enormous drug trade into chaos. And the situation shows little sign of improving amid tense relations between the two countries.

Before her package arrived last week, Ying had less than a month's supply of imatinib left. Many other leukemia patients she knows are in even worse positions.

"I'm really lucky," says Ying. "Few of the patients in our chat group have received drug deliveries from India. Many placed their orders long before me — in July."

It's unclear exactly how many people in China buy cancer medication from India, but anecdotal evidence suggests the number is in the hundreds of thousands at least.

He Xiaobing, CEO of Beijing Memorial Pharmaceutical, a Chinese firm that specializes in coordinating clinical trials, has 14 years of experience dealing with cancer patients in the Chinese and Indian markets. He tells Sixth Tone demand for India-produced drugs among Chinese patients is enormous, especially among those with liver cancer, prostate cancer, non-small-cell lung carcinoma, renal carcinoma, and chronic granulocytic leukemia — the condition from which Ying suffers.

Each year, around 500,000 people in China are diagnosed with liver cancer alone. He estimates around half of them use generic drugs for treatment. The situation is similar with patients of many other conditions, he adds.

Chinese patients buy off-patent medication from several sources, including domestic manufacturers, but India — the world's largest producer of generic drugs — is a major supplier. When discussing treatment options, many in China simply refer to nonbranded products as "Indian drugs."

A black market for made-in-India pills first emerged in China due to the massive gap in drug prices between the two countries. For many Chinese families, the increased availability of cheaper overseas medication was life-changing.

Ying was diagnosed with leukemia in her early 20s, just as Novartis was bringing Glivec to the Chinese market. The exciting new treatment, however, cost 23,500 yuan ($2,800) per month — far beyond what Ying's family could afford.

For the next decade, Ying's parents managed to keep their daughter supplied with Glivec thanks to assistance from a nonprofit called the China Charity Federation, which subsidized 75% of the treatment costs. But the 70,000 yuan annual expense was an enormous drain on the family, who lives in a small county in the eastern Zhejiang province.

"This was a big burden for my parents," says Ying. "After my diagnosis in 2000, I didn't work for an entire decade and lived with the support of my parents, who were average wage earners in our small county. In the early years, I frequently suffered from headaches and fevers — I wasn't able to pick up any kind of job."

In 2013, Ying's condition worsened. Her doctor advised the family to increase her dosage of Glivec, but they couldn't afford the extra pills. It was then that Ying decided to explore the possibility of buying medication from India.

"My trust in Indian generic drugs came from chatting with other patients in a QQ group (an online messaging platform)," says Ying. "They had used them and shared their positive feedback."

A QQ contact passed Ying an email address. To order up to four boxes of imatinib, she just had to send a message with her address and requirements, and then wire the money. The cost was just $100 per box — less than one-tenth the price of Glivec in China.

Ying had no idea who the supplier was — she speaks little English — but the service worked like a charm. Within a week or two of placing the order, the imatinib would arrive via EMS, the cross-border express mail service.

At the time, what Ying was doing was illegal. China labeled any unapproved pharmaceutical imports "fake drugs," and those caught selling them were harshly punished — sometimes with long prison sentences.

But many Chinese cancer patients didn't care, and the market for Indian drugs flourished. Jin Ni, a resident of the eastern city of Taizhou, recalls speaking with many families in the hospital after her mother was diagnosed with lung cancer in 2009.

"They were all using Indian drugs," Jin tells Sixth Tone. She adds the targeted drug used to treat non-small-cell lung cancer — gefitinib — cost 15,000 yuan per month in China at the time. "It's unaffordable for average Chinese families, no matter urban or rural."

Eventually, the Chinese government appeared to accept the benefits of generic drug imports and began to semi-legitimize the trade. In late 2019, China removed the "fake drugs" label from generic drugs widely available overseas and relaxed punishments for those caught distributing them.

By this point, made-in-India drugs were flooding into China via two main channels. Many patients, including Ying, relied on EMS, which is cheaper and less closely monitored than commercial delivery services like DHL and UPS. Others relied on professional buyers — known as daigou in Chinese — to get packages across the border.

"In seven years, I'd never encountered any difficulties accessing my drugs via EMS," says Ying. "I was never required to provide any documents to any authority."

But things have changed radically in 2020.

As COVID-19 began to spread through China in February, India canceled the visas of Chinese citizens and stopped issuing new entry permits. A month later, China introduced its own travel ban preventing foreign citizens from entering the country.

The visa restrictions cut off daigou services almost entirely, forcing most cancer patients to rely solely on EMS to obtain their medication.

Express deliveries, however, have also been severely disrupted. Ying says she was forced to turn to fellow leukemia patients with large stocks of imatinib to supplement her own supplies during the first half of the year, due to the difficulty obtaining boxes from India.

Then, on July 23, India took the unprecedented step of removing China from its list of EMS delivery destinations, citing the limited availability of flights.

The Indian authorities reversed the decision two weeks later, but the move unnerved many in China. Many patients are still waiting for packages to be shipped from India.

"Patients are generally very anxious," says He. "But as many keep one to three months' worth of drugs at home, I haven't heard about a patient running out of drugs yet."

Cancer drugs have become much cheaper and more readily available in China over recent years, but a large number of Chinese are still reliant on imported pills.

In Ying's home province of Zhejiang — one of the wealthiest in China — Glivec is now included in public insurance schemes that provide patients with up to an 85% subsidy. This has reduced the cost of the drug to 18,000 yuan per year or less for most patients.

Even this price, however, is too much for some patients. And many Chinese provinces can't afford to provide patients with such a high level of remuneration on drug costs.

A new shipment of made-in-India generic drugs offered by a Chinese "daigou" agency.

From the agency's online advertisement

According to He, most of the patients using Indian drugs he has encountered are elderly and based in rural areas, where income levels are lower than in the cities.

"They're heavily dependent on their children to pay for these drugs," says He. "They won't have much spare money to spend on purchasing more drugs for future use."

Ying is fortunate enough to be able to switch to branded drugs if necessary. As her condition has stabilized, she has started working at a local hospital, earning up to 5,000 yuan per month. But she's reluctant to pay more for her medication.

"My parents sacrificed a lot due to my disease ... It's cost my parents almost their entire life savings," says Ying. "If I can save some money, I'd like to spend it on improving their lives."

She's also hesitant about switching drug suppliers for health reasons. This year, her condition has remained stable. But for chronic granulocytic leukemia patients, there's always a risk that a genetic mutation could cause a sudden acceleration in the disease.

"The Indian medicines have worked on me very well," says Ying. "I don't dare just change to another brand."

Unless the travel disruptions ease, patients may be left with no choice. According to Ying, most of the leukemia patients she knows are running out of supplies.

For now, Ying continues to order fresh batches of pills via email. Others, however, are exploring alternative channels, such as agencies that claim to have large stocks of cancer drugs stored in Chinese warehouses.

One agency reached by Sixth Tone says the firm bought large quantities of drugs from Natco Pharma — a major Indian pharmaceutical firm — before India suspended its EMS services to China. It charges less than 500 yuan per box of imatinib — even less than the price Ying pays.

"It took up to 35 days for them to arrive; now it takes almost forever," says a staff member from the agency. "If you don't trust us, you can find a lab to test the ingredients before you take them."

He Xiaobing, however, urges patients to exercise caution when buying from daigou. Given the unpredictable situation, it's likely the number of counterfeit drugs on the market will rise.

"Patients should stay alert whenever a daigou service promises to send them Indian generic drugs," He says. "Fake generic drugs exist in both India and China."

The subject for the above story is chosen for her typicalness. Unlike Gou Jing in the identity theft story, Ying Junjing, the profile subject, is not a news maker herself. The news here is the travel bans between China and India that threaten to cut off the supply of life-saving pills for Chinese cancer patients. Ying, a leukemia patient dependent on the cheaper generic drugs bought from India, is presented as one of the huge group of cancer patients using and buying generic pills out of India. The profile subject is more of a narrative device, used mainly to illustrate a rather complicated issue. Her long experience with both cancer and the targeted drug therapy coincides with the history of the India generic drugs in China from its first appearance as fake illegal drugs to its eventual popularity as officially recognized generic pills. Along the same line that a war could be depicted through one soldier, the story is told through the prism of this one patient.

Notice the way the story moves back and forth between Ying's life and the wider setting. The story begins with a brief scene in which Ying receives her long-awaited medication. The story then shifts to the news peg, the news event that forms the basis of the story that the travel ban is threatening the lifeline of cancer patients. In paragraphs 9 to 13, the scope of the story is given. Ying is not alone in her worries and concerns; there are at least "hundreds of thousands" of people trapped in similar situations. The story then returns to Ying and describes, in chronological order, her experiences with "Indian drugs." In this major part of the story, the role of the profile object as a storytelling tool is made explicit. Ying's life is not fully explored, but only to the extent that it can illustrate the history of these generic drugs in China. Certain family details are revealed: her parents depleted the family's savings to pay for medical treatment, and Ying was out of work for a long time, only finding work after her health had greatly improved. These details are highly relevant to the theme of the story, as it was partly financial constraints that led to a reliance on cheap "Indian medicine." Again, we can see from these biographical details that the subject was chosen because of her exemplary value. Other less fortunate patients are also profiled, in contrast to Ying, who comes from Zhejiang, "one of the wealthiest regions in China, where Glivec is now included in public insurance schemes that provide patients with up to an 85% subsidy." The fact that the story ends not with the subject of the profile, but with a quote from He, one of the industry insiders, warning of the dangers of fake drugs in desperate situations, gives away the instrumental role the subject of the profile plays in the story, whose real subject is the issue rather than the person.

7.3 The personality approach

There is another group of profile subjects that make good stories. They are not chosen for their representativeness of certain issues, but for their uniqueness. They are interesting people in their own right, and their life stories are themselves legendary and fascinating to read. English-language profile stories of such subjects add interest to the portrait of China. The following feature article is such a story① from *Shanghai Daily*. It tells a fascinating tale about an "amateur" who beats the highest mountain in the world.

The Untrained Herdsman Who Beat Everest

By Wang Qin'ou, Li Jiaxin and Cao Aifeng

FIFTY-SEVEN-YEAR-OLD Tibetan herdsman Gesang owns a house with the most unique mountain views. On sunny days, the top of Mount Qomolangma, the world's highest peak, is framed in his doorway like a wooden picture on his wall.

"Mount Qomolangma? That's it," Gesang pointed at the peak to the assembled journalists. Then he continued to calculate his village's income last year. He is now a member of the village committee.

"I've been up there," he said.

Gesang lives in Zangpu Village in Zhaxizong Town of the Tibet Autonomous Region. It is one of the closest administrative villages in China to Mount Qomolangma, with an average altitude of 5,000 meters. Gesang has lived in this highland pasture for decades.

It is a legend to many that an untrained nomad has climbed atop Mount Qomolangma.

"I've heard of this man but never seen him myself. Is there such a man?" Solang, an official of the Mountaineering Association of the Tibet Autonomous Region, said.

According to Solang, multiple qualifications are required to climb up Mount Qomolangma from the north slope in China. Applicants must be led by a professional guide and have climbed at least one snow-capped mountain more than 8 kilometers above sea level.

"The north slope of Mount Qomolangma is definitely not open to people with such qualifications," Solang said.

But Gesang's Qomolangma certificate clearly states that he reached the summit in 2001.

At that time, Qomolangma expedition had been commercialized, but the mode of operation was very different from that of today. As the cradle of high-altitude mountain guides in China, the Himalayan Mountaineering Guide School of Lhasa (formerly Tibet Mountaineering School) had been established

---

① Wang Qin'ou, Li Jiaxin and Cao Aifeng. The untrained herdsman who beat Everest[N/OL]. Shanghai Daily. (2020-07-25) [2021-08-04]. https://archive. shine. cn/feature/The-untrained-herdsman-who-beat-Everest/shdaily.shtml.

just two years previously. The local guide team and the management of mountaineering were still in their infancy.

Moreover, the guiding job on the north slope was completely controlled by foreign companies.

Gesang said he had reached the summit with a team of foreign nationals led by New Zealander Russell Reginald Brice. Brice organized commercial expeditions to Mount Qomolangma every year between 1996 and 2007. Many of Tibet's first commercial guides have been interns in his team.

In 1997, Gesang began to serve Brice's team, transporting supplies with his own yaks like many of his fellow countrymen. In 2001, the company chose Gesang as the temporary porter to move supplies to the summit.

"Probably because I was in good health," Gesang said.

Normally it takes two days to transport goods from the base camp (5,200 meters) to the advance camp (6,500 meters), but he only needed five to six hours. He also picked up quickly from the Tibetan guides how to walk on crampons on the icy paths above 6,500 meters.

Gesang felt a sense of pride and confidence since no ordinary villagers had ever had a chance to make a summit attempt. But he admitted that he started to have regrets as the journey began.

"I could barely stand in the gale after reaching 7,000 meters," Gesang said.

On the day of the summit, when they were passing the "Second Step," at an altitude of around 8,600 meters, a client urinated in fear on a near-vertical rock.

"My legs were weak, too. I grasped the rope and was afraid to look down," Gesang said, adding he had been thinking of his wife and children, thinking that he really "shouldn't have come!"

Fortunately, he reached the top after dawn. Standing at the summit, he saw "the clouds below are flat and wide, stretching far away." He was so joyful, because he was finally "going home."

Back to the mountain

Some villagers said Gesang is awesome, while others thought him crazy. He still went to work on Mount Qomolangma the following year. People knew that he had been to the top, but he never became a star. The Himalayas have not been short of legends of farmers and herdsmen turning into mountaineers, and the Sherpas from Nepal had long made their mark.

Gesang spent 10 years with Brice's team. In 2008, Brice moved to the south slope on the Nepalese side.

That same year, the Beijing Olympics torch made its way to the top of Mount Qomolangma. By escorting the torch to the summit, the Tibetan guides trained themselves to build their own commercial climbing model.

Afterward, they took over the annual road-rope laying task at an altitude of more than 6,500 meters, which marks that their technical skills have won the trust of international teams and that they are increasingly dominating the north slope climbing season. But with increasingly strict mountaineering regulations, ordinary villagers are only allowed to travel up to 6,500 meters to transport supplies and clean up trash, earning money in much safer ways.

After 2008, Gesang went back to being a herdsman in the pasture, year in and year out. In 2018, he was elected to the village committee, giving him more time to stay in the village. Each year around April or May, the villagers would still help mountaineering teams transport supplies with their yaks. He gave this chance to his son.

It was not until this year, when temporary workers were needed to build 5G network in conjunction with Qomolangma's elevation measurements, that Gesang returned to the mountain.

"My health is failing. I don't go to the mountains much now," Gesang said. His younger son later went to Tibet Mountaineering School. Gesang was a bit envious, but he said "different periods feature different ways of living. It's fine the way it is now."

The meaning of climbing

Almost every Qomolangma conqueror has been asked what it means to climb the mountain.

"I am happy to make it. It proves that I am in good health," Gesang said.

"Why climbing?" This is the ultimate question in the circle of mountaineering. It is hard to say if Gesang has not pondered it over, or if he has thought it simply and clearly.

"I guess some people want to be famous. But I'm just curious. I want to see what's up there," he said. "And I've seen it now."

In the end, a journalist wanted to see a picture of Gesang at the summit. He searched for a long time but could not find it.

"Maybe I lost it while moving," he said and pulled out a suit of down jacket from the room, which was given to him by Brice's team that year.

"You've kept it as a souvenir all the time?" the journalist asked.

"Sort of. The jacket is warm, suitable for blustery winters on the pasture," Gesang said.

The life led by the subject depicted in the above story is somewhat removed from the world that ordinary readers are familiar with: Tibetan pastures, snow mountains, herdsman employed to assist in mountain climbing, these scenes are far away from the run-of-the-mill, and may pique the reader's curiosity for their outlandishness. Gesang, the profile subject, is attractive in his own right. Scaling the highest peak in the world is no small feat, not to mention such a feat was accomplished not by a trained professional climber, but by an amateur herdsman. Therefore, Gesang, the herdsman who made to the top of Mount Qomolangma, qualifies as the kind of subject that captures the reader's imagination by his innate interest. At the beginning, the story places the readers in the snowy world of the mountaineering by zooming in on an unusual view: the top of the highest peak in the world framed in Gesang's doorway "like a wooden picture on his wall." Then the story moves on to introduce briefly the owner of the doorway, Gesang, the profile subject, and his main achievement, the conquering of the Qomolangma. After that, the story continues chronologically to recount Gesang's experience with the highest peak in the world. This main section of the story is rich in information, where the reader gets a glimpse not just into the subject's life, but into the distant and mysterious world of mountaineering, where Gesang, the protagonist in the story, actually plays a periphery role as a porter in charge of "transporting supplies with his own yaks." The porter became a local legend when he made to the top. However, the story doesn't end with the moment of achieving summit, but continues with the life of Gesang who had remained working as porter and later a herdsman in the pasture, only to return to the mountain to help with the elevation measurements of 5G network. Gesang's role in helping build the 5G network is the news peg for this profile story. Beating the Everest constitutes the impressive achievement central to the story, but it is the latest construction of 5G network that brings Gesang back to the mountain and into the focus of the readers. The story ends by a discussion of the meaning of climbing, to which Gesang answers that he is just curious and wants to know what is up there. The simple feeling reflected by the reply defines the subject for the readers: Gesang is different from the other climbers not just in the fact that he is not professionally trained but in that to him, reaching the summit, working as a porter, being a herdsman in the pasture, calculating his village's income, all are the same, just a natural part of his life. Last but not least, as a necessary part of the puzzle that makes up the profile, Gesang's family details are given and the reader understands that his son is training for the mountaineering, a different way of living for the Tibetan young in a different period.

The above profile subject is from the distant snowy world, however, more profile subjects can be found near home, in the familiar world of modern life. The following story① portrays an old woman who bursts onto the scene through, among other things, lifting weights in an urban gym.

Age is no barrier to Achieving Body Fitness

By Chen Huizhi | 00:26 UTC+8 September 9, 2020 | Print Edition

"A peach bottom, ant waist and swan neck." Chen Jifang, 68, isn't talking about some 25-year-old model. She's talking about herself. Though her physique may not quite match that ideal, she has undergone an extraordinary change in the last two years.

With sweat and perseverance in a local gym, the Minhang District resident shed 12 kilos, toned her muscles and bid farewell to belly flab. She says she never felt better.

Chen dispels the notion that gym workouts are only for the young. Her online videos of easy workouts on an ab wheel have drawn "oohs" and "ahs" from netizens.

Chen, **a Shanghai native, worked as a food shop assistant before retirement.**

"My health went downhill after I gave birth to my daughter," she said. "I would say I was constantly living between life and death and always in low spirits."

She did enjoy playing badminton until bad knees forced her to give the game up. Lacking exercise, she began putting on kilos.

A physical exam in 2018 was a wake-up call. It showed she had hyperlipemia, high blood pressure, excess uric acid and a fatty liver.

"The doctor told me to move my body or it would get worse for me," she said.

She sought advice from Zhang Li, a woman who owns a fitness studio about 4 kilometers from her home, and decided to undertake a fitness course.

---

① Chen Huizhi. Age is no barrier to achieving body fitness[N/OL]. Shanghai Daily. (2020-09-09) [2021-08-06]. https://archive.shine.cn/metro/Age-is-no-barrier-to-achieving-body-fitness/shdaily.shtml

"I asked for a private coach because I always trust professionals," Chen said.

Liu Luyao, a 30-year-old former armyman with a decade of experience in fitness coaching, took her on.

She was his oldest client. People over 60 are a rare sight in gyms, he said.

"She looked unhealthy physically when I first met her," he said. "Badly injured knees and knee pains, and weak kinetic ability."

Liu said her first training sessions focused on mobilizing her joints and muscles. Her years of badminton playing had left her with a slightly hunched back and unbalanced body strength.

After 24 one-hour classes with Liu, Chen was advised to take group classes because she was physically prepared for more intense training.

"I lost 5 kilos after the first month, and after three months, I was a changed person," Chen said. "People often admire me, as if I had to endure something terrible to look like this now. But I enjoyed every minute."

She is now standing up straighter, adding 2 centimeters to her height and is able to do deadlifts with a 45-kilogram barbell. Liu said the feat is remarkable for a person of her age because many people in their 30s and 40s can't lift that weight or do it with such precise technical detail.

Diet was also a part of her program. Zhang, who is also a nutrition consultant at the studio, took on that task. She also said Chen was **her oldest-ever client.**

"At her age, food needs to be easily absorbed by the body, and she needs extra nutrition for her bones and eyes," she said.

Nowadays, Chen works out two to three hours in the gym every day, with a dietary lunch there. She walks to the gym and back home.

Chen had a physical check in summer last year. It showed she no longer had a fatty liver and her blood pressure and blood fat levels were stabilized. She has become a partner in the gym and runs a health consulting firm.

Many of her clients are senior citizens with neck pain, strained lumbar muscles and other bone and muscle ailments. However, few of them are interested in regular gym workouts.

"My fellow retirees usually would rather take part in 'commercial events' where they can get dozens of eggs for free than invest in their health," she said. "They have yet to understand that money spent in improving physical fitness could eventually pay off in fewer hospital bills."

How to exercise appropriately

Zhang Xin, a specialist at Shanghai Medmotion Rehabilitation Clinic who specializes in geriatrics and athletic orthopedic injuries, said **Chen sets an example** for senior citizens who are often uninformed about the benefits of regular physical training.

"The human body has great potential, and even patients who have suffered rather serious heart disease can restore their physical activeness," she said. "If you train regularly, your muscles will grow after two to three months, and your cardiopulmonary function will be improved after one to two months."

Older people often have pain in the knees, usually not from ligament injuries but from loss of muscle mass, she said. In 80 to 90 percent of the cases, the pain can be reduced by training the muscles around the knees.

Here is Zhang's advice to seniors:

• Find out if you have any diseases of the heart, lungs, liver or kidneys. If your blood pressure is 160 or higher, you should avoid intense physical activity until you bring your blood pressure down. If you're diagnosed with heart disease, you need to seek advice from your doctor and try rehabilitation on professional training equipment at hospitals.

• Take it step by step and don't overwork your body. It's recommended that a healthy person do aerobics at least five times a week and at least 30 minutes per session of mid-range intensity. That is, when you're slightly panting but can still talk normally. If you're able to monitor your heart rate during training, your heart rate usually shouldn't surpass 130 beats per minute. Progress slowly in raising the intensity of training.

• Don't ignore pain. Your training should be painless. If you have pain in the knees even when you're not working out, you can allow slight pain when you start out and continue after two or three weeks if the pain doesn't grow stronger. Otherwise you should reduce the intensity of your training.

• Improve your balance and build your strength. As people grow older, their body balance deteriorates and their bone mass drops. To prevent falling and bone fractures, which are not unusual in older people, balance training by means of tai chi, yoga and badminton, for example, is recommended. Besides jogging and swimming, strength building is very important for the health of older people but often ignored. Start from 20 to 30 percent of the maximum weight you can take and add more progressively.

• Train under professional guidance. People who haven't done training for a long time usually have weak body control, and working out under guidance can reduce the chance of injuries.

Chen Jifang, the main character in this story, is at first glance no different from any other elderly person in our daily lives. Retired from a tedious job and suffering from various common ailments of old age, Chen Jifang is unlikely to be the subject of a full-page newspaper story. In fact, Chen was featured after a video of her working out at the gym went viral online. The whole story therefore focuses on the health aspects of her life, and Chen was chosen because of the important role she plays, as she "sets an example for senior citizens who are often unaware of the benefits of regular physical training." Details about her family and herself are presented, but only very briefly. The story is not about Old Lady Chen, an ordinary retired Shanghai resident, but about the fact that she has maintained exceptional health through exercise and training under professional guidance. In this sense, the profile story fulfils an important function unique to feature writing: by describing the real-life stories of others, the feature article shows us how to live better ourselves. As the first Chinese city to have a third of its population over 60, Shanghai is plagued by a variety of problems specific to its growing elderly population, the most common of which is evidently poor health. Chen's story certainly offers a solution to this common problem of ageing. As such, the story not only provides the reader with an interesting read about an inspiring character, but it also provides a service by informing the reader of a healthy lifestyle. In the aforementioned article, Chen's story ends with a quote from the young 68-year-old, who advises the elderly that they would be better off if they invested more in their own health and spent their dwindling time more wisely than in queuing for free eggs. The article doesn't end there, however, as it goes on to discuss the relationship between knee pain and muscle loss and provides a list of tips for dealing with safe exercise in old age. This additional "information box" at the end, more commonly seen in service stories, clearly demonstrates the dual purpose of this profile story discussed above.

7.4   The celebrity approach

Another staple source of profile subjects is found in the world of art, culture, and entertainment. Film directors, movie stars, singers, musicians, painters, writers, and artists of various sorts get profiled frequently in the media. The following story from *Shanghai Daily* on a documentary maker and his latest acclaim-winning film[①] is one of the many that, by painting vivid portraits in words, brings that refined and glamourous world to people's life.

Gritty Documentary Focuses on Miners With Black Lung Disease

Ma Yue

Independent documentary filmmaker Jiang Nengjie turned his lens on his own hometown in Hunan Province to record a heart-rending story about the plight of coal workers in illegal mines. It's entitled "Miners, the Horsekeeper and Pneumoconiosis."

The horsekeeper in the film is Jiang's own father Jiang Meilin, and the dying miner Zhao Pinfeng who is a central character in the film is a fellow villager. Pneumoconiosis in coal miners is more commonly called black lung disease.

Jiang, 35, released the 83-minute work free online, and it has become an instant hit among those who prize documentary films.

Jiang admitted to surprise about the reaction the film has generated.

"The attention and viewership the film has received in the past month exceed anything I ever experienced before in my career," Jiang told *Shanghai Daily*.

"It's a film of public interest, and it becomes meaningful only when it gets spread and viewed. Considering that it won't reach cinemas, I decided to air it for free."

Independent documentary making in China is a relatively small industry, compared with commercial documentaries. It focuses on less-followed themes and has limited distribution channels.

Jiang's film began to draw attention in late March, after he contacted a few documentary fans with links to his film via a file-sharing site. The fans added the film to their want-to-watch list on Douban. com, which could be tracked by Jiang. Several "celebrity" users on Weibo also promoted the film.

"I encouraged viewers to share it with others," he said. "I want to focus attention on the plight of miners who suffer poverty after losing their ability to work because of an occupational disease."

Black lung disease is caused by long-term exposure to coal dust. It

---

① MaYue. Gritty documentary focuses on miners with black lung disease [N/OL]. Shanghai Daily. (2020-05-080) [2021-08-06]. https://www.shine.cn/feature/art-culture/2005087714/.

progressively builds up in the lungs, leading to fibrosis and often death.

As of this week, 72,000 Douban users have added the film to their want-to-watch lists, and some 19,000 have already watched it. The film has received an average rating of 8.5　in the site's 10-point system.

"I give 7 points to the film, and one more point to the director's sincerity in bringing this subject to a wider audience," viewer Shen Mi wrote in her comment. "The camera captures typical rural village life, which is often overlooked by mainstream audiences. Our era and its stories can be remembered only if they are recorded."

Jiang was an industrial design major student in college, but he refused to follow the career path envisioned by his parents. Instead, he followed his creative passion for free expression and a desire to highlight marginalized communities.

"My childhood dream was to become a writer," said Jiang. "I moved toward filmmaking in college, but no filmmaking companies were impressed by my resume when I graduated in 2008. So I had to do other jobs and save up money to pursue my real interest."

Jiang spent 10 months working as a cashier in a chain store in the southern city of Guangzhou before returning to his hometown in Xinning County of Shaoyang City.

"I was told that the primary school in my hometown was facing imminent demolition," he said. "Most of the students in the school were 'left-behind' children. I wanted to film them because I too was a 'left-behind' child when my parents left for jobs in the big city."

Jiang's first digital video camera cost him 5,800 yuan (US $820) — money half saved and half borrowed. He worked as mathematics teacher at a primary school in Xinning for three months, during which he filmed the daily life of the "left-behind" children.

He started work on "Miners, the Horsekeeper and Pneumoconiosis" in 2010. The project was an on-again, off-again endeavor for eight years, during which the self-funded director had to take on other jobs to finance his filmmaking dreams.

"I spent no more than 100,000 yuan on this film, which was not a particularly big investment," he said. "But the amount of time I put into it can hardly be calculated. By 2018, an illegal mine operated by my cousin had been closed for years, and my main character Zhao Pinfeng had died. That was when I decided to end the film and make it public."

Jiang comes from a mining family. His grandfather was a victim of a mine accident nearly 30 years ago. Two of his uncles suffer from black lung disease, and his own father became a horse porter for miners' goods after he was diagnosed with the disease when Jiang was 11 years old.

Most miners in the area of Jiang's hometown suffer from some level of black lung disease. Many of the illegal mines where they worked to feed their families have since been closed by the government.

When Jiang started to shift the focus of his film to Zhao in 2016, the miner was already in the late stages of the disease and had to breathe with the help of a ventilator. Zhao died when a village power blackout in 2018 shut off his oxygen supply. He is survived by two children and a wife who is mentally retarded.

Jiang last visited the Zhao's family during the recent Labor Day holiday. Charitable foundations have helped the family, including tuition for the children's education, he said.

Warm-hearted viewers have donated books to children featured in Jiang's film, and the filmmaker himself has established four libraries in his hometown.

"I hope attention is focused not only on this one family but also on the large number of black lung sufferers who need medical attention and government support," Jiang said. "Employers should be held responsible for workers who contract occupational diseases like this."

In addition to his films on miners and "left-behind" children, Jiang has also documented the plight of veterans of the War of Resistance against Japanese Aggression.

He is now working on two new documentaries. One focuses on the LGBT community; the other on people with mental disorders. Will he again share the films for free? Jiang said that with a film about lesbian, gay, bisexual and transgender people, he may have no other choice.

"An LGBT-themed film has very little chance of getting to domestic cinemas," He said. "These kinds of works are often shown at underground locations. Some works can be released at independent film exhibitions and festivals."

Despite restricted distribution channels, Jiang said he has no plans to give up his current work or alter his films to make them more socially acceptable.

The above story is a typical achievement profile: Jiang, the documentary maker is profiled because of his latest work. After a direct lead that contains the news peg, explaining the newsworthiness of the subject, the story proceeds to the central achievement, Jiang's documentary that offers an unflinching look into the world of the black-lung patients. After that, details about Jiang's family life and professional work are provided to illuminate how Jiang's achievement is brought about as well as to present a rounded personality. The brief chronology of Jiang's work history, his film-making, brings the story naturally back to the documentary that's the focus of the story and the story lingers for a moment on the surviving family of the leading "actor" in the tragic film. Then the article ends by looking into Jiang's determination and his future work plan.

Jiang the documentary maker is caught in the media spotlight because of his compassionate work promoting the disfranchised and the alienated. Dancer Wang Jiajun swirls into it because of his stunning performance in a renowned revolutionary role. The following profile[①] on the performing artist starts with the dancer's daunting schedule — 10 shows in 11 days, which illustrates both the popularity of the dancer and the musical drama that depicts a true story of a revolutionary couple. Then the story moves naturally to the nut graf where the drama, Wang's latest achievement, is introduced in details. After that, the story turns back to Wang and gives a chronological account of his professional career starting from the age of ten. At the ending part, the time line leads the story back to the dancer's present achievement again and the story finishes off with the dancer's hope for further career development in the future. In addition, the story is very focused: Only the professional aspect of Wang's life is narrated.

This profile on the dancer is part of a series of people stories by *Shanghai Daily* on Party members from all walks of life, ordinary or famous, to mark the 100 years of Communist Party of China.

Dancer Inspired by His Revolutionary Role

Ma YueMa Xuefeng

15:31 UTC+8, 2021-06-28

Wang Jiajun, Shanghai Dance Theater's principle dancer, has had one of his busiest schedules this month. Playing the lead role of revolutionary martyr Li Xia in the dance theater's "The Eternal Wave," he had 10 performances

---

① Ma YueMa Xuefeng. Dancer inspired by his revolutionary role[N/OL]. Shanghai Daily. (2021-06-28) [2021-08-06]. https://www.shine.cn/news/in-focus/2106281209/.

scheduled in 11 days.

For the 36-year-old, the tight schedule was a challenge to mind and body.

"I'm glad that the audiences liked this production," said Wang. "I know some audience members made a special effort and flew to Shanghai from other cities to watch the performance. It was probably their first time and only time to watch it, so I had to show my best form."

"The Eternal Wave" is based on the true story of martyr Li Bai and his wife, who risked their lives for 12 years to secretly pass information to forces led by the Communist Party of China. While sending intelligence on the Kuomintang's Yangtze River defenses in 1948, Li was arrested and later executed in Shanghai.

Since the premiere of "The Eternal Wave" in 2019, Wang has played the role in some 160 performances.

"For artists, repetition can be painful sometimes. But I'm always trying to find new possibilities for improvement when playing the role and keep myself refreshed," he said.

Wang started learning dance at the age of 10 in 1995 when he was recruited by Shanghai Theater Academy's dance school.

"I had a relatively weak body in childhood. My parents sent me to learn dancing, hoping that it would help improve my health," Wang recalled. "I still remember I did a set of gymnastic exercises during the entrance interview instead of presenting a piece of dance like a lot of others. The recruitment teacher told me later that they considered me a blank paper with a great potential."

Wang joined Shanghai Dance Theater in 2007 and gradually became a key member. His first lead role was as a zebra in the theater's original production "Wild Zebra."

"That was in 2004 or 2005 when I was still a student," said Wang. "Firstly I completed a pas de deux well in that work, and was therefore given an opportunity to play a solo role. More chances came after that, so 'Wild Zebra' was quite an important work for me."

Today, Wang plays the lead role in both the theater's signature productions — "The Eternal Wave" and "Crested Ibises." But the most meaningful stage experience for him was when he performed as a guest dancer for the Zhengzhou Song and Dance Theater in its production "Goddess of Luo River" in 2010.

"I left my dance troupe and arrived at a strange city, and was pushed to learn and grow quickly," Wang recalled. "I had to study the role and take care of other things myself instead of relying on my own troupe. That experience helped me grow mentally and become a good dancer able to think on his feet."

In "Goddess of Luo River," Wang played the role of Cao Zhi, a prince of Wei in the Three Kingdoms Period (AD 220-280). Cao was also an accomplished poet in his time.

"He was like me, young and handsome," Wang joked. "I read a lot of poems he wrote to understand how he felt about the goddess. When dealing with the role, I thought much about how to present the character for audiences instead of concentrating on techniques like I used to."

Since then, Wang cultivated the habit of studying the role and character in advance with any material he could find.

"Only when the performer knows the character by heart and even gets touched by the role himself, he can really have the audiences engaged," he said.

Before playing the role of Li Xia in "The Eternal Wave," Wang visited the martyr's former residence.

"I was born in the 1980s. The major challenge for me is to find similarities between myself and my role," said Wang. "I visited Li's former residence and got the feeling that the couple lived a simple but happy life. I imagine that Li wanted to protect the happiness of all families like his own, even at the expense of his own life. The more I play the role, the more my empathy with him grows."

The role also aroused Wang's patriotic passion, and he became a reserve member of the Communist Party of China in May. (It usually takes about a year for a reserve member to become a formal Party member.)

Like most dancers, Wang often encounters physical discomfort. Due to the many lifts he has to do in "The Eternal Wave" and "Crested Ibises," he has been bothered by lumbar muscle degeneration.

"I try to protect myself as much as possible by doing stretching thoroughly before and after each performance," he said. "I will try to increase my career span and meet audience's expectation.

"Physically, a dancer reaches his best form at the age of 25—30, but tends to focus on techniques and ignore the characterization of the role. After 30, a dancer becomes creative and richer in mind. I think 30—40 is the golden age for a dancer."

When Wang has a day off, he attends performances to relax and learn from other stage artists.

"I watch not only dance, but also musical concerts and dramas. I can get inspired and learn from all other performers," he said. "I also hope to do more crossover performances in the future and present new things for audiences. As for dances, I want to try some negative characters which might be a contrast to my appearance."

As the above article illustrates, a newspaper profile story typically consists of five parts: an introduction, a news peg, a core achievement or event/incident that makes the subject newsworthy, family history and personal information, and a conclusion. Such feature articles are usually 750 to 1,500 words in length. There is no set formula for the structure of a profile story. However, it is best to avoid a strict timeline. The profile story is about the individual, but the focus should be on the central achievement. Note that in each of the above stories, the author avoids turning his or her story into a biography or a full chronology. Instead, a thematic storyline is used, and each story is accordingly organized around the central news event that forms the basis of the feature story. The biographical details in the above stories are provided in short paragraphs that give a brief insight of the subject's personal life.

Exercise

1. Read the following character sketches carefully, which one do you think would work as a subject for a newspaper profile and which one would not work at all? And why? Please give your criteria and reasons for your judgement.

   1) Mimi is a famous singer and she captured the public's attention with her first album ten years ago. Since then, she has worked and sung like a professional singer, uneventfully, never coming up with more exciting songs. But she earns a steady income, gives performance on various stages regularly, and still enjoys a loyal group of fans.

   2) Ruru is a straight-A student at a famous college. She works very hard and is admired by many fellow students for her exemplary academic records. And lately she was admitted by a graduate school from an even more famous university. As a result, she is even more admired by more people in her college.

3) Cici is an elderly woman who spends her time creating art works by cutting, patching, and pasting small pieces of fabric. She learned this cloth collage technique in a course offered by a local college for the elderly after having retired from teaching primary school. Now she keeps innovating to create more interesting fabric works out of rags.

4) Yoyo is a big sister to a brother who fell victim to substance abuse. Yoyo gave up her white-collar job in a big city and returned to her hometown, a small village, to help her brother to get clean. When her brother succeeded in doing so, she started a pig farm with him to help him stay on the right path.

5) Sisi is a cat-lover who feeds the stray cats in her neighborhood every day. She knows every cat and even gives them individual names. She spends a fortune on the cat food because she believes the cheap cat food will hurt these nimble furry balls. Not all her neighbors like what she does. Sometimes she becomes involved in quarrels with neighbors who view the stray cats as a nuisance. They believe her feeding act attracts even more stray cats into the neighborhood.

2. Read the following profile story① depicting a "village girl" giving back to her hometown. Who is the subject? What makes the subject newsworthy? What's she like? Can you find answers in the story to these questions? What details allow you to form your current impression of the main character in the story?

Village Entrepreneur and Her Happy Elderly Village

By Zhang Jiaqi

"If it doesn't work out, we can always use it for our own retirement!" Jiang Qiuyan said, sipping a cup of tea in a yard decorated by her team with discarded planks and tires.

For the last 16 years, starting with an online charity section at Rongcheng Forum in 2005, Jiang has devoted herself to programs that serve the public. She is one of the three founders of Shanghai Yexie Community Yanjing Elderly Care Home, known to locals as the Happy Elderly Village. Instead of high-rise buildings with modern facilities, the place is composed of several compact houses that blend quietly into their surroundings, like ordinary homes.

---

① 　Zhang Jiaqi. Village entrepreneur and her Happy Elderly Village[EB/OL]. Shanghai Songjiang APP. (2021-04-10) [2021-08-23]. https://app. sjmedia. net/App/content/detailshare. html? contentId＝5459230&appId＝110139&projectId＝12&shareAppId＝110139&channelType＝4.

Arriving, it is easy to mistake the retirement home for a kindergarten. Creative handiwork is displayed everywhere and trash cans in the shape of cute Doraemons and minions line the road.

"Things that work in a kindergarten are fine for the old people here," Jiang said. "Old people fight, just like children. Sometimes we see them whacking each other with walking sticks! So you have to give them something to do." Jiang said that they had a Village Hall where old people take the role of monitor, deputy monitor and group leader. One elderly man has a special fly-catching role. "He collects all the dead flies and faithfully reports his performance every day," Jiang said, with a smile.

To her, mental health is key. Old people need attention and recognition. Village residents do finger gymnastics and square dance every day. They also take singing and handcraft lessons. Special events such as contests for peeling edamame or antique clothes fashion shows are held every year and everyone takes part. Trial and error has allowed Jiang and her team to identify the most popular and successful activities.

Jiang started the project with two other kindred spirits, a lawyer and an architect. Together, they invested a total of 4.5 million RMB in the Village. "We knew from the outset that we wouldn't make a profit. It was impossible and we never planned on that. We prepared for the worst," Jiang shrugged. "So when we received a subsidy from the government, it felt like a windfall."

"Nothing was easy!" Jiang replied, when asked about the obstacles she had had to overcome. She pointed at the 100-meter footpath outside the yard and said, "We spent two months paving that road." Road construction infringed on villager's private plots and many people were resentful of it. Jiang and her team went door to door to negotiate, did a lot of talking and compensated people for their loss.

Jiang calls herself a village girl and is proud of her resilience. To apply for a catering service license, she went to the local Industrial and Commercial Bureau 24 times and one time got into a quarrel with the staff. The site could not be qualified because there was no secondary sewage network in the village. Putting one in meant an investment worth tens of millions of yuan. They finally solved the problem by introducing an off-grid sewage disposal system, which added an extra 2 million yuan to the original budget. Jiang and her partners joked that the money would have turned over multiple times if they had used it to buy a property.

"We three are the key," Jiang said. "The other two partners take care of money and I manage the whole operation." The architect planned and designed the Village layout. Each time she was on the brink of a breakdown, the lawyer encouraged her to carry on. Her partners never interfered, giving her a lot of leeway to try out new ideas. "They always tell me to give it a shot and when things go wrong, they comfort me and say, if money can fix it, nothing is a problem."

In the beginning, few people believed in them, throwing cold water on their enthusiasm. Villagers instinctively distrusted their aims, suspecting them of being profiteers. Jiang and her team had to start everything by themselves. "There is not a tree or a stone I don't know here." Jiang said that she would work in the Village in the daytime and edit their official WeChat account at night. For two years, she never went to bed earlier than 2 am. "It's what I expected. I was prepared for it." She talked lightly of the workload, as though she was talking about having breakfast.

"Luckily, my husband gave me unqualified support. He believes that we accumulate merit and virtue by our acts. Virtue is its own reward. He asked his parents to close their family store to help raise our son so that I could have more time."

Jiang's mother backed Jiang up in her own way. She thought the idea was too demanding and thankless, and made no bones about her opinion, but would nevertheless show up whenever needed. Since the Village was officially opened, she is fully supportive. The other day, when one of the cleaning staff suffered a fracture, she volunteered immediately. "And yet she hardly wipes a table at home!" Jiang laughed.

No one came to the Village when it first opened. "So I used my family members as guinea pigs. I asked my parents' relatives to move in and recruited my uncle to be the security guard. Then word got around and people gradually came in," Jiang said.

Now there are 45 residents in the Village with an average age of 87. About 80% of the residents are local villagers. They are well taken care of and appreciate the fact that they do not have to leave behind their familiar spots. Some have known each other all their lives. "They watched me grow and I watched them age." Jiang said.

The Village has now made a name for itself across the country for its practical, homely and adaptable mode of old-age care. Recently, it has received government support and the model will be replicated and scaled up.

Jiang proudly regards her project as part of the national strategy for rural revitalization. She is planning on expanding and pooling resources. Her ambition is to build a mini pastoral complex, combining old-age care with tourism and leisure services. She wants more people to learn about the countryside and wants to inject more verve and vitality into rural areas.

"Always prepare for the worst and then you'll find a way to think through many things," Jiang said, turning to wave at an elderly woman walking by.

Chapter 8　Travel Stories

Wanderlust is as ancient as any other human desires. Mark Twain states，"Travel is fatal to prejudice，bigotry，and narrow-mindedness，and many of our people need it sorely on these accounts. Broad，wholesome，charitable views of men and things cannot be acquired by vegetating in one little corner of the earth all one's lifetime." Indeed，people travel to get away from the mundane routines，to seek leisure and pleasure，and not the least，to enrich and broaden their mind. Moreover，with increasing mobility brought by modern boom of both technology and economy，people travel wide and far by increasing frequency for all kinds of reasons. Traveling has become an intrinsic part of modern life. Tourism has grown into a pillar industry as vital and thriving as any other trade. The industry contributes greatly to the national economy by serving the needs of people on the go. The statistics yielded by the leisure industry are impressive：the China Tourism Academy estimated that in 2019，the year before the pandemic breakout，the number of domestic tourists would reach 6.015 billion，inbound tourists would reach 144 million，outbound tourists would reach 168 million，and total tourism revenue would reach 6.6 trillion yuan.[①] Xinhua reported that during the National Day holiday in 2020，with the COVID-19 pandemic hanging over，China saw a total of 97 million domestic tourist trips made on the first day of the eight-day national holiday. The figure was 73.8 percent of the trips made during the same period last year. Tourism revenue reached 76.65 billion yuan (about 11.26 billion U.S. dollars)，a recovery of 68.9 percent of the revenue gained in the same period in 2019.[②] It is worth to note that operating revenue of China's rural tourism sector exceeded 850 billion yuan (about $130 billion) and a total of 3.3　billion trips were made to rural areas in 2019，according to Xinhua.[③]

[①]　杜希双：服务业发展提质增效[EB/OL]. 中国经济网. (2020-01-19) [2021-08-06]，http://www.stats.gov.cn/tjsj/zxfb/202001/t20200119_1723779.html.

[②]　China sees 97 million domestic tourist trips on National Day [EB/OL]. Xinhua. (2020-10-02) [2021-08-06]. http://www.china.org.cn/business/2020-10/02/content_76773131.htm.

[③]　China's rural tourism revenue tops 850 bln yuan in 2019 [EB/OL]. Xinhua. (202012-07). [2021-08-06]. https://www.chinadaily.com.cn/a/202012/07/WS5fcd9a4ba31024ad0ba9a44f.html.

Travel stories, a popular type of feature article, serve this niche market targeting both those bitten by the travel bug and people on business trips, travelling out of necessity. The niche market is actually huge, grown out of a variety of human needs and developing into a kaleidoscope of forms and shapes. Accordingly, travel stories take on a hodgepodge of shapes. Roughly speaking, travel stories can be further divided into two major categories: a news feature that examines the nuances of the tourism industry or a destination piece that presents the myriad shades of a tourist attraction. Tourism industry has become as complex as it is immense. There are a million issues that a feature writer can explore: the policies, laws and regulations, money issues, safety issues, the various products, the tourists themselves, to name just a few. The travel stories with some aspect of the tourism industry as the subject are often written in the same way of an issue-based feature story. On the other hand, a destination piece focusing on one tourist attraction is written more as a travel log, though not quite the same. Different from a regular travel log marked by the first person point-of-view and the immersive experience, a destination feature is first and foremost a journalistic article and it should be written like one. Whether it is a news feature examining a tourism issue or a destination story narrating a travel experience, both assume the same structure, consisting of a lead, a news peg, a nut graf, a body, and an end. In addition, both should ideally inform as well as entertain.

8.1   Destination story

8.1.1   Thematic plot

The following story from *Shanghai Daily*[①] is a typical destination piece. The article on a trip made to Saudi Arabia offers a peek into the desert country just opening up its tourism. The story is in first person and reads like a travel journal. However, the story is distinctively different from the kind of diary kept by a random traveler on foreign voyage. First, it boasts a news peg that broadcasts the policy of opening up of its tourism industry adopted by the desert kingdom. The news peg makes legitimate both the author's trip and her story.

---

① Yao Minji. Desert kingdom of contradictions is opening up tourism[EB/OL]. Shanghai Daily. (2020-05-29) [2021-08-06]. https://www.shine.cn/feature/travel/2005299145/.

Second, the story develops and revolves around its newsworthy theme, the contradictions of a country only recently opening its gate to the tourists around the world. Far from a simple account of what happened each day of the journey, a clear story line sticking to this theme can be detected. Third, background information such as explanation and analysis is duly provided, alongside description and narration of the travelling experience. In a word, the travel story is not just a personal diary where a writer may indulge individual penchant and private quirks. Instead, it is a journalistic article with all its fundamentals in place.

The opening of the story, depicting the preparation on the eve of the journey, seemingly promises a chronological story line that turns out to be thematic. In fact, the difficulties in getting information about the destination country spelt out in the lead illustrate the "contradictions" that are central to story. Saudi Arabia is launching its service sector yet clearly with an ill-conducted promotion campaign. In paragraph 11-12, the author sums up her travelling experience as "surprises abounded:" "The more we tried to "blend in" with locals, the more disparities we encountered." This theme statement captures the conflicting elements of a traditionally veiled country determined to unveil its leisure industry but rusty in the job. And in the following story, the author portrays with conscious observation a country out of practice in dealing with the curious peeks that its budding industry has brought. The ancient desert kingdom is clearly still young in playing the host to outside visitors. Moreover, the incongruities depicted in the story are more likely of a type perceived by a professional reporter rather than the average tourist. For example, the reporter observed no female drivers but did see women working "in all kinds of jobs." The second half of the story presents the tourist attractions which are mainly the various UNESCO heritage sites Saudi Arabia boasts. However, the author offers few descriptive details about these places but plenty of useful information on ticketing, visiting hours, and accessibility. The point is less to show the reader what the famed sites look like than to tell the reader what they need to know if they plan a trip themselves. This is a basic function of the travel story: graphic description is great, but solid information is better. The story looks forward at the end with a piece of new information that shows the direction the country is going, the non-alcoholic drinks the writer and her friends missed being an optimistic sign of the future of the opening up.

8.1.2 The first person

One further point of note is that the *Shanghai Daily* story is written in first person. Most journalistic articles, especially news stories and news features, are still ruled by third-person objectivity. However, the story on Saudi Arabia is presented as personal experience and the author herself becomes the principal source for the story. Indeed, travel story is one area where the employment of the first person approach is common, and its advantage is clear. The writer, by using the first person, offers a kind of substitute immersive experience and assumes an informal tone as if the account were an intimate exchange with friends. This follows the long tradition of travel logs. Personal insights, funny anecdotes, even embarrassing stumbles are conveyed in a natural manner, as if the reader were there with the writer, the latter conferring with the former freely and continuously at every turn and twist of the trip.

8.1.3 Descriptiveness

In addition to the use of first person, the *Shanghai Daily* story is rich in descriptive details that convey "what it felt like" "what it seemed like" and "how it struck people." The reporter relies heavily on her own impressions: "I was there and this is what it was like." And exact, vivid but simple words, many being simple nouns and verbs, are used to bring the scene to life. No open-mouthed exaggeration, no breathless overstatement. The tone is calm, almost cautious, befitting the description of a country whose tourism just emerging. Good description is always for a purpose, which in the case of travel writing is to serve the storytelling as a whole. Never describe just for the sake of description. The story on the desert kingdom centers on the contradictions, and all the details in the story are provided to illustrate that. The readers see old house-turned-café offer roof seating, a commonplace in any popular tourist site, but also see shops "where mannequins in different poses all had on the same black robes." The details speak loudly, every one of them resonating with the motif of the story.

The story runs as follows:

Desert Kingdom of Contradictions is Opening Up Tourism

Yao Minji

On the eve of our departure on a flight to Saudi Arabia, four friends and I were still agonizing over whether to cancel our long-planned holiday.

It was the end of January. International flights in and out of China were being canceled daily, and policies related to Chinese tourists in different countries were changing equally rapidly due to the coronavirus outbreak.

Virus aside, it had been a most difficult trip to plan. Saudi Arabia didn't offer a general tourist visa to non-Muslims until last September.

It took about 15 minutes to fill out an online visa form with basic information, and the e-visa was sent by e-mail within hours.

That was the easy part.

Without knowledge of Arabic, we found very little online information in English or Chinese about the country, except for the cities of Riyadh and Jeddah.

Even Chinese Muslim friends who went on the Hajj couldn't offer much help. Like many others, they didn't travel extensively beyond the holy sites of Mecca and Medina.

Online comments from the few who had visited Saudi Arabia were often contradictory. Was it safe for a foreign woman to travel? Could men wear short pants? Was it necessary to cover one's body from head to toe for the entire trip? Were UNESCO sites open to the public?

Those who had returned all agreed on one point: The trip was worth it. In the end, we took the trip and I ended up agreeing with them.

Our three-week tour included five-star hotels in large cities like Riyadh, filled with expatriate workers and foreign businesspeople, and local breakfast-and-bed hostels in smaller places like Taif and Zee Ain.

The trip certainly ticked off all the boxes for a good holiday: heritage sites, distinct culture, hospitality, good food and plenty of serendipity.

Surprises abounded — some pleasant, some not so. The more we tried to "blend in" with locals, the more disparities we encountered.

When we disembarked at the airport in Jeddah, the west coast commercial hub of Saudi Arabia, I didn't even dare to take out my mobile and grab a selfie. I felt a bit intimidated about what was acceptable.

So I took my cue from photos on the Saudi official tourism website, and by the time we arrived in Al Bahah, 410 kilometers away, two weeks later, I was already in jeans and shirt, wearing a pink headscarf.

"So much has changed in the last two to five years, but that depends on where you go," a Pakistani worker at a McDonald's in Al Bahah told us. "It is more conservative here in Al Bahah, but there are still obvious changes. For one, you would not be walking down the street like this if you had come two years ago."

We had heard that the kingdom was now allowing women to drive, but we didn't see any of them behind the wheel. However, we did see women working in all kinds of jobs, including those speaking fluent English in pharmacies. And we encountered a few women secretly begging for money or food on the street.

Encounters with individual Saudis were both reassuring and sometime odd. An older woman of conservative demeanor "protected" me in a crowded queue, when I had accidentally lined up at the wrong entrance for a sacred site. A young man speaking broken English in a shopping mall told me: "Respect my country."

At the same mall, I came across an abaya shop, where mannequins in different poses all had on the same black robes. Across from that shop, a lingerie shop allowed only females inside.

We were kindly offered coffee and dates by a local family on a bullet train. The husband was curious about us and eager to communicate, using translation apps and body language. He even showed us videos about China that were trending locally.

We were kicked out of a local eatery because there was no "family section" where groups with women could eat. Admittedly, the restaurant staff looked upset at having to refuse us service.

Saudi Arabia had recently unveiled new rules about breaking down the barriers between singles and family sections in restaurants, stirring a debate and opposition from conservative forces.

For most of our trip, people stared at us, openly or surreptitiously, but I found most of them just curious, not hostile. I could see smiling eyes peering out of veils.

We might have been the first young Chinese tourists they had ever seen. Chinese construction workers are common in the kingdom, and there are older Chinese Muslim families visiting there, but tourism is just emerging.

We didn't see many tourists from any country while there. At times, we were the only visitors at a UNESCO heritage site.

Saudi Arabia has five such sites. Madain Saleh, a desert archeological site of the Nabataean kingdom, is quite similar to the popular Petra site in Jordan. It was the first Saudi site to be given UNESCO designation. Other sites are under construction as part of the Saudi Vision 2030 plan to diversify the economy away from oil dependence.

It was unclear whether Madain Saleh was actually open on a winter weekday. However, the official tourism site and many online comments pointed us to the Winter at Tantora Festival that was held at the site. It's an eight-weekend series of music festivals to promote the site.

When the festival began in December 2018, its list of performers included Andrea Bocceli and Yanni. A short-term, festival-specific tourist visa available with each set of tickets. The festival was a sort of trial balloon for opening up the tourism sector.

Indeed, photos filled with colorful hot balloons floating above grand ancient tombs were stunning. I wanted to see this place of pre-Islamic civilization, filled with tombs and rock art.

We found tickets still available at a plaza equipped with an outdoor rest area and fast-food booths. All visitors are taken from the plaza to four ancient sites on fancy buses. The only other tourists on our bus was a young local couple, who kindly offered us chocolates.

They and we were the only visitors at each site. A tour guide, fluent in English, told us about the Nabatean kingdom, which had its capital in the modern archaeological site of Petra.

This area sat at the crossroads of an important trade route in incense and myrrh, which brought great prosperity at that time.

The place is still under excavation by foreign archeology teams. Four sites are open now — a religious area and three congregations of rock-carved graves.

The tour starts at the religious area, with a narrow corridor casting sunlight in between high rocks inscribed with ancient pictures and scripts. On one side, a government edict was carved out of rock, showing where and how the highest-ranking inhabitants gathered.

Most graves were carved, in rows next to each other. Names of the occupants were inscribed at the entrance, some for women. Phrases warning visitors from entering can also be found on some graves.

Carved staircases found in most of the later tombs indicated a pathway to heaven, according to the tour guide. Birds, flowers, imaginary beings and even human faces were carved on other graves, though some faces were badly weathered.

The most iconic grave is the Lonely Castle. Carved on an isolated rock outcrop, it is the largest and has four columns with Nabataean crowns on the front. Most of other graves had only two regular columns, but the guide told us there were no traces of burial sites inside the one with crowns.

The Saudi capital Riyadh is a cosmopolitan city filled with skyscrapers and modern shopping malls.

We found the UNESCO heritage site Al Turaif on its outskirts closed for construction. Our Uber driver took us around the walls to give us a glimpse of a small section of original architecture left from the kingdom's first capital in the 18th century. It has been largely restored, with new buildings around it. The driver also told us luxury hotels and malls would be built there.

We went to a traditional village called Zee Ain, located on a mountain in Al Bahah. Dating back about 400 years, the village has some 300 stone houses, a small mosque and several fortifications that display how village people lived and defended themselves. Facades have been restored but most interiors await reconstruction.

On the mountaintop, we discovered the underground spring water that gave the village its name.

The city of Jeddah and its Al Balad historic old town, also a UNESCO heritage site, had a lot more tourists. We encountered an elderly couple who looked local, the husband pushing his wife's wheelchair. They told us they had moved to Canada 30 years ago but returned to their native land last year, after relatives told them about the huge changes in the country.

The zigzag alleys in the old town house dozens of historic coral stone and wooden buildings, some dating back 500 years and many still under repair.

The homes are distinctive, with secluded wooden balconies and windows. We visited the interiors of houses turned into museums and found tea sets on the secluded balconies, indicating that women in the households could get some fresh air and street views in their indoor clothing without being seen.

Some old houses have also been turned into cafes, providing rooftop seating that affords a panoramic view of the entire area.

Jeddah was also the only place in Saudi Arabia where we had seafood. We ate in a fancy seashore restaurant where the most popular seats were those by the window, allowing patrons to view the Jeddah Fountain, the tallest of its type in the world.

After we left Jeddah, we read that a new bar was offering non-alcoholic drinks in the city. It was a pity we missed it.

8.1.4　Cultural heritage

Not all destination stories are written in first person. The following story[①] also from *Shanghai Daily* is in third person, in accordance with the journalism tradition. However, the story is still written by following one tourist who provides a personal point of view. This deviation from a usual feature story is surprisingly fitting for travel writing. This one tourist acts like a tour guide, showing the readers the attraction through her eyes.

The story glimpses into a Chinese village famous for its paper fish lantern festival, a local tradition buoyed by its 200-year-old folk handicraft. China has long been a popular destination for tourists around the world. The country's long and splendid history has given birth to gems of heritage and culture all over the land. Travel stories like this one are the perfect medium to present these jewels steeped in Chinese customs and traditions to the foreign audience. Moreover, it plays a uniquely effective role in nurturing the kind of cross-border goodwill scarce in today's polarization, for the goodwill fostered this way has deep roots nourished by understanding of each other's cultures.

8.1.5　Human element

This is all very well in theory. But how exactly to bring out the heritage gem and make it truly shine? First, focus on the human element. Just as a worthwhile travel experience should not just entail "counting the cats in Zanzibar," a worthy travel story is not just about the scenic spot or the curious rituals. The story on the fish lantern festival is as much about the fish lantern parade (the curious ritual) as about the people living in the village. How the villagers' way of living dates back to the pre-internet era, as the village itself looking "pretty much like it did a century ago;" How the villagers adapted under the 2020 COVID-19 pandemic; these human-centric details about the villagers themselves are as interesting and newsworthy as the traditional festival they held.

---

① Lu Feiran. As tourist stops go, one village is a different kettle of fish[N/OL]. Shanghai Daily. (2020-11-04)[2021-08-06]. https://archive. shine. cn/feature/As-tourist-stops-go-one-village-is-a-different-kettle-of-fish/shdaily.shtml.

The structure of the story is thematic, similar to the previous one on Saudi Arabia, though it employed the point of view of an outsider/tourist, functioning as a kind of built-in thread to tie the story together. The headline of the story suggests the motif of the story by a clever pun of the word "fish". The phrase "a kettle of fish" means a difficult, awkward, or bad situation, alluding to the pandemic halting tourists and darkening everything in the year 2020, but it also could be the fish pertinent to this story whose shape the local lantern has assumed for over 200 years. The leading paragraphs of the story go to the central point straight away. This is a story about a small Chinese village with an interesting tradition. The rest of the story revolves around this central idea. The villagers, composed of a mostly elderly population, live as they have ever lived before, seemingly oblivious to the change of time. They visit each other in their houses built in the traditional Hui style. They live a clannish life, worshipping their common ancestors and practicing their ancient rituals dutifully every year. They leave their doors open during the day and have little experience with tourists —"only one family running an inn", despite the fact that its fish lanterns keep piquing outside curiosity. Moreover, almost a microcosm of today's China, the village is far from a mere relic of its long history. It is very much alive, vibrant with a surprising renaissance of its ancient folk handicraft. The revival of the old art is boosted by the Internet-savvy young Chinese who assert their cultural identity by shooting videos in which they deck out in Hanfu (traditional Chinese clothes), with the exquisite fish lantern an essential prop in completing the latest fashion.

8.1.6   Cultural proximity

The boom of the local handicraft is the real focus of this travel story. By zooming in on the latest aspect of the 200-year-old tradition, the story provides a viable approach to sketching a microcosm of a culturally specific portrait of China to a foreign audience. However, the unique customs and special rituals, such as the fish lantern parade, may attract but a few curious souls broadminded enough to show an interest in different cultures. It is presumptuous to catalogue every reader a potential outlandish-culture-lover. In order to draw a larger audience, the writer must find and present some mutual elements that would be interesting and newsworthy to the general audience. In other words, elements of Chinese culture that are unique while at the same time have a broad appeal. In this particular story, the combination of the elderly villagers' tradition and the young Chinese's fashion statement is that element which is both idiosyncratic and general. A bunch of old villagers walking around while waving lanterns in fish shapes may be a bit strange. But for young people to "choose different types of fish lanterns to go with various styles of garments, then share their photos and videos on social media platforms" is a familiar enough act globally.

On a more technical level, the story also tries to achieve what can be summed up as cultural proximity. Specific terms are interpreted and the local legend is explained in a way that makes sense to a foreign reader. For example, in paragraph 24, the special Chinese traditional architectural term "Jin" is translated as rings of houses. And in paragraph 8, the narration of the ancient legend emphasizing the contradicting elements of fire and water explains why the lanterns used in the ritual parade are in the shape of fish. There are other examples in the story. The point is the culturally specific terms and concepts should be explained in a way that's both succinct and accessible.

In the last two paragraphs, the story veers from the theme and turns its attention on the local delights that might be enjoyed by a tourist seeking quiet away from the hustle and bustle of urban life. Then story ends with a quote on the local delicacies from our dutiful guide, Zheng. However, there are two more appending paragraphs, serving as the obligatory information box that usually goes with a travel story. The "If you go" paragraph provides transport information and other helpful tips for readers who may contemplate a possible trip after reading the story.

One more point to note is that this destination piece is also highly descriptive. The village described here is charming in its primitiveness and attractive for people who are mired in the chaotic hubbub of urban life. This impression of primitiveness is created and heightened throughout the story with descriptive details focusing on the simple life almost frozen in time. The villagers still drop by one another and keep an unlocked door during the day, which is a bygone custom in rural China. Even the old village temple building that boasts "one of only two Mao statues left in Anhui Province" missed renovation and "looks its age." The details chosen serve a unifying purpose. The imageries painted are as vivid as consistent. The words used are simple but apt. All these are ingredients that form a recipe for good description.

The story runs as follows:

As tourist stops go, one village is a different kettle of fish

Lu Feiran

18:54 UTC+8, 2020-11-05

When Peggy Zheng first stepped into Wangmantian Village in Anhui Province, she was amazed by how primitive it was.

Hidden deep inside a mountainous area 40 kilometers away from the nearest bus station, Wangmantian attracted Zheng, a handicraft enthusiast from Beijing, because of its fish lantern parade, a folk custom dating back more than 200 years.

"The parade is actually held every year around the Lantern Festival, which falls on the 15th day of the first lunar month, but this year because of the coronavirus epidemic, I missed the event and didn't get to visit the village until June," she said.

The village still looks pretty much like it did a century ago. Ancient buildings and bridges are constructed in typical Hui-style architecture, a Chinese style that has prevailed in the ancient area of Huizhou, including what is today's Anhui.

People still live in a pre-Internet era, communicating with each other by dropping around rather than texting or using mobile phones.

"All the families are more or less related to each other, mostly surnamed Wang," Zheng said. "It is so safe here that the villagers don't bother locking their doors during the day."

Although Zheng didn't get to see the fish lantern parade this year, local people told her a lot about the event and showed her some of the classic fish-shaped lanterns.

Villagers for centuries believed that a huge stone, smooth as a mirror, fell from the sky onto a nearby hill. Superstitious residents believed it was the source of all fire-related accidents. Because water is the antithesis of fire, they organized a fish-lantern parade every Chinese New Year to pray for a safe 12 months ahead.

In bygone days, all the men in the village would parade with fish-shaped lanterns for three successive nights.

The most prominent lantern, a "king fish," is 7 to 8 meters long and 3 meters high. Its frame is constructed of bamboo and its body is made of tissue paper, with hand-painted scales. Candles are lit on the inner side of the fish body, and it requires about 20 men to carry it.

The traditional procession is accompanied by lion dancers, a gong-and-drum band and people carrying other lanterns. Children often carry the much smaller lanterns at the back.

Legend has it that the fish lanterns should "wag their tails" three times when passing ancestral temples to pray for a flourishing population.

On the last night of the parade, after reaching the stone, or the "fire mirror" site, all the fish lanterns "wag" their tails and villagers bow to the stone, praying for a safe year.

Like many other small rural villages in China, most of the remaining population in Wangmantian are older people. The young leave for cities to seek a better life.

Nearly all the seniors in the village know how to make a fish lantern. Zheng said she wants to promote this unique lantern culture far and wide.

"Before visiting the village, I had already seen people posing with fish lanterns while wearing traditional Chinese garments go viral on the Internet, so I knew there must be a need beyond the village," she said.

Easier said than done. Making a fish lantern takes at least two days for an experienced craftsman — one day to make the frame from bamboo collected from the mountains, and the other to make the body and paint the scales. But the lanterns, as they are currently constructed, might be too fragile for shipping elsewhere.

Zheng was undaunted. She managed to persuade some of the older villagers to make lanterns during slack seasons and then sold them, earning some extra income for the village. Some adjustments in construction materials had to be made, and a small team was recruited to handle orders, packing and shipping.

Most of the customers are enthusiasts of traditional Chinese garments called hanfu. They choose different types of fish lanterns to go with various styles of garments, then share their photos and videos on social media platforms. It is popularizing a culture unknown to most Chinese even today.

"I hope that one day we could offer more design options so that customers can order fish lanterns by color and size," Zheng said.

The popularity of the fish lanterns, particularly among younger Chinese, has drawn attention to the village. Wangmantian is welcoming more visitors than ever nowadays, despite its lack of tourist amenities. Only one family runs an inn.

Visitors can participate in local activities, like digging bamboo shoots and picking tea leaves in the spring, or harvesting from Chinese torreya, or nutmeg yews, in the autumn. Because the local economy is reliant mainly on tea cultivation, trying a cup of freshly picked tea is always recommended.

Meanwhile, the ancestral temple dating back hundreds of years, where the fish-lantern parade passes, is also worth a visit.

The building, consisting of seven jin, or rings of houses, is officially called Yongmu Hall, which means "harmony and solemnity." The temple has not been extensively restored or repainted. It looks its age.

Inside, the memorial tablets of the Wang family are worshiped, attesting to the history of the village.

A huge statue of Chairman Mao Zedong is also worshipped in the hall, among all the mottled paintings and cracked carvings on doors, columns and beams.

The statue was a grand prize, granted to the village in 1968, for building a tea farm on a mountainside. It is believed to be one of only two Mao statues left in Anhui Province, a testament, of sorts, to the degree that the village has been bypassed by contemporary life.

"You will never get bored in Wangmantian," Zheng said. "You could hike up 1,400-meter-high Shangyangjian Mountain to enjoy a splendid natural view or marvel at the authenticity of the Hui-style buildings."

She added: "What's more, the farm food such as local ham, free-range chickens, dried bamboo shoots and preserved vegetables are so delicious that they alone are worth the visit."

If you go

There are direct high-speed trains from Shanghai to Shexian County, the nearest station to Wangmantian Village. From there, it's best to book a taxi because bus transport is sporadic at best.

Source: SHINE   Editor: Zhang Liuhao

8.2   The industry story

Both the above stories are destination articles with one focusing on a foreign country and the other on a Chinese village. The following story[1] doesn't portray a particular tourist attraction, but examines how small innkeepers cope with the empty beds caused by the COVID-19 pandemic. The story belongs to

---

[1]   Lu Feiran. Beds empty, small innkeepers turn to stop-gap measures[N/OL]. Shanghai Daily. (2020-04-15) [2021-08-06]. https://archive. shine. cn/feature/Beds-empty-small-innkeepers-turn-to-stopgap-measures/shdaily.shtml.

the other major category of travel feature articles, news features with the tourism industry as its subject matter. Specific to this story, the central idea, the ingenuous and courageous efforts made by small business owners to fend off the pandemic, is especially apt and timely in view that the world is combatting the scourge and China is evidently leading the battle. One question that has always been on the minds of Chinese journalists when reporting on China to the world is how to do so effectively. This travel feature article offers a possible solution by focusing on ordinary people facing adversity that affects the entire world. Tourism is one of the hardest-hit sectors in national economy and the pandemic strikes at all levels of the industry. This story focuses on one of the most vulnerable groups of people low on the industry chain. This underdog approach, telling the story at the micro level, is in line with the reading preferences of Western readers. Moreover, these little guys did not let the readers down; the innovative and instructive "stop-gap measure" minted by them obviously works. The impressive resourcefulness and creativity displayed by these small innkeepers also make the story an interesting read.

In terms of structure, the story is organized around three illustrative profile subjects. The story starts with a contrast lead, comparing the prosperity and depression of small inns business before and after the pandemic. Then the story flows naturally along the cause-effect chain to the nut graf (paragraph 4) where the gist of the story is summarized concisely in a one-sentence paragraph: Facing empty beds and nonexistent guests, the inn-keepers explores other avenues for profit. Afterwards, the story moves to illustrate that by depicting three business owners in Yangtze River Basin that were mired in similar difficulties but refused to be beaten. Each of them came up with unique solutions to lift themselves from the quandary. It is noteworthy that these three characters are portrayed to varying degrees, some at greater length, some only scantily. The decision is apparently based on each individual's situation and how that situation is pertinent to the story. The story ends with a quote from the last profile subject, promising that more innovative ideas are on the way.

Beds Empty, Small Innkeepers Turn to Stop-gap Measures

Lu Feiran

00:00 UTC+8, 2020-05-20

Bed and breakfast operators in Chuansha Town in the Pudong New Area were overjoyed when Shanghai Disneyland Resort opened in 2016. Business boomed. But now, the beds and breakfast tables are empty.

Disneyland announced a temporary shutdown in January due to the coronavirus outbreak, and B&Bs relishing the prospect of a prosperous Spring Festival holiday hit rock bottom.

Room reservations and company team-building retreats were canceled.

Even now, as the epidemic abates on the Chinese mainland, there is no immediate sign of recovery for B&Bs, so some operators are looking for new business avenues to help them weather the crisis.

Suyu Inn in Lianmin Village is a typical case. Before the epidemic hit, it was one of the most popular B&Bs in the area.

"By the end of January, canceled reservations cost us 230,000 yuan (US $ 32,620), and there were no reservations at all in February," says Chen Yumo, an official with Suyu. "Although we had several reservations in March, there are still no team-building events on tap, and those events account for half of our income."

What to do?

After seeing that stores and scenic sites were resorting to live stream to keep afloat, Suyu latched onto the concept of reminding visitors what they are missing and what they can expect when life returns to normal.

The inn has a ready team capable of doing baking, pottery crafts, painting and the weaving activities provided for guests during their stay.

The idea was to showcase that expertise.

Zhang Yangyang, a "butler" with Suyu, is also an experienced baker. In the live stream, he shows how to make cakes and pizzas at home.

"Live stream is a new thing for me," Zhang says. "But I believe that showing what we have to offer guests may spur some people to say, 'I want to have such a weekend.'"

Another live stream features strawberry tasting. Staff with the inn show viewers the ripe, juicy strawberries grown in the village.

"It's started out well," Chen says. "During the baking live stream, we sold five room reservation coupons. And during the strawberry live stream, we sold more than 200 boxes of strawberries."

The same kind of transformation is also happening in the neighboring province of Zhejiang. In Changxing County there, B&B owners are using e-commerce to make up for the loss of revenue.

Before the coronavirus epidemic, the county was popular as an idyllic tourism destination of green tea fields, ancient temples, quiet old streets, U-pick orchids and specialty local cuisine.

It earned the nickname "Shanghai Village" because of the large number of visitors from the city.

B&Bs are a pillar industry there. Residents redecorated their houses into small inns, receiving guests with a cozy environment and homemade delicacies.

Song Chaofeng, one of the earliest householders in the village to become a B&B business, is now making money selling farm products online. Free-range chicken and duck eggs, ducks and salted meat are among the most popular items in his online store.

"I try every one of the products before I sell them to make sure that they are worthy of the price," says Song. "Sometimes I give buyers extra gifts, such as fresh bamboo shoots, to go with salted meat."

Nearly half the 580 B&Bs in the county have launched online stores, and every day more than 1,000 orders are dispatched.

Meanwhile, many B&Bs are taking advantage of the slack time to redecorate the rooms and gardens to welcome guests back in a better environment when the pandemic is finally over.

"We've cleared up the yards and planted a lot of new flowers, hoping that when the flowers are in full bloom, business will pick up again here," says Song.

B&B operators are optimistic that the crisis will end and visitors will return as soon as possible.

"Many people have been cooped up at home for more than two months, and they will crave a getaway as soon as the epidemic subsides," says Zhou Jia, owner of Past to Future Inn in Zhoupu Town, which is located in the vicinity of Disneyland Resort.

In the first months of the epidemic, B&B operators were pretty pessimistic, she says. But she is prepared to return to normal and is promoting pre-order coupons that people can use anytime within the year.

"We need to expand our source of customers," she says. "In the past, we relied on visitors to Disneyland, but now that the resort is still closed, we must develop something else to attract customers."

Source: SHINE   Editor: Zhang Liuhao

Strong news values

As the above story shows, COVID-19 hit the world economy hard, with tourism industry right in the epicenter, and since then the world has been fighting an uphill battle to get back to normal. Hubei Province was hit the hardest in Chinese combat against the plague. In the middle of 2020, a story[①] from *China Daily* takes a bird's eye view of how the province was recovering in terms of its tourism industry. This travel feature contains strong news values. It is timely and significant, answering important questions when Hubei's approach could provide a viable model for a world grappling with the pandemic. This news feature/travel article is also substantial, offering telling details and solid numbers, presenting both the signs of revival as well as the restrictive measures still in place out of necessity. Most of all, the comprehensive and balanced report acts as a perfect antidote to the misinformation and disinformation rife in the international media amid the pandemic. The story serves to remind us of the important roles feature writing can and should play in China's efforts to communicate with the outside world. The front-page stories are eye-catching and have their shock values. However, it is the "soft" story, the people angle, and the human experience that enables effective exchange and fosters real understanding.

The news feature opens with a summary lead, getting straight to the point of the story: tourism in Hubei is recovering. Then the lead is immediately borne out by more details of the precaution measures necessary for the reopening tourist attractions. After the general introduction of the overall situation in Hubei, the story goes on to review a few tourist hot spots in Hubei to give an up-close look in further details at how these famed attractions revive with their own ingenuity and help from government. The first hot spot, Shennongjia, whose signature pencil-like mountains were featured in the blockbuster Avatar, is distinctive in that it is an open-air scenic spot, which makes social distancing easy to keep. The second hot spot, Yichang's Tribe of the Three Gorges scenic area, "has suspended its indoor performances and closed a cave that contains narrow spaces." These telling details show a practical picture of the tourist attractions making the most out of what's available to revive business. The third spot belongs to Wuhan, the heroic city that just came out of her ordeal and welcomed visitors with meticulous precautions. The landmark of the city, the Yellow Crane Tower, partially opened with strict precaution measures. The

---

① Xu Lin and Liu Kun. Hubei's tourism resumes, cautiously[N/OL]. China Daily. (2020-05-19) [2020-08-06]. http://www.china.org.cn/travel/2020-05/19/content_76063230.htm.

reopening of the Yellow Crane Tower was a landmark event itself, symbolic for the tourist industry for the whole country. After the glimpse of the Yellow Crane Tower, the story continues to present the last tourist site, the indoor provincial museum that was forced to remain closed though asserted a proactive online streaming existence. The last part of the story introduces the situation of the travel agencies, hard-hit but optimistic. The story ends with a quote from an industry authority, giving sound advice on how to pull through, bringing the story to its full.

The tone that underlies the whole story is matter-of-fact. The feature article reads almost like a news story. This no-nonsense unsentimental tone somehow resonates with the theme of the story well and naturally brings out the resilience of Chinese people in the face of great adversity.

Hubei's Tourism Resumes, Cautiously

By Xu Lin/Liu Kun | China Daily | Updated: 2020-05-19 08:24

Attractions in the province most affected by COVID-19 are gradually reopening while employing strict infection-prevention measures, Xu Lin and Liu Kun report.

The tourism industry in Hubei, the province hit hardest by COVID-19 in China, is gradually recovering.

Scenic areas, museums and hotels have been actively marketing themselves through livestreams and short videos. They're also offering discounts for visitors with extra consumption coupons provided by the government.

Travelers must make reservations so that attractions can limit visitor numbers in real time.

They must also present their health QR codes and undergo temperature checks at the entrances. And they're required to wear masks and practice social distancing. Dining facilities require customers to eat separately and use serving chopsticks.

Hubei's Shennongjia National Park reopened its scenic areas on March 25 with daily visitor numbers limited at 30 percent or less of its capacity.

"Shennongjia is known as a natural oxygen bar. This is typically its peak visitor season because of the blooming flowers and good weather. Visitor volumes are recovering," Shennongjia's culture and tourism bureau's deputy director Ming Lei says.

"Visitors enjoy the unique fauna and flora. Many ride horses, practice archery and see cute spotted deer."

Many visitors drive themselves. Most are from Hubei, especially Wuhan, Yichang and Xiangyang cities. Some independent travelers arrive by motorcycle or bicycle, he says.

The park received over 184,000 visits between the reopening and May 12, a 50 percent decrease over the same period last year.

Before May 1, travelers could visit Shennongjia's six scenic areas for free.

From May 1 until June 25, visitors can buy a ticket for all these zones at the reduced price of 169 yuan ($24).

Yichang's Tribe of the Three Gorges scenic area has suspended its indoor performances and closed a cave that contains narrow spaces.

Tourists can still enjoy open-air performances of ethnic Tujia wedding ceremonies and folk-culture shows.

"We're cooperating with online influencers to market the scenic spot... It's an efficient way to promote the stunning scenery and cultural items that tourists like to buy as souvenirs," says Qu Jiachun, assistant to the general manager of the company that runs the scenic area.

He hopes greater government support and media exposure can accelerate the tourism industry's recovery.

The province hosts such resources as magnificent landscapes and ethnic culture. And its central location ensures convenient transportation to other places across China.

These advantages can support local tourism's revival, he believes.

Wuhan's tourism recovery started later than other cities' in the province because of its situation during the epidemic.

Its landmark Yellow Crane Tower reopened on April 29, with indoor areas remaining closed.

The site received around 5,400 visitors during the five-day May Day holiday. About half were annual-membership-card holders or enjoyed free admission, such as medical workers and people older than 65. The number is nearly 2 percent of the same period last year.

"Most visitors are locals. Many are in their 30s and 40s, and bring their children to enjoy the outdoors. Our current visitor numbers are still low because most people feel uncertain (about going out)," says Wang Hongnian, head of marketing of the tower's management.

Hubei's tourism resumes, cautiously

Tourists can visit the corridors of the 51.4-meter-high tower, and the halls of each floor will reopen incrementally, since they're well ventilated. The attraction will also be meticulously disinfected.

In April, the Yellow Crane Tower started to ask staff members to host livestreams showing the attraction's views and introduce its history. Each averaged over 1 million views.

"Netizens across the country are interested in the historical tower and comment that they want to visit in the future. The livestreams also enable some locals to learn more about the tower and entice them to visit," she says.

"But the key is to make visitors feel safe... There's still a long way to go."

She expects numbers will recover gradually until September, when the fall semester begins.

"The tower's fifth floor offers marvelous bird's-eye views of the city, including the bridges that span the Yangtze River. My favorite is watching the sunset."

Visitors to the tower can also head to nearby Hubuxiang to enjoy local snacks and stroll through the Tanhualin historical and cultural block. Or they can hop a ferry across the Yangtze to explore Hankou district.

The city's indoor attractions, such as the Hubei Provincial Museum, remain closed.

Hubei was part of the powerful Chu kingdom during the Spring and Autumn Period (770-476 BC) and the Warring States Period (475-221 BC).

"Our online exhibitions and livestreams promote Chu culture and history, and its people's strong spirit and character," says the museum's curator, Fang Qin.

"The internet offers new opportunities to popularize museum culture, and we should continue to use this approach."

Chinese travel agencies' interprovincial and outbound services remain suspended. CTG Travel resumed its business in Hubei on April 26.

Its packages offering attraction tickets and accommodation are popular among travelers who drive themselves.

The company also organizes small-group tours. Buses are regularly disinfected, and at least half of seats are required to be unoccupied.

Wuhan's authorities initiated ongoing testing of all residents after new cases of COVID-19 were diagnosed, raising concerns over its tourism recovery.

"The new cases will affect Wuhan's tourism and interprovincial travel in the short term. But over the long term, the influence will ebb as confidence in the market is gradually restored," says Yan Qi, who's in charge of CTG Travel's business in Wuhan.

China Tourism Academy associate research fellow Zhan Dongmei says Hubei's tourism industry, especially Wuhan's, is recovering at a slower pace than its counterparts.

But she's confident it'll catch up over time.

"Chinese, and especially people from Hubei (now), tend to postpone their travel plans because of safety concerns," she says.

"The epidemic may have influenced their psychology. Tourism players should be patient and prepare for the recovery during this period in such ways as developing products that appeal to visitors."

8.3   The listing story

We have reviewed two major approaches to writing travel stories. The destination story concentrates on one tourist site and the writer tries to bring out the charm of the place and the authenticity of the experience with carefully-chosen descriptive details and a use of personal point of view. The travel news feature, on the other hand, examines some newsworthy aspect of the tourist industry. The story contains strong news values and focuses on the latest happening in the service sector in contextual details. Apart from these two usual approaches, another organizational method, the round up approach, is often used when the writer intends to enumerate the tourist spots of a place or to give a recommended list of scenic spots of some common characteristics. For example, in the story headlined "Tis the season to venture out and relish[1] the year's last, loveliest smile" from *Shanghai Daily*, the reporter reviews the best places in the city to take an autumn walk that will "fill you with the joy of nature's palette." Three places in Shanghai are introduced one by one and all possess stunning twilight color of the year. At the end of each introduction, transport and admission information is provided. A photo showing the glorious fall color accompanies each introduction. Another story from *Shanghai Daily*

---

[1]   Lu Feiran. Tis the season to venture out and relish 'the year's last, loveliest smile[N/OL]. Shanghai Daily. (2020-10-28) [2021-08-06]. https://www.shine.cn/feature/travel/2010288605/.

titled "Sanya a tropical paradise packed with scenic delights"[1] gives a summary of the tourist spots of the tropical city Sanya at the southernmost of Hainan Island. Each of the four tourist spots is presented in the same format, a brief introduction followed by "if you go" information and a photo showing the beauty of the delight. In a word, the listing story, following the invisible bullet points, gives the travel writer an efficient way to organize and present a group of scenic spots or tourist sites with a unifying theme.

8.4　Summary

Travel feature articles serve a unique need of the readers. It is popular with the general audience as we can see that the webpages are flooded by recollections of and tips on trips and voyages. However, newspaper travel features provide readers with much more than mere reminiscences and advice.

First, the newspaper travel features, including the destination story, takes a news peg, a news event that justifies the sudden interest in the place. The story is fundamentally newsworthy, though some, mostly destination stories, focus more on entertaining the reader, and others, frequently the travel news features, lean towards informing the audience. A travel feature writer should treat the subject as any other: do the usual research, conduct proper interviews, select and organize the gathered materials based on the central theme. Like any other feature story, a good travel article results from thorough reporting as well as careful writing.

Second, travel features, especially destination stories, often use the first person. The first person approach is in keeping with the long tradition of travel account of firsthand experience. The rendered style is friendly and casual: The writer tells the story to a friend at leisure over a cup of tea rather than to an obscure mass audience. The experience accounted feels real and the readers are brought along naturally.

Third, travel features are heavy in description and color. This requires substantial observation power on the part of the writer. Effective observation is conscious. It is a process of summing up the place and recognizing the defining details. It is a dialogue between the observer and the surroundings observed. All

---

[1]　Yu Hong. Sanya a tropical paradise packed with scenic delights[N/OL]. Shanghai Daily. (2020-11-05) [2021-08-06]. https://www.shine.cn/feature/travel/2011059053/.

the five senses of the observer are assailed by the place while the place is meticulously catalogued and analyzed. Later, when actual writing begins, words that are simple and precise should ideally be used. Good description consists in exact factual sketch, not adjectives-filled hyperbole.

Last but not least, travel writing plays a unique role in telling stories of China to the world. China has always been a popular tourist destination. Her rich tourism resources formed in the country's eons of history have their roots in the nation's splendid culture. By presenting to the world the country's spectacular sceneries, unparalleled craftsmanship, famous cuisines, and hospitable people, travel features help naturally bridging the cultural gap and promoting the nation's image. A travel writer should pay special attention to dealing with cultural specific matters that tend to congregate in stories focusing on China's long history and splendid culture. Necessary contextual information must be provided and cultural specific terms must be explained further. The goal after all is an intelligible story.

Exercise

Let's consider a campus as a tourist destination. Suppose you are to introduce your campus to the general public as a place worth visiting. Discuss with your classmates, and decide on what scenic spots there are on your campus, what are the uniqueness of each attraction, and what approach is best to present your campus to outsiders. Should your story be a destination piece, a news feature, or a listing story? What kind of research and leg work are necessary to adequately report such a story?

Chapter 9　Reviews

The best judge of a feast is the guest, not the cook, says Aristotle. The role of this grating and ungrateful guest in journalism is fulfilled by feature writers as they review and critique movies, theatre, books, food, art, music, and other cultural events. "Criticism" and "reviewing" are two terms we use to refer to explaining, interpreting, appraising, and evaluating an artistic work or a cultural event. However, the former often refers to the more formal and comprehensive analyzing based on professional knowledge. The latter is what we see every day in newspapers and magazines, not so much professional evaluation as informative reporting of the event. This chapter will concentrate on how to write reviews, which, compared with criticism, is less academic and more a quick taking of the pulse of the fluid contemporary culture.

A review article is essentially a piece of opinion. This is one of the few areas that a reporter is allowed his or her opinions in journalism. For any other type of feature stories, the reporter's opinion should be kept strictly from the story. The reporter's role is confined to presenting all the facts and letting the readers draw their own conclusions. In fact, ideally a writer should refrain from voicing personal opinion in any kind of non-fiction writing. E.B. White decrees "do not inject opinion" because though "we all have opinions about almost everything", the demand for them is not "brisk". In addition, "in any event, (the opinions) may not be relevant to the discussion."[1] Very sound advice indeed. A feature story inflated by personal opinions is biased and lacking, because it is more likely a product of the reporter's equally inflated ego than serious reporting. Reviews are the exception to the rule. The writer is supposed to give opinion in order to aid the audience in their appreciation of the artistic work or cultural event. The opinion is supposed to be fair, though it is sometimes difficult to specify what's fair and what's not, especially considering the inevitably different premises taken by the reviewer and the reviewed author, creator, performer, or cook. So the proper approach to writing a

---

[1]　William Strunk JR. and E.B. White. The Elements of Style (illustrated) [M]. New York: Penguin Books, 2005:114.

review is to do sufficient reporting and then make sure the opinion is based on the facts gathered. In this way, rather than merely personal, the opinion is a kind of intelligent conceptualizing supported by gathered evidence. Once the opinion is formed, it must be stated boldly and confidently. Wishy-washy reviews won't work. Readers expect confident and certain advice. The reviewer must be sure or at least appear to be sure.

Review writing has its own ethical issues. The subject of a review, whether it is the latest movie or a new restaurant opening nearby, is often a business as well as a product. This requires review writers to take extra care in their writing and to remain independent. Their job is to report on events and give an unbiased assessment, in the hope that the audience will make an informed decision. It is not to promote it by singing its praises. It is often unwise for reviewers to have too close a friendship with their reviewed subject, for fear that their reviews will become meek. On the other hand, reviewers must also be fair. They should make bold comments and offer strong opinions, but without malice. Inappropriate attacks without solid evidence can put people out of business. Furthermore, it is bad taste to use the work under consideration as a take-off point to launch the reviewer's own view of the world, or to criticize the work for not being what it was intended to be.

Review writing is a process of reporting expertly alloyed with assessing. Reporting is essential to all reviewing. Through reporting, the reviewer is able to answer some basic questions like what it is about or why it was written/ painted/made. Assessing, on the other part, answers questions like whether it is worth the time and money, whether it is interesting/moving/entertaining, or how it compares to previous or similar work. Generally speaking, a review is supposed to cover the following points.

（1）To introduce the work that is being reviewed.

（2）To give an informed judgement as to whether it is worth the reader's time and money.

（3）To support with evidence and convincing argument that is based on knowledge and experience.

（4）To interpret the work under consideration, connecting the artist(s) and the audience.

（5）To give basic if you go/ if you watch information.

Review writing is one area of media at all levels that is dominated by external contributors. Douban, a popular media platform known as China's

IMDB，rates films and posts reviews mostly created by users. In music apps such as WangYiYun，users often check out reviews left by other fans. Thousands of short videos and articles flood social media platforms offering advice on how to enjoy restaurants and food. Professional and amateur opinions are freely offered，and everyone seems to have an opinion. However，it takes professional knowledge and insight to provide informed commentary. Reviews of such subjects as art，theatre and music obviously require special knowledge and expertise. Even a food review，being on a common and arbitrary subject，requires extensive knowledge of food ingredients and preparation，aesthetic judgement，and an understanding of how a restaurant operates as a business. As such，freelance writers with expertise in a particular area can provide noteworthy commentary. A professional feature writer working on such stories also needs to draw from experience and knowledge gained over time.

Despite its "soft" approach，reviews play an irreplaceable role in telling China's stories to the world. Books，plays，films，TV，concerts，art exhibitions，and other cultural expressions are a kind of universal language that naturally goes beyond actual vernacular barriers. The valuable service reviews provide is to explain and interpret the subtleties of Chinese art and culture，the meanings of which are often buried in layers of tradition. These nuances may be hard to convey in the coverage of the large events that appear on the front page. Indeed，reviews on miscellaneous cultural events and artistic works form a significant part of China's English-language reporting. There are as many kinds of reviews as there are viable subjects. This chapter will focus on introducing three most common types of reviews：movie reviews，art reviews，and food reviews.

9.1　Movie reviews

Newspaper movie reviews are rich in information and aim for the middlebrow or popular market. The article plays an essential service role by informing the audience of what's on and what's worth watching. It is often shorter than movie criticism，which is professional，learned，almost academic evaluation，offering，for example，a comparison of the reviewed work with the director's previous works or other works in the same genre. Either approach，the reviewer must have a basic understanding of how the medium works and of how to tell a story employing images.

Review writing often takes the essay approach and has a clear beginning, body and ending. It starts with a declarative statement that sums up the film. This opening paragraph is similar to the nut graf in a regular feature story. Then the review goes on to give a variety of evidence to back the opening statement up. A movie can be reviewed in terms of the quality of the directing, the performance of the actors and actresses, the cinematography, the soundtrack, the script, the adaption if it is adapted work, the special effects, the general reception of the movie so far, or anything of note concerning the making of the movie. Of course it is ill-advised to judge every small point and write a laundry list of review. It is unbecoming to be this boring when offering comment on entertainment. So it is rather obvious that one should focus on the parts that have been highlighted in the opening summation. There's no fixed way to end a review. A quote from the director or a key actor often is a good choice. In addition, make sure such service information as the release information, the running time, and ticketing are given at the end. Last but not the least, the reviewer should review the film without exactly giving the story away.

The following movie review is from *China Daily*.[①] The article critiques a documentary telling stories from "the early days of the novel coronavirus outbreak in Wuhan, China." It opens with a declarative statement that sums up the documentary as "raw and gritty." Then more basic information about the making of the film is given in the next two paragraphs. After that, the review moves on to give examples illustrating the "raw and gritty" quality of the film in support of the opening statement. The review also provides key contextual information on Wuhan and the world to help put everything in proportion. There are some spoilers in the article but it does not give the entire film away. The scenes recounted in the review are chosen to demonstrate the unflinching look the documentary film takes: For example, the article reveals a telling scene where "the mobile phones of dead patients ring unattended in a storage container as worried relatives try to contact them." The film director is quoted several times in the article explaining the thoughts and considerations leading to the making of the film. Towards the end of the article, the reception of the film by the international audience is reported.

---

① Belinda Robinson. Wuhan film tells stories of hope and kindness[N/OL]. China Daily. (2020-10-08) [2021-08-06]. http://www.chinadaily.com.cn/a/202010/08/WS5f7f364da31024ad0ba7d84b.html.

Wuhan Film Tells Stories of Hope and Kindness

By BELINDA ROBINSON in New York | China Daily Global |

Updated: 2020-10-08 23:54

A raw and gritty documentary captures the chaos and trauma of the early days of the novel coronavirus outbreak in Wuhan, China, and lays bare how dedicated nurses and doctors battled to save thousands at the start of the global COVID-19 pandemic.

76 Days, a film by the US-based Chinese director Hao Wu, uses rare footage from two filmmakers, Weixi Chen and one dubbed Anonymous, who were both on the front lines in Wuhan. It was filmed during the city's 76-day lockdown, which began in February and ended April 8. It had its debut at the 2020 Toronto International Film Festival last month to widespread acclaim.

"I needed to tell a story about hope, about the human experience living through a common tragedy, about our shared humanity in this divided and scared world, in order to survive this pandemic myself," said Wu.

In the opening scenes of the film, a desperate medical worker runs toward the intensive care unit inside a hospital where her father lay dead.

"I want to see my papa off! I want to say goodbye!" she says. She is wrapped head-to-toe in personal protective equipment, including plastic goggles to cover her eyes, and encouraged not to cry by nurses.

She lets out a yell of despair. "Let me see my papa for the last time!" The woman weeps uncontrollably. Her father is soon taken out of the intensive care unit in a body bag. His daughter is overcome by grief.

"I'll never see him again!" she shouts through tears as an ambulance drives off with her father inside. It was just **one example** of the immense loss experienced by thousands of families in Wuhan due to COVID-19.

In a city with a population of 11 million, at least 3,869 people died from the coronavirus and 50,333 were infected by April 17, authorities said. The novel coronavirus was first detected in Wuhan.

The World Health Organization declared the virus a global public health emergency on Jan 30. As of October 2020, the global death toll from COVID-19 is more than 1 million people, and over 35.9 million have been infected worldwide.

The early days of tackling the virus were an uncertain time for frightened patients and overworked doctors in Wuhan. Filmmakers capture a crowd of 30 patients gathering outside the front of a hospital's epidemic disease section after becoming infected. Some were too weak to stand. All were anxious.

"I admitted 27 patients," a nurse dressed in plastic yellow personal protective gear said on a mobile phone. "There are still 36 outside. That's more than 50 already."

"People are dying. Open up!" a patient shouted from outside.

Hospital staff assured the sick that they'd be admitted in stages, but it was not enough to quell their fears.

After they were admitted, the film showed how medical professionals worked diligently to help them breathe with ventilators.

Their compassion and professionalism were on full display even when one elderly patient with dementia wept and begged to die because he was "old" and thought it was his time.

Another female patient described how she'd woken up and realized her mom was dead next to her. She thanked nurses for saving her and her dad.

Doctors held up mobile phones to allow families to talk to sick loved ones. Many patients were elderly and afraid.

Amid the chaos, a pregnant woman had a cesarean section alone. She could not be with her family over fears it could spread the virus. That baby girl, patient number 98, was separated from her mom, but eventually went home after her parents underwent quarantine.

Said Wu: "I have huge admiration for my co-directors, who risked their own lives to film in the hospitals, especially when the danger of the coronavirus was little understood in the early days of the Wuhan lockdown.

"Every night after filming they would go through a disinfection ritual and go back to rest alone in hotels reserved for front-line workers. Their existence during the lockdown was an exhausting one, both physically and emotionally."

Back at the hospital, the old man with dementia wandered through the hallways impatiently. Agitated, he tells staff he wants to go home. They try to calm him down, though the man's strong dialect makes it difficult for them to understand him at the beginning. Weeks later, he gets better and is discharged. But not everyone was so lucky.

In one heartbreaking scene, the mobile phones of dead patients ring unattended in a storage container as worried relatives try to contact them.

Every day, hospital staff had the grim task of contacting the relatives of people who had died. They kept the belongings of the deceased, like a grandmother's bracelet, so that they could reunite it with heartbroken relatives.

"Rich or poor, revered or despised, fate befalls all. What a tragedy no one can escape," a nurse said as she disinfected the identity cards of those who had died.

By April, life in the city began to return to normal. Some patients recovered and were released. A nurse promised to share a local delicacy with her co-workers when it was all over — hot dry noodles. (back to normal)

Wu, an award-winning documentary filmmaker, producer and writer who divides his time between the US and China, has directed a host of documentaries, including Beijing or Bust, The Road to Fame and All in My Family. His documentary People's Republic of Desire, about China's livestreaming culture, won the Grand Jury Award at the 2018 South by Southwest film festival. (The cv of the director)

He put together 76 Days in Atlanta as coronavirus ripped through the United States. After its debut in Toronto, it received international praise. The Washington Post described it as "a riveting documentary filmed during the shutdown of Wuhan, (an) astonishingly candid and deeply wrenching portrait of death suffering and compassion ... the first movie of its kind to emerge from China". (world reception of the documentary)

The Hollywood Reporter added that it was a "hidden gem". And Rolling Stone said "harrowing doesn't even come close to describing some of the more intense sequences in here. It's an invaluable look at the early days of a global catastrophe".

Wu said: "As much as I have been horrified by the human toll of this pandemic and the failures of different societies to mount a cohesive and effective defense, I have also been encouraged by the ample evidence of human tenacity and kindness."

Newspaper movie reviews sometimes take the round up approach and take an inventory of the latest movies or movies of a special genre. This type of review is essentially a listing story, introducing the movies on the watch menu one by one and giving a panorama of what's going to be on. The following review from Shanghai Daily① is such a listing story. Published on December 7, the review focuses on unveiling the films about to grace the festive silver screen. Of all the 50 movies vying for the new year box office, nine are introduced in details. At the end of the story, the reporter summarizes the season's movies by

① Xu Wei. Latest festive films ready to be unleashed [N/OL]. Shanghai Daily. (2019-12-07). [2021-08-06]. https://www.shine.cn/feature/entertainment/1912077548/.

recognizing a shift in Chinese audience' taste from the eye-candy blockbuster to the story-centric feature films.

Latest festive films ready to be unleashed

Xu Wei

00:00 UTC+8, 2019-12-07

Latest festive films ready to be unleashed

"Ad Astra"

Chinese cinemagoers have a bumper month of highly anticipated movies to watch during the festive period.

By the end of November, China's box office had already exceeded 59 billion yuan (US $ 8. 4　billion), almost reaching last year's box office revenue of 60.9 billion yuan. And, with new movies slated for Christmas and New Year release, a new record is expected to set for 2019.

Around **50 movies** from home and abroad will be presented, covering the **diverse** genres of comedy, sci-fi, romance and suspense.

Award-winning Chinese filmmaker Diao Yinan, known for his crime thriller "Black Coal, Thin Ice," presented his latest crime drama **"The Wild Goose Lake"** yesterday.

Starring Hu Ge and Liao Fan, the film tells a story about the self-redemption of a wanted man. The movie takes you on a rollercoaster adventure, which also unveils the destiny of ordinary people and the truth about love and humanity.

Sci-fi blockbuster movie **"Ad Astra"** was also released in China yesterday.

The film, starring Brad Pitt, Tommy Lee Jones and Liv Tyler, follows an astronaut who tries to find his missing father in space.

On his journey to the Moon, Mars and Neptune, he is aware that the Solar System is under the threat of a dangerous experiment. The film was entered at this year's Venice International Film Festival.

"Downton Abbey" will hit cinemas across China on December 13.

Based on the popular romantic British period drama, the film gathers the full, original cast, including Michelle Dockery, Maggie Smith and Hugh Bonneville.

The screenplay is written by Julian Fellowes, who created the original drama.

The film has already made US $ 180 million at the global box office.

With more lavish scenes and exquisite costumes, the cinematic extension of the TV series records the unprecedented challenge to the Crawley family, thanks to an official state visit by King George V and Queen Mary in 1927.

The film conveys the power of family connection and the diversity of humanity. It also portrays the growth of Lady Mary and Lady Edith, and the sisters' mutual understanding and compromise.

Director Dong Runnian presents the sci-fi fantasy **"Gone With the Light"** on December 13. A strange light takes many people in love away from the Earth. Their separated partners then have to face up to life without them and learn the true nature of themselves and love.

Dong said the film was inspired by his own imagination and wondered what if the tranquility of people's lives and the rules of society were, all of a sudden, broken.

On December 20, **"IP Man 4,"** the final installment of Wilson Yip's popular martial arts franchise, will hit cinemas across the country.

Kung fu star Donnie Yen told fans the film series has witnessed the growth and breakthrough of his career over the past 10 years. He revealed it will be his last kung fu movie.

Based on the life of Wing Chun grandmaster IP Man, the film follows his experience in San Francisco, where he and his student Bruce Lee surprise the local martial arts community with Chinese kung fu. Several scenes pay tribute to the revered martial artist and actor Bruce Lee who died at an age of 32.

The fight scenes in the movie were designed by award-winning martial arts choreographer Yuen Woo-ping. The audience will be amazed at the combat between Wing Chun, Tai Chi and Karate.

Filmmaker Feng Xiaogang will present **"Only Cloud Knows,"** which is a movie based on a friend of Feng.

The film tells the touching story of a middle-aged man who embarks on a journey to fulfill his wife's last wishes.

Malaysian director Quah Boon-lip will screen his crime film **"Sheep Without A Shepherd"** on December 20.

Set in a small Thailand town, the film is centered on a father who tries to protect his family after a confrontation with local cops. It is a remake of the Indian film "Drishyam."

Quah's short flick "The Free Man" was nominated in The Oscars Live Action Shorts Category in 2015. The talented director has superb skills in cinematography.

On New Year's Eve, director Yang Zi will offer **"Adoring,"** a film with six heartwarming stories about pets.

With the help and company of pets, people of different ages learn to love and cherish what they already have.

"**Begin, Again,**" also out on December 31, points the lens at the difficult and inspiring lives of urban white-collar workers who leave their hometown to pursue a dream.

Compared to movies released in the same period last year, most of the homegrown films have a strong realistic flavor and feature ordinary people.

Film industry insiders have noted that blockbuster movies are not always the preferred choice of Chinese movie buffs. Productions with original stories always resonate in the hearts of viewers who like to see an "underdog" or "dark horse" triumph over adversity.

9.2   Art reviews

According to Britannica. com, art is a visual object or experience consciously created through an expression of skill or imagination. The term "art" encompasses diverse media such as painting, sculpture, printmaking, drawing, decorative arts, photography, and installation.[①] This umbrella term represents all manner of expressions of aesthetic emotions and impulses. In turn, art reviews cover a variety of subjects and frequently report on an art exhibition or a cultural event. It is often written as an essay, careful evaluations presented with solid evidences.

The art world is capricious and temperamental. To review the unpredictable artistic expressions takes more courage. Generally speaking, a reviewer should present her thesis confidently. For an art review, the writer must assert her conviction with extra assuredness. Moreover, to review intelligently and fairly, the reporter must at least have some professional knowledge. However, though the reporter is strongly advised to make herself an expert on the reported subject, she is equally advised against flaunting that expertise at the readers. A condescending piece is annoying. What the reader wants is fair summation based on evidences turned up by sufficient reporting.

A prosperous cosmopolitan city, Shanghai enjoys a robust cultural and art scene. Every day the city hosts various exhibitions featuring art, vintage and

---

① Britannica[EB/OL]. [2021-08-06]. https://www.britannica.com/art/visual-arts.

contemporary, home and abroad. The following art review① published on *Shanghai Daily* introduces an exhibition on traditional Chinese bird-and-flower painting "with a modern twist." The art form is an obvious Chinese specific subject that's unfamiliar to a foreign audience. The introductory paragraphs try to decode the ancient eastern art: The bird-and-flower paintings symbolize Chinese people's longing for a good life. Then the artist herself is quoted to clarify the "modern twist" on the traditional painting. The rest of the story is a blend of declarative generalizations, anecdotes and quotes, all contributing to explaining the art and helping the prospective visitors to get an intelligent as well as enjoyable experience. At the very end of the review, if-you-go information is given.

Traditional Chinese bird-and-flower art with a modern twist

Shi Hua

00:00 UTC+8, 2020-08-28

Throughout history, Chinese bird-and-flower paintings have featured birds resting or flying amidst blossoms, leaves, branches and occasionally rocks and rippling waters. Exuding beauty and liveliness, these paintings reflect Chinese people's yearning for happiness and harmony.

A colorful paradise flycatcher appearing with peaches symbolizes longevity. Magpies resting on plum blossom branches herald future happiness, fortune or good luck. A graceful egret frolicking amidst lotus flowers in a pond implies great career advances.

"I wanted to carve out a path of my own off the beaten track," said artist Wan Fu, 61, at her exhibition's opening ceremony earlier this month at Jin Space Gallery in Shanghai.

The professor at Shanghai Art & Design Academy has been working on traditional Chinese bird-and-flower paintings for decades, but her goal is to create a completely new style.

Dubbed "contemporary urban gongbi bird-and-flower painting" by collectors and art critics, her recent paintings are replete with masterful Chinese brushstroke and ink-wash techniques. Yet they look contemporary and modern, different from conventional Chinese paintings.

The birds are tiny and lifelike, as in a traditional Chinese gongbi (fine,

---

① Shi Hua. Traditional Chinese bird-and-flower art with a modern twist[N/OL]. Shanghai Daily. (2020-08-28) [2021-08-06]. https://www.shine.cn/feature/art-culture/2008285000/.

meticulous line) painting. Yet, the flowers and leaves are scattered around the rice paper as if floating through the air.

Backgrounds consist of blurred squares and rectangles, abstract and non-descriptive, with a mixture of white and different shades of gray and black or colors reminiscent of both city skylines and reflections of buildings in a pond.

By incorporating constructivism from the West, Wan has dismantled integral parts of traditional Chinese bird-and-flower paintings and created her own unique style, an ethereal realm of flora and fauna.

"I absolutely love these pretty, cute birds and flowers," she said. "In each painting, I want to create a surreal yet natural realm that is serene, harmonious, secure and beautiful."

Art critics say Wan's paintings reflect her mind-set and yearning for peace, love and beauty in modern life.

The flowers are arranged in an independent yet interactive fashion, and the birds are depicted in a carefree, secure, fairy tale-like setting with blurred backgrounds adding a touch of modernity and sophistication.

To capture the most realistic, vivid bird postures, Wan once raised a pair of finches and even witnessed one coming out of its egg. Ten days later, she began feeding the infant bird using a recipe from a book.

She still has one finch that flies around her studio when she paints. Sometimes it dips its claws in paint and leaves its claw prints on paper.

"My paintings stem from real life," she said. "I have been living and working in Shanghai for decades, so naturally I have put my love for and understanding of the city landscape in my paintings."

Apart from a few large paintings, most of her works are small in size. They must be viewed closely to see the birds properly, offering an intimate experience to visitors.

Exhibition info

Date: Through September 25, 9:30am-6:30pm

Venue: Jin Space Gallery

Tel: 186 1681 6519

Address: 2F, 1191 Nanjing Road W.

The following art review[1] from *Shanghai Daily* acquaints the readers with

---

[1]　Tan Weiyun. Capturing motion when beauty strikes a chord[N/OL]. Shanghai Daily. (2020-09-05) [2021-08-06]. https://www.shine.cn/feature/art-culture/2009055470/.

an Iranian-British artist coming to town with her works that are highly current. The story starts with a straightforward introduction of the exhibition, followed by a declarative statement summing up the show. The body of the review divides between providing biographical and professional information about the artist and shedding light on the "deeply personal and philosophical" exhibition. Again, general evaluations and factual statements are spliced together to render the story informative and useful. At the finish, the story is appended by exhibition information.

Capturing Motion When Beauty Strikes a Chord

Tan Weiyun

01:26 UTC+8, 2020-09-05

What's On

Iranian-British artist Shirazeh Houshiary's first exhibition in China "As Time Stood Still" is to open next Saturday at Shanghai's Lisson Gallery, featuring a series of new works inspired by her experience in the United Kingdom during the coronavirus lockdown.

The exhibition is deeply personal and philosophical, exploring profound questions about perception and imagination, as well as the fundamental power of beauty.

"As time stood still through the lockdown and with death all around, it's beauty that strikes a chord with most of us," Houshiary said. "Beauty in nature and the movement of trees as the breeze ruffles its leaves. Beauty is the awareness of life and our ephemeral existence."

The exhibition follows the artist's trip to China in 2018, including a visit to Dunhuang's Library Cave, a UNESCO World Heritage site on China's Silk Road.

During the trip, Houshiary was invited by the Central Academy of Fine Arts to an in-depth dialogue with artist Yu Hong, where they discussed the history of this artistic and religious site, the significance of Silk Road and Houshiary's early interest as a young child in stories from this region.

Since the 1980s, she has sought to embody profound abstract concepts, namely the very essence of existence — transcending any form of perceived identity from nationality, language, culture or beliefs — through her work. The mediums she works with include painting, sculpture, installation, architecture and film

Born in Shiraz, Iran, in 1955, Houshiary moved to London in 1974. In the 1980s, galleries around the world began exhibiting her work — from the Venice Biennale in 1982 to a 1994 nomination for the Turner Prize, considered the British art world's highest honor.

Her first solo exhibition at Lisson Gallery took place in 1984. In 2018, Houshiary was awarded the Asia Society's Asia Game Changer Award, which honors people making positive contributions to Asia's future.

Her work is included in prestigious public collections worldwide, including New York's Metropolitan Museum of Art, Museum of Modern Art and Guggenheim Museum, the Centre Pompidou in Paris, and London's Tate.

"As Time Stood Still" is a pertinent reflection of our current state of existence, with visual commentary on this period of global transformation but from an alternative perspective. The exhibition presents a rare opportunity to observe what has arisen in the pandemic's wake — a sense of appreciation and gratitude for natural surroundings.

"As the lockdown has continued, I haven't been distracted by events and have found solace in looking through the window of my studio into the woods beyond," she said. "Here, all relationships and ideas that make up the cosmic process can be seen, and I am reminded how shortsighted humanity can be."

In five powerful new paintings created this year — "Swell" "Parable" "Mind and Matter" "Chimera" and "The Big Picture," Houshiary mirrors the passing nature of the atmosphere around people, overlaying markings with fleeting patterns that dance and weave around each other. Along with these works, a new sculpture "Duet" uses a wall as its stage. Its red and dark blue ribbons recede and advance, gesturing to draw the viewer closer.

"I am trying to capture motion in continuous movement rather than in a static, solid form," she said. "Light and transparency play a big part in this, where the immaterial becomes the invisibility of the material."

Houshiary also noted the similarity of the intertwining ribbon motifs in these works to those found in Dunhuang's Mogao Caves that depict wind or star gods, as well as flying apsaras and celestial beings that charge across the many murals.

Exhibition info

Date: From September 12 to October 24 (closed on Sundays and Mondays), 11am-6pm, or call 6333-9296 to make appointments for special tours given when the gallery is closed to the public.

Venue: Lisson Gallery

Address: 2/F, 27 Huqiu Road

Source：SHINE   Editor：Zhang Liuhao

As the above examples show，newspaper art reviews come from a combination of art appraisal and journalistic reporting. The targeted audience is the general readers as well as art lovers. Hence the story is as much about educating the public on the merits and faults of the given artistic work as about providing cultural information as a regular news story. It is clearly distinctive from art criticism which features longer from and demonstrates much expertise and professional knowledge. The newspaper art review，though often written as an essay，is essentially a piece of news reporting with an aesthetic subject. Besides，some art reviews also adopt the round-up approach，instead of offering detailed appreciation of one show，provides a to-do list of upcoming exhibitions for the interested art patrons.

9.3　Food reviews

Food entices and soothes with taste，smell，and look. It connects with human emotion in a way that's unlike anything else. Food satisfies hunger，cures homesickness，and brings people deep pleasure. It is a universal language everybody understands. Home cooking has nostalgic connotation of comfort and familiarity，and local cuisines are a powerful source of regional pride and a mighty impetus for tourist interest. Food reviews are an important part of lifestyle features and make enjoyable reading. English-language food reviews unveil to the world the sophisticated charm of Chinese cuisines which have mellowed and perfected in Chinese long dietary tradition and food culture. These are stories that appeal to the palate and drip with culture.

Like other types of review，food reviews are written mainly in essay form. It is one area that opinions rule. Food is a very personal thing. As the saying goes，one man's meat may be another's poison. However，the challenge in writing food review is not being firm when voicing one's view，but the mastery of enough words to do justice to such a delectable subject. A food reviewer works from a rich and lush word bank to brings out the color，aroma and flavor of the cuisines. Have a look at the following passage[1] and take note of how words are put together，scrambled and stirred to present the richness of both the

---

① Donia Bijan. The last days of Café Leila：a novel [M]. Chapel Hill：Algonquin Books of Chapel Hill，2018.

food and the family tradition.

> In the thirty years sine Yanik had tied an apron around her belly and shown Nina how to separate eggs, she had explored countless recipes, decoded the subtleties of Persian food, its ancient alchemy of sweet and sour, hot and cold, its deference to plants and herbs, soliciting Naneh Goli's palate to measure and fine-tune. What triumph to turn out a pot of rice with a golden potato tadig— that magic crust beneath the steamed rice.

Writing about food appears easy. Most people eat three meals each day and everybody has something to say about their diet. However, the story idea for food review has to be carefully examined and shaped. Adequate research and sufficient reporting should be carried out. A suitable story structure must be decided upon, with a clear focus and a workable story line. The opinion must be as fair as possible though allowing for the personal bias that's inevitable in such a story. As to the writing topics, there is a wide range of choices. A newly-opened restaurant is certainly worth investigating. A novel dish of the seasonal ingredients may pique the reader's curiosity. An expert explanation of a special ingredient, a way of cooking, or even a unique presentation of the food, may serve as an interest read. When international communication is concerned, food stories are typically both entertaining and informative. The local cuisines are often presented with emphasis on both the flavor and the stories or the lore behind it.

The following story[1] from *Shanghai Daily* takes the round up approach and enumerates several distinctive local dishes under a unique Chinese dietary concept: *Xiafan*, which means to go well with the rice. The story manages to give a sweeping view, through a specific prism, of the extensive and profound home cooking culture of China. Traditionally members of an agricultural society, Chinese people have great attachment to the soil and the rice and grain that grow on it. Staple food is held in utmost respect in Chinese culture, as the saying goes *Min Yi Shi Wei Tian*, literally translated as "the people considered the food as heaven." Xiafancai, an essential part of home food, is prepared to make the staple food more delectable. These dishes are made from common ingredients and saltier than the ordinary dish, thus a little is enough to go with

---

① Li Anlan. But does it go well with rice? [N/OL] Shanghai Daily. (2020-11-04) [2021-08-07], https://www.shine.cn/feature/taste/2011049015/.

the rice. In a very real way, *Xiafancai* is a microcosm of the life of an ordinary Chinese family: simple, unpretentious, frugal and flavorful.

Also, it is worth to note that the story is not a string of recipes despite the detailed attention on how the various source dishes are prepared. The story has an angle and all the descriptions contribute to its arching concept: the dishes presented here are not fancy, but every day food boosting the appetite and cooked at any Chinese household.

The story runs as follows:

But does it go well with rice?

Li Anlan

Xiafan, the Chinese expression that translates as "go well with rice," is a unique standard people often use to rate the deliciousness of savory dishes — the dish that makes a person eat more rice is a winner.

A hot bowl of rice is the basic staple choice especially in the southern provinces where rice is planted. With its light aroma, a hint of natural sweetness and ideal texture that's not too hard or too soft, rice has the power to absorb sauces and flavors instantly while balancing out saltiness and richness.

The concept of xiafan also applies to other foods like noodles, steamed buns and baked flatbread, as delicious dishes always encourage people to eat more staples. Hence, there's a category of dishes called xiafancai, dishes that go well with rice, and within its range, there's xiafanjiang, which is sauce-based dishes that are designated to pair with staples.

One of the most iconic xiafanjiang dishes is Beijing-style zhajiangmian, noodles served with a stir-fried dark sauce with a base of soy bean paste. It's often ranked among the top 10 most famous noodle dishes in China, and as an everyday staple in Beijing, the recipe varies in different households.

The basic composition of zhajiangmian consists of thick, al-dente noodles, a salty dark sauce and thin shreds of fresh cucumber, carrot and cooked bean sprouts. The vegetables used as toppings may change according to seasons.

The key to the dish is the dark sauce, which is essentially a stir-fry made of soy bean paste sauce, sweet fermented flour sauce (tianmianjiang) and minced pork with the optional of tiny bites of shitake mushroom and dried tofu. The proportion of the two sauces varies depending on taste. Some people prefer to have more soybean paste while some love to split it evenly. The soybean paste is a very salty condiment while the fermented flour sauce is milder and sweeter. The latter is the sauce served with the Beijing roast duck to balance out the richness of the duck skin and meat while adding more flavor.

The basic process of making zhajiang, the fried sauce, is stir-frying the minced pork (preferably with more fattier meat) until the fat is rendered out, then adding minced garlic and ginger to neutralize the meaty taste before adding cooking wine, spice of choice (like star anise) and the sauces.

The ideal texture of the fried sauce should be thick but not dry with a glossy finish. It's then simply poured over freshly cooked noodles with vegetable toppings to complete the dish. The best noodles for zhajiangmian are the thicker handmade noodles that are chewy and can be coated by the sauces very well.

In Shanghainese cuisine, a similar signature dish is babaolajiang, or eight-treasure spicy sauce. It's not as sauce-like as the kind in zhajiang and more of a stir-fried dish with cubed ingredients cooked together.

Though it's named eight-treasure, this dish can feature a dozen ingredients including both meat and vegetables. Traditional recipes usually use pork, chicken, shrimp, chicken or duck gizzard, pork tripe, green peas, shitake mushroom, bamboo shoots, dried tofu and fried (or toasted) peanuts. The larger ingredients are chopped into small cubes for even cooking and texture.

The stir-fried sauce uses the same combination of sweet fermented flour sauce and soy bean paste, but in moderate amounts.

The time-consuming part of making babaolajiang is preparing all the ingredients accordingly, like blanching the peas and shrimp in water, boiling the other meat and vegetables before lightly frying them in hot oil until about 80 percent cooked.

The meat, bamboo shoots, mushroom and tofu are stir-fried with garlic, ginger and scallions with the sauces, sugar and a drizzle of red chili oil. Peanuts are added last while the peas and shrimps are for garnish.

Babaolajiang has a sweet, salty and spicy flavor profile, and the evenly cubed ingredients are perfect as a topping for noodles, or a standalone dish that can also pair with rice.

Egg sauce, which is a recipe popular in northeast China, is a much easier stir-fried sauce that can be ready in minutes. It's very salty, flavorful and a great alternative to the meat-based xiafanjiang dishes. The idea is stir-frying the scrambled eggs with intense flavored sauces like soy bean, soy or oyster sauce to make it almost like a gravy. Chopped green chilies can be added to boost the spiciness.

Egg sauce is usually served with rice, noodles or hot steamed buns. The staples can absorb the sauce very well, which can also be used in various wraps and sandwiched flatbreads.

The popular and versatile mushroom sauce, on the other hand, is a bit oilier than the ones above as more fat is needed to make extra flavorful mushroom sauce.

Mushroom sauce is usually made with the most easily accessible mushrooms, shitake and abalone varieties are perfect for this sauce as they are very meaty and can be cut into small cubes easily. Meat is optional in this case.

The key to stir-frying mushroom sauce is to blanch the mushrooms briefly and squeeze out the moisture so they won't become watery when stir-fried. The soy bean sauce is added after sauteing the mushrooms in oil together with some water. The sauce is ready when the moisture evaporates and can be stored in the fridge for a couple of days to serve with congee, buns or noodles.

Yaozhu, or dried scallops, is a very umami ingredient used in a wide variety of recipes from soup to staples. The intense seafood flavor of dried scallops also makes great stir-fried sauces, and an all-purpose recipe is garlic chili sauce with dried scallops.

The cheaper small dried scallops are sufficient to make this xiafanjiang, it should be soaked in water for 30 minutes to regain moisture, then torn apart in shreds for later use. It takes about six tablespoons of minced garlic and six to eight extra spicy small chilies that are finely chopped.

Using the double amount of oil as common stir-fries, cook the garlic and chili until the fragrance comes out, then add the dried scallops and season with oyster sauce and soy sauce. Toss a handful of toasted white sesame seeds in at the end to boost the richness of the sauce. The garlic chili sauce with dried scallops is a great companion to rice, buns and vegetables.

It's very spicy, yet not as bold and rich as the sauces made of fermented flour sauce or soy bean paste.

Source: SHINE   Editor: Fu Rong

Exercise

1. Do you have a favorite dish? Is it your mom's home cooking? What cuisine

does it belong to? What does it look like? What does it taste like? Is there a story behind it? Write a passage to describe this dish and recommend it to your friends. Don't forget to ask your friends for feedbacks. Are they tempted by your writing?

2. Write a review on the latest movie for your school magazine. Make sure your review contains such basic facts about the movie as the title, the genre, the director, and the cast. Give your opinion and support it with evidence, but do not give away the film. Also remember to tell the reader the time it runs.

3. Pay a visit to your local museum and write a story on it. Is there a new exhibition which can serve as the new angle for your story? Or is there any new feature added to it you can take advantage of? What attracts you as you tour the museum? Should what attracts you become the focus of your story? If so, how can you make it as interesting to you as to your readers?

Chapter 10   Writing Feature Stories
On Suburban Shanghai

Media convergence has been all the rage in recent years. It happens at all levels and to all kinds of media organizations. In China, the media landscape, especially at the county level, has been tremendously transformed by this converging trend. Traditionally small in size and weak in influence, the county-level media has been converging the former disparate newspapers, television, radio and websites into one conglomerate to offer better and more efficient news service to the public at the grassroots level. This convergence of the county-level media has generally leveraged external resources, forming extensive partnerships with other media organizations, local companies, research institutions, and universities. The school I am in, the School of Journalism and Communication (SJC) of Shanghai International Studies University (SISU), has formed such partnership with the local county convergence media center, Songjiang Convergence Media Center (SCMC). And this innovative collaboration provides my students and me opportunities to participate in the reporting on one suburb of Shanghai. The collaboration works in the following patterns: The SCMC helped open doors to different communities and negotiating access to various sources. The students went on reporting trips covering villages, neighborhood communities and local businesses, gaining a panoramic in-depth view of the county life that is close to them yet somehow inaccessible before. If the stories produced are good enough, there's a chance they will be published on the English-language channel on the App of the SCMC. This English-language channel publishes English news and feature stories in the form of texts, photos, and video, and is the first of its kind in the country as English news media are often city-level and nation-level endeavors and SCMC belongs to a suburban district of Shanghai.

10.1   The so-what question revisited

From the previous chapters, we understand that any meaningful discussion of English feature writing should be conducted within the framework of international communication and a constant concern that we need to be sensitive to throughout is why our readers would want to read our articles. In other words, it is the so-what question: what you have written so far is all very interesting, but so what? Why should I care about it? In my students' reporting of the local affairs to an international audience, they run into the same so-what question: the story is about so and so, but so what? Why should my readers care about something happening in a suburban district in Shanghai? What can I do to make my story accessible to this ambiguous readership? Does what I have written really make sense to a foreign reader? If not, how to make it so?

10.1.1   Making it matter

One answer to the above challenges my students have come up is to present the local story in a larger context, making clear the connection between the seemingly slight incident they covered and the much bigger issue driving it. For example, in the coverage of a neighborhood community in Songjiang, the initial story idea pitched is to do a profile story on the head of a neighborhood committee and to give the readers a glimpse into the life of such a community worker. In the class discussion, we put this story idea against the so-what question. Why should our readers care about the life of a community worker in a Shanghai neighborhood? We found the question hard to answer. Then the story idea was modified to including interviews of a number of community workers on carrying out the national campaigns at the grassroots level, such as the COVID-19 pandemic prevention and the national census-taking. In this way, we intended to focus the reality of the community life on a specific issue that has bearing beyond this particular community. So the eventual story would naturally connect the life of these community workers to that of the nation. This approach uses this neighborhood as a microscopic example to present a noteworthy aspect of social life in Shanghai and China. Hopefully, in this way, the eventual story would be informative, providing a miniature with local flavor of something important and newsworthy in the whole country.

The following story[1] on census taking is one of such stories the students produced. The story starts with depicting a specific item, the work kit of Zhang

---

[1]   Pang Yuxia, Yuan Tianyun. A Day in the Life of a Census-Taker. Shanghai Songjiang APP [EB/OL]. (2020-12-03) [2021-08-26]. https://app. sjmedia. net/App/content/detailshare. html? contentId = 4952833&appId=110139&projectId=12&shareAppId=110139&channelType=4

Yanjun, a volunteer census-taker from the aforesaid neighborhood community, and then quickly shifts to presenting the bird's eye view of the national effort of tallying the population. After giving an interesting look down the long history of China tracing the origin of both ancient head-counting and contemporary census-taking, the story explains the purpose and scale of the national population studies, before going on to discuss the more effective ways to carry out the census-taking in the digital today. This discussion of digital census-taking gives the story an opportunity to turn naturally back to the neighborhood community at hand and refocus on the digitalized endeavor undertaken by Zhang and her fellow volunteer workers. In this swing back and forth between the local life and the national engagement, the neighborhood community is treated as a sample and studied at length to present a slice of the national life.

The story runs as follows.

A Day in the Life of a Census-Taker

By Pang Yuxia, Yuan Tianyun

A face mask, a white vest, an ID card and a khaki bag crammed with folders and papers——this is basic kit for Zhang Yanjun, a 70-year-old woman who volunteers as a census taker in Shanghai.

Zhang Yanjun used to be a college professor. After retiring, she was involved in voluntary service in Jiuyangwenhua——a local community in the southwest of Shanghai. "I've been involved in community service here for a long time, so I'm quite glad to be a volunteer" she said.

China has deployed millions of census takers for the country's seventh census this year, and Zhang is one of them. Whenever there is a big event in China, volunteers and officials in local communities step up to do their bit and that's how a nationwide event is divided smoothly into smaller parts.

The prototype for the national census can be traced back to the Han Dynasty. According to *Han Shu*, a history book from ancient China, in 206BC, after court officials had made a careful study of the number of weapons collected from prisoners taken in war, the emperor was informed that the national population had fallen from 30 million to 13 million.

Things have moved on since the days of Ban Gu and Ban Zhao (the authors of *Han Shu*). China's first national census was conducted in 1953. Mobilizing over 2.5 million census takers, the government gathered information from 50 million citizens.

Following the 1953 exercise, China has carried out three more national censuses up to 1990. The government then decided to routinely conduct the national census every decade, obtaining information such as name, gender, age, ID number and ethnicity. It's fair to say that today's census is much more comprehensive than the somewhat sketchy investigations conducted in ancient China.

The demographic information collected aids policymakers. In 2000, the fifth national census added a survey on housing conditions and that helped the government reallocate public facilities as needed.

Meanwhile, methods for data collection and records have improved over the years. In the first two censuses, census takers collected and recorded all the data by themselves. It wasn't until 1982 that computers were used to analyse data. A code number is attached to every statistic and the data is transferred to municipal computing stations. However, personal information records still relied on census takers (visiting each residence to ask questions and collect the information).

But in 2020, for the first time, citizens are able to submit their information via a mini app on WeChat.

In Jiuyangwenhua, the seventh national census is a top priority for the second half of this year. There are 1701 households in this community. Twenty-six volunteers will visit them to collect data.

A census requires a lot of preparation. In September, census takers in Jiuyangwenhua were trained on how to collect information for the national census. "We were taught what to ask and how to talk to residents in an appropriate way," said Zhang Yanjun, "Also, the older volunteers have to learn how to use the new apps. That takes time!"

After their training, Zhang and her colleagues began with a preliminary data collection. "First of all, we recorded the information collected in the last national census. This really boosted our efficiency," said Zhang.

A lot of publicity about the seventh census appeared in the local community. Posters popped up on every bulletin board and staff members in neighborhood committees sent brochures to residents so that they wouldn't be taken unawares when the census takers visited them. "I was worried about people showing up unexpectedly," said Mrs. Xu, an elderly resident in Jiuyangwenhua, "But the pamphlet explained things clearly. It really helped me understand this year's census."

On Nov. 1, Zhang Yanjun and 7 million other officials started their visits to families all over China. Zhang has to collect data from 96 households.

"Thanks to smartphones and apps, it only takes about 5 minutes for them to fill in the form." Zhang said, with a smile on her face.

Everything went well at first. Zhang visited more than 15 families on average each day, and it only took her a week to collect all the data from 93 households. However, the remaining three could not be located.

"We made every effort to get in touch with them ——phone, email and even letters," Zhang said, "but there was no response."

Citizens' concerns over issues of privacy was another difficulty Zhang faced during her work. "Young people were perturbed when they found out that we knew a lot about their private affairs," said Zhang, "And they were very suspicious of us."

Despite all these frustrations, Zhang is still optimistic about the national census. "It's not surprising that residents are suspicious because they don't know us," Zhang said, "but with new technology they'll be able them to fill in the form by themselves on their mobile phones, which will be more convenient and efficient."

10.1.2　A geographical beat

Covering a suburb of Shanghai is actually reporting a beat. Songjiang, where SISU has a campus is treated as a geographical beat by the class, a beat that allows us to focus on the region on an ongoing basis, gain an in-depth knowledge through prolonged immersion, make friends and accumulate sources along the way, dig deeper into local stories and eventually learn to present China well to the world through the microscopic local life.

To accomplish that, the key word is to dig deeper, which means striving for a thorough and accurate understanding of the issue to the heart of the intended story. This command may sound self-evident. But in our practice, we found it easier said than done. Take a profile story[1] we produced about the only young person working in a local neighborhood committee. Traditionally a Chinese neighborhood committee is filled with middle-aged matrons, so when the class pitched story ideas, they naturally found the only young man there an

---

[1]　Yu Peixin, Wang Zizhen. A young man on track in community work. Shanghai Songjiang APP[EB/OL]. (2020-12-01) [2021-08-26]. https://app.sjmedia.net/App/content/detailshare.html? contentId=4941507&appId=110139&projectId=12&shareAppId=110139&channelType=4

interesting subject. The ensuing article in turn focuses on the challenges the young man encounters entering a field traditionally dominated by older personnel. To highlight the challenges, the story uses several anecdotes and one runs as follows:

> But chatting up strangers is the easy part of the community work. During the COVID-19 pandemic, one resident whose neighbor was observing home quarantine called the committee and showered Xu who answered the call with curses. "He was afraid of being infected by his neighbor," Xu says.
>
> Though Xu tried to explain that strict controls had been undertaken and there was no fear of being infected, the resident continued to hurl abuses. "I felt insulted but I didn't shout back, because I realized he must have been truly frightened at that time." To his surprise, the resident called him later after calming down and apologized. "I get tearful when I think back to that moment," Xu says. "When you try really hard to understand others, it is such a comfort that they understand you eventually."

As discussed in previous chapters, anecdotes are an essential ingredient in writing a feature story and is particularly effective in presenting vividly both the person and the issue. But for anecdotes to be effective, they must be clear at first. There is a problem with the above anecdote where Xu, the young community worker, deals with a difficult resident who lodged an irrational complaint about his home-quarantined neighbor. It is understood that the incident is included in the story to show the difficulty of the seemingly trivial work done by the members of the most elementary government organ. However, the anecdote suffers from vagueness and ambiguity because it is treated in a rather skimpy way. The turnaround of the nameless resident who started all the trouble for Xu was too abrupt to be believable. A few moments ago this man was storming around, verbally abusing Xu, and a few moments later, he was calm and apologetic. What exactly had happened concerning the sudden change of mind? This point should have been clarified. As the story goes, the way this resident behaved doesn't make sense.

The most likely reason that the above question goes unanswered in the story is that it was never raised in the interview. Here, the student reporters might have failed to dig deeper. Digging deeper doesn't have to mean the reporter will be faced with great adversity and will have to unearth tightly-guarded secrets at great expense and risk. More often than not, it simply means to ask necessary follow-up questions to get the details that will help the reader make head and tail of what exactly happened. No matter what the fact is, important or trivial, it is necessary to get it right. Particularly in the field of international reporting, the targeted readers already have the cultural and language barriers to tackle. It is highly advisable not to burden them with obscurities that could easily be cleared up by digging deeper.

10.1.3 Accuracy rules

Our reporting beat, the Songjiang District of Shanghai, is known for its proactive development of industries. Once we had the opportunity to visit and report on a leading science park in the district, our first attempt at producing serious business feature stories. Business stories have always been a challenge to the class who lack professional knowledge and experience in the field. To make that up, we were provided with background materials and encouraged to read all there is about the enterprises we were to write about. We were also presented with access to sources who are decision makers and thus possess both information and expertise. Armed with results from prior research and set interviews, we felt that we had gathered enough numbers and information to give it a go. However, when the stories were produced, a common problem emerged: many stories were vague and inaccurate in important places.

The inaccuracies take many forms. Two stories give two different numbers on the land coverage of the same science park. A story gives some interesting fact about tax relief policy during the pandemic without identifying the source for this important information. Another story gives statistics about the number of people suffering from lower limb disability and that of people paralyzed from spinal injuries respectively. However, by using the rather ambiguous word "and" to link the two figures, confusion arises over the relationship between the figure given before the conjunction "and" and the one after: Is the number of spinal injuries part of that of the lower disabilities? In that case, "including" should be used. Or are the two numbers independent of each other? Then "as well as" is the more accurate word. Yet another story mistakenly adds a string of zeros to the number indicating the coverage of the third phase of the park, making the third phase still under construction in Songjiang, Shanghai, almost as large as the whole land area of China.

Accuracy is the most fundamental requirement in all journalistic writing.

For business stories in particular, accuracy simply reigns. Every bit of research, every piece of fact must be checked out. Every number must be right both in RMB and in dollars. The notes taken from interviews must be diligently pored over and the recorded interview must be listened to word by word. All the quotes must be examined to make sure that no meaning is twisted or lost in the translation. Every piece of cited contextual information must be traced to a source that carries the authority needed to ensure authenticity and significance. In short, a reporter must dig deeper to ensure the accuracy of her stories.

The above decrees the class has already learned about in previous lectures. But this time the grasp of the rule was put to test in a real situation. And from all the blunders and errors we made in the coverage of the science park, we started to understand that the vagueness and confusion, more often than not, resulted from sloppy research and superficial interviews during the reporting process. Reporting and writing are inseparable. They are not two processes but one. Nothing else but thorough research and careful interviews are the key to the success of the story.

One company in the science park we visited is a start-up that designs and manufactures assistive robots for people with lower limb disabilities. The pre-arranged interview assisted by SCMC is for student reporters to have a half-hour talk with one of the young cofounders of the company. The young cofounder appears to be an ideal source for a story on the young innovative company. The interview was arranged at an unassuming room on the sixth floor of the company, another ideal choice affording us the flavor of the place and the opportunity to observe the interviewee in her work environment. What's more, the plain-looking room turned out to be the lab for their R&D team to develop their key robots. So the room alone is worth writing about. However, the disadvantage of the interview is also obvious: it was a group one and turned out to be also rather rushed as the subject's phone kept ringing and she herself was called away after a brief talk. However, in a way, such an interview is a valuable experience for us to learn to work and adjust in an authentic situation. Considering the sudden shortened time, the students needed to rise to the occasion and make the most out of it by asking such questions that would elicit answers not to be found anywhere else.

However, generally lacking in experience, most of the students stuck to the list of questions they'd prepared before and wasted precious time asking general questions with answers that can be easily found with a little research into the company. They asked questions like when the start-up was launched and why it came to Songjiang. They asked the busy manager to explain a PPT publicizing the company. Few questions were asked about the personal involvement of the interviewee or what was new about the company or the interesting room they were in. As a result, the stories produced faithfully reflected our want of experience in conducting interviews. Most of the stories made little use of the interview but were written almost purely with information gathered from research. Major anecdotes are all from videos or stories published previously. In one story, the interview subject only made a brief appearance at the very end, whose words were used to finish the story off. One could almost say that these stories on this promising start-up company that is setting the standard of the industry could have been written without conducting the interview with one of its cofounders at all. The consequence is that although the eventual stories contain a lot of information, but the facts are rehashed, stale, nothing new. And it all can be traced back to a flimsy interview where we failed to dig deeper.

10.1.4   How does a normal human being speak?

Another lesson we learned from this valuable all-authentic reporting and writing experience is that it is no easy task to make one's human sources sound like a normal human being. For example, in the coverage of the science park, one interview subject is an Egyptian man working in a company in the park. The students were curious to find out how an expat lives and works in Songjiang. The story turned in starts with an anecdote where the profile subject attended a team building activity which involved Karaoke singing. It runs as follows:

> Ayman Tarek went to karaoke with his Chinese colleagues after taking part in a team building activity. The 28-year-old Egyptian man couldn't sing any Chinese songs but he soldiered on till almost midnight.

So far so good. Then our student reporter wanted to follow the anecdote with a quote from the subject. Very reasonable thinking. It is highly advisable to put a voice on the face of the primary actor in a story. However, in the first draft, the quote added immediately after the above incident is as follows:

> Ayman Tarek went to karaoke with his Chinese colleagues after taking part in a team building activity. The 28-year-old Egyptian man couldn't sing any Chinese songs but he soldiered on till almost midnight. **He said, "I wish to spend the rest of my life in Shanghai."**

There is nothing inherently wrong with the quote professing the subject's love for the city he lives in. However, placed where it is in the story, the quote feels abrupt and makes the subject sound like a publicity tool rather than a normal human being. The opening anecdote may elicit a chuckle from the reader as the subject is put in a slightly comical situation: a foreigner who can't sing any Chinese songs sticks it out in a Chinese Karaoke bar. But the following quote quickly turns that chuckle off. So the student reporter was asked to read the interview notes again and she found another quote that contains words a normal person would have said on such occasion and thus more suitable. She decided to save the "love Shanghai" one for later in the story. The revised lead runs as follows:

> Ayman Tarek went to karaoke with his Chinese colleagues after taking part in a team building activity. The 28-year-old Egyptian man couldn't sing any Chinese songs but he soldiered on till almost midnight. **"I liked keeping company with my Chinese colleagues," said Tarek. "But I am glad we are about to leave and I need to sleep."**

The expressed desire for sleep after so much team building in a foreign language somehow makes the subject more believable and delivers home the comical moment.

Another interview subject also sounds like a publicity pamphlet in the initial version of a student's work. The subject is the manager and founder of a campus-born start-up in Shanghai. During the interview, the subject repeatedly prized business sense above everything else in his venture of innovation based on the technology of Internet of Things. Discerning this, the student reporter decided to weave her story around this belief and to make clear this theme by quoting the subject as saying "Only business can make a good technology benefit mankind and society." The original passage reads as follows:

> Yunyi Electronic Technology Co., Ltd is another start-up that started in a college campus before moving to the Park. Its main business is the Internet

of Things(IoT), which is the technology that connects daily things to the Internet. Lu Hao, a founder of the Yunyi Electronic Technology Co. Ltd., said entrepreneurship is his dream. **"Only business can make a good technology benefit mankind and society,"** **Lu said.** His company produces IoT products to facilitate people's lives.

The above passage is afflicted by several problems: the explanation of IoT is vague, the company's products are not introduced properly, and the quote suffers from overstatement. When quoting people, especially with translation involved, a writer should do her best to make sure that the quote assumes a conversational quality: the source talks to the reader as if he is talking to his friend or family over a cup of tea. When one speaks to one's mate, one tends to use simple language marked by plain words. And it is not customary for big words like "mankind" and "society" to find their way into a casual conversation with a friend. The subject in the above passage sounds too formal to be endearing to the reader, even pompous. In the second draft, after careful study of the interview transcript and further research, the passage was revised as the following one.

Shanghai Yunyi IoT Technology is another start-up that began life on a college campus before moving to Tus Caohejing Science Park. Focusing on the Internet of Things (IoT), the aggregate collection of network-enabled devices, the company launched a series of high-tech products including a sonic fire extinguisher powered by 3D printing technology and lithium battery, a smart stroller and a smart suitcase driven by intelligent road-following system, and a successfully-commercialized shared oxygen generator.

Lu Hao, founder of Yunyi, started his research when he was still a graduate student in Donghua University, a Shanghai-based university only 15-minute ride from the Tus-Caohejing Science Park. In the process of putting together a startup team, Lu quickly became aware of the importance and the role of business sense in commercialization of the R&D in college. **"Only business can bring out the practical values of good technology,"** **Lu said.**

In the revision, the technology "Internet of Things" is explained in clearer terms; the main products of the company are presented to give the reader a concrete idea of Lu's company; and the quote is retranslated into plain language. Compared with the platitudes in the first draft, the second version is not just plainer in choice of words，but also clearer in meaning. In the initial version，Lu claims business can make technology benefit society and mankind. But how? In the second draft，the question is answered：by bringing out the practical values.

10.2   A new rural reality

Recent years，the development of the countryside has been a focal point of the growth of the whole country. According to the National Bureau of Statistics，the seventh national census-taking[①] reveals that the population living in rural areas was 509.79 million，accounting for 36.11%. The central government has implemented various effective measures to raise the living standards of people in the countryside and eradicate extreme poverty. Stories on combating poverty and the construction of the new countryside have repeatedly made headlines. English-language stories depicting the life of the Chinese villages help to present to the world a full picture of the exciting and dynamic changes occurring in the new rural reality. The English-language media in China has understood and taken on the task enthusiastically. For example，*China Daily*，the national English-language newspaper，has established a reporting base at Huichang County，Jiangxi Province since 2015 and has been treating the small county known for its citrus fruits lying at hilly southeastern China as a microcosm in reporting how rural China is developing in all fronts and at full speed.

Strategically based in Songjiang，a traditionally agricultural county，my class also wants to do our bit for telling Chinese rural stories to the world. The opportunity came when we were granted a visit to a small village named Yaojing. It is located in the southwestern Shanghai and about 50-minute drive from our campus. The village is listed as one of China's top ten model villages of beautiful rural construction and has received a number of accolades for its vibrant development，leading the way in Shanghai in both rice cultivation and waste separation. Thanks to its ideal location，a secluded corner of one of China's busiest cities，the village also serves as an incubator that's especially green，attracting a variety of young talents. These young people，seeking

---

① 第七次全国人口普查主要数据情. 国家统计局［EB/OL］.（2021-05-11）［2021-08-07］. http://www. stats.gov.cn/tjsj/zxfb/202105/t20210510_1817176.html

tranquility and career opportunities in the village，represent a new trend in contrast to the more common situation where young people flee villages full of 'left-behind' elderly people for the big cities. All in all，the small village is a perfect starting point for us to learn to report on the new countryside that heralds the future of rural China.

Upon their own investigation around the village，the students soon found that the village was experimenting with standardized collective farming. The key word is standardized. Rice planters（individual farmers）forming the cooperative must comply to strict green standards of planting. The result is that the rice they planted becomes a famous organic local brand and sells well all over the country. The following story[①] explores this new farming mechanism which represents the trend of farming when the farming population is getting old and farming itself becomes increasingly concentrated with urbanization roaring on. The article adopts the multiple profile approach and gives stories of three people，a farmer joining the cooperative，the manager of the cooperative and the daughter of the manager，the third choice representing the rarely-seen young person finding work and worth in the countryside. The three people represent three key groups of people who complete the picture of the new farming mechanism that points to the way of agriculture for the future. The theme of the story is the common prosperity that this new way of farming brings.

Though the story is structurally sound and interesting to read，its shortcomings are clear：it doesn't provide enough background information to render depth to the story. In other words，it lacks the big picture. The stories of the farmers are presented and then it stops there. Many questions remain unanswered. What's the scale of the new cooperative farming? Is it just a creation of this village，of Shanghai，or a widespread practice in China? The manager Fan is making money and believes he will continue to turn profits，but what about the general prospects of this new farming? Are other managers of family farms making money like him? As to the green standards，how did they come about? Where did Fan learn about them? What about the local government? What kind of role it has played in this experiment? Both Ding and

---

① Zhang Chenjia，Zhou Yao. Family farmers in Songjiang enjoy prosperity working in tandem. Shanghai Songjiang APP［EB/OL］.（2020-10-19）［2021-08-26］. https：//app. sjmedia. net/App/content/ detailshare. html? contentId ＝ 4775796&appId ＝ 110139&projectId ＝ 12&shareAppId ＝ 110139&channelType＝4

Fan's daughter are selling rice via new media. Is that the new way of marketing for farmers in the village? How widespread is the practice? And so on.

As a first attempt, the cooperative farming story is informative but regrettably incomplete, lacking key background information. Apart from the technicalities in story organizing and writing, this reporting experience also taught us a very practical lesson: covering the seemingly idyllic countryside requires expertise and knowledge, especially when the economic side of the rural life is the reporting subject. And we are ignorant in this regard. We quickly realized that covering the village is a real learning experience in every way.

The story runs as follows:

Family farmers in Songjiang enjoy prosperity working in tandem

By Zhang Chenjia, Zhou Yao

Ding Houqin shows the audiences on Douyin the scene of golden rice gently swaying in the autumn breeze, in the background a female voice singing "The wind that shakes the barley": the rice field in Yaojing Village is ready for harvest.

Ding started a family farm in 2018 in Yaojing, a small village in Songjiang District, Shanghai. She grows green rice with the help of her parent-in-laws. The rice behind her on the Douyin video will be harvested, processed and sold as "Songjiang Rice" which is the only national brand of rice in Shanghai for now.

"I should learn from the seniors," Ding said. Born in the 1980s, she is relatively young among the other farmhands in this village. Few young people can be seen in the village as most of them have left for the allure of the big city.

As a mother of two, farming is an ideal option for Ding - not just to take care of her kids but also to put food on the table - the 17 acres of farmland earns her close to $15,000 each year, which is about the same as the average wage in Shanghai.

However, Ding's family cannot afford to count on income from the farm alone, especially with the increasingly high cost of child-rearing in Shanghai. So her husband works elsewhere for a salary.

But Ding is not alone in her farming. She joined Huimin farmers' specialized cooperative to broaden her market.

Fan Huifeng, who owns a larger farm of 87 acres, is the manager of the Huimin Cooperative, which is one of the eight firms in Shanghai permitted to use the label of "Songjiang Rice".

Family farmers who joined the Cooperative must grow rice in a standardized way. The harvested rice will be bought by the Cooperative if the produce passed the quality inspection conducted by Fan. Then the rice will be processed, packed and sold as brand of "Songjiang Rice". In 2019, Huimin Cooperative sold over 1,030,000 kilograms of rice, which is enough to feed nearly 5,000 people for a year.

Unpolluted, safe and of high quality, rice honored as "Green Food" by national institutions are typically harvested only once a year. To get the strict quality certification, farmers must fulfill 33 planting criteria, including weeding the field frequently and using less fertilizers and pesticides.

Fan checks the crop before buying to make sure the eventual products with his logo are all of high and uniform quality. "Farmers welcome the inspection," Fan explained. Joining his cooperative and meeting the requirements is profitable for farmers, bringing an extra ten dollars per acre of income.

Fan's white painted factory sits opposite his office, with various machines roaring inside. "We have the best rice polisher in China," Fan Huifeng said.

From planting, growing, reaping to processing, machines are an integral part in almost every procedure in the production of rice, and this has improved the quality and efficiency of his organization. He planned to purchase a new dryer and processor to further save manpower.

Thanks to the machines, the coronavirus pandemic raging in this year has had little impact on rice production. But Fan still had difficulty in finding a market for stored rice as well as upcoming fresh rice.

In Fan's plant, a super-short-haired girl wearing gold accessories is sealing the rice deftly. "That's my daughter," he introduced, with a smile.

Fan Yiting, the only child of the family, graduated from college last year and decided to stay home and help her father to run the farm. In addition to the ordinary work in the plant, she runs their Taobao shop and the official account on Wechat.

No one knows young people better than the young themselves, said Fan Yiting, whose job is to bring the farm up to date.

This September, she put "SongJiang rice" onto the screen - Dragon TV - and introduced their products on a TV shopping program. Five thousand kilograms of rice were sold out quickly and fetched them $14,000 dollars in sales within 15 minutes.

"It's meaningless to make fortunes alone ," said Fan Huifeng, who makes over 50,000 dollars a year. "I will keep leading villagers to create wealth together by growing and selling rice."

Apart from family farming, another thing that has struck the class's fancy is that though the village population is dominated by older farmers with young villagers leaving for the city nearby, young talents from outside do come here, attracted by its eco-friendly environment, favorable policy, job opportunities, and the ideal location of the village lying in a secluded corner of the most prosperous city in China. The class visited such a young talent, a ceramic artist in his 20s who moved his career from Jingdezhen, the ceramic capital of China, to the village for a commercially viable operation. He taught the young kids coming in over the weekends while continued to learn the craft after getting a degree in a college specializing in ceramics in Jingdezhen. The village provides the space needed for doing ceramic crafts as well as substantial help in making his studio profitable. The class treated him as a microcosm example of the urban young coming to the rural area for better opportunities and wrote several profiles on the young man.

The following[①] is one of them. This story contains real substance as it manages to go beyond Lin, the ceramic artist and gives a relatively comprehensive portrait of the young people of the village. The story begins with a scene in which Lin, a ceramic artist, is immersed in his work. The story then shifts from Lin to his studio, which is supported by the village running a program aiding these young makers. Naturally, Pang, another major character of the story, enters onto the scene here, being a staff member of the "Rural Entrepreneurs Association" set up by the village to help these young entrepreneurs in realizing their start-up dreams like Lin's. In this story about Lin, Pang's story is featured for several paragraphs, a wise editorial decision that provides the necessary background information to help readers understand the story as a whole. Of course, Lin is not alone in his search for a career in the countryside. There are other makers and artists roaming the countryside. However, apart from more outsiders like Lin seeking a better life in the village, the village young also benefit from the talent incubator drive and some of them

---

① Chen Yufan, Liu Yuhang. Young people follow startup dreams in countryside. Shanghai Songjiang APP [EB/OL]. (2020-10-16) [2021-0826]. https://app. sjmedia. net/App/content/detailshare. html? contentId=4775943&appId=110139&projectId=12&shareAppId=110139&channelType=4

like Pang decide to stay at home for a different career than farming. The lives of these two young men are almost mirror images of each other, completing the picture of young people in rural areas. At the end, the story returns to Lin, the profile subject, ending with a quote that restates his enthusiasm.

Young people follow startup dreams in countryside

By Chen Yufan, Liu Yuhang

Lin Yongxiang gently touches the clay on the ceramic throwing machine, a machine that is used when making porcelain, as if touching the petals of a flower. He is shaping one of the bowls for a batch of customized tableware.

In Lin's studio, bottles, pen holders, various daily necessities and gadgets made of ceramic can be seen everywhere.

Ceramics seem to be an intrinsic part of his life.

Lin's studio is called "Yinhe Nishe", and it's located in Yaojing Village in the southwestern Songjiang District of Shanghai. The green and quiet village enjoys convenient transportation, abundant land resources, and charming sceneries.

"When rice is planted, the egrets come here in groups," Lin says. "The morning and evening scenery in the countryside is beautiful, and there are many craftsmen in the village."

Yaojing Village has attracted many craftsmen and artists to start their own businesses. In 2019, they established the Rural Entrepreneurs Association. This association provides entrepreneurs with a large platform and many opportunities, allowing them to share resources.

Pang Haixian from Maogang Village, Songjiang of Shanghai, is a staff member of the Rural Entrepreneurs Association. He says that the association can help entrepreneurs establish connections with the government and often helps them with the preliminary communication.

For example, if an entrepreneur wants to organize an activity and needs a venue, the association will find a contact for him.

The Rural Entrepreneurs Association holds at least one or two charity events in the village every month. Children, people from and outside the village can come to learn paper-cutting and pottery. The government is supportive of such non-profit activities.

Before the arrival of entrepreneurs, most of the residents in the village were elderly people. Now, the studios of entrepreneurs and their activities have attracted many young people to visit, bringing new vitality to the village.

"No matter how beautiful the village is, if no one knows about it, no one will appreciate it," Pang says. The entrepreneurs have brought a lot of popularity to the village, and this tiny paradise has begun to receive praise from the outside world as well.

Pang Haixian has always lived in the countryside. "I am used to it, and I especially like the countryside," he says. Pang used to work briefly in a big city but he couldn't get used to the rhythm of the urban life at all. He returned to his hometown after a mere two days.

In the future, he will continue to work here.

"If I really wanted to leave, I would have left," he says softly, but firmly.

Through the activities held by the Rural Entrepreneurs Association, Pang has the opportunity to meet, communicate, and even become friends with many people. "I often go to Lin's studio now. I have many ideas and topics in common with him," Pang says.

Lin Yongxiang graduated from Jingdezhen Ceramics University and came to the countryside just after graduation. In his eyes, the Rural Entrepreneurs Association "is just like the center of a spider web, connecting all the dots."

Lin's current cooperation with this association is to set up not-for-profit courses in the village, teaching people to make ceramics and popularizing knowledge about ceramics.

Usually, Lin receives some guests who come to experience making ceramics, and cooperates with some calligraphers or painters to complete their customized potteries. When there is no other work, he creates his own ceramics.

Being able to make ceramics is why Lin stays in the country. In the crowded city, he finds no room for the needed bulky machinery. In Yaojing Village, he can make ceramics as much as he wants. He even met an experienced teacher who often guided him.

He says that he wants to make his own unique style of work, but he is still exploring. He has made many rustic potteries such as chopstick holders in the shape of carrots and fish.

"I'm not interested in doing anything else, but I like making ceramics," he says, eyes sparkling.

The village visited by the class has an amazing cultural life, characterized by the existence of a poetry society. The farmers are encouraged to express their feelings and perceptions in their lives in poetic terms. The poetry society is led by a former English teacher who has been assigned to the village to help organize leisure and cultural activities for the villagers, such as lectures on Sinology and free pottery classes. The students had a long chat with the organizer of the poetry club and visited the one-room exhibition hall displaying the arts and crafts made by the villagers.

The following story[①] on the poetry society is one of the stories produced but has obvious drawbacks. On the one hand, despite a second visit, we didn't get to interview farmer poets. There are not enough sources for the story. On the other hand, there are some unanswered questions in the story. How many villagers have joined the poetry club? What did the poetry club mean to the farmers? How do the common villagers view the club, or poetry? How was the idea of the poetry club first conceived? How did the farmer poets actually create? These questions were not answered, partly because of a lack of relevant sources; there were only two original sources in the report. The official voice of the society chairwoman is authoritative but far from enough. Another reason might be again we failed to dig deeper, not realizing the importance of these questions and not asking them in the first place.

Despite the regrettable editorial decisions and the inadequate reporting, the coverage of the poetry society brings us an inspiring discussion on the cultural life of the village. The students initially were not convinced of the significance of poetry clubs for ordinary villagers, and they pondered over and argued about the relationship between highbrow poetry clubs and the comparatively lowbrow farming life. It is understandable to have such doubts, as the value of the poetry club may not be apparent at the moment, with the club members being an educated minority, distant from the routine farming life and the village leisure life traditionally dominated by games like mahjong. However, as the previous stories show, it has become increasingly common for the village young to get a good education and meaningful work at home. Against this backdrop, the poetry club, though appearing to be elitist at present, represents an important part of the future of the new countryside. Even now, the cultural activities spear-headed by the poetry club offered in the village provide an interesting alternative as people face more leisure time with the mechanization of

---

① Bai Jinshuang, Teng Yutong. Egret poetry society returns to village. Shanghai Songjiang APP[EB/OL]. (2020-10-13)［2021-08-26］. https://app. sjmedia. net/App/content/detailshare. html? contentId＝4761297&appId＝110139&projectId＝12&shareAppId＝110139&channelType＝4

agriculture. So we may say that the value of the poetry club is beyond itself, pointing to a possibility of transcending the traditional stereotypes of Chinese village life. This discussion and contemplation is a constructive part of our reporting and writing process. This is what makes such fieldwork so valuable. The coverage of the villages goes beyond a few stories. It is a valuable opportunity for us to understand and, more importantly, to reflect on the development of the new countryside.

Egret poetry society returns to village

By Bai Jinshuang, Teng Yutong

Standing in front of the wall created by the Egret Poetry Society, Song Huanjie read the Seeds of Hope passionately, which was the first poem she wrote in her life.

Song Huanjie, an instructor of Yaojing village, is reading the Seeds of Hope aloud.

"I used to be an English teacher but I never tried writing poetry; it was only after I joined the Egret Poetry Society that I began to write poetry gradually," she said.

In September of last year, Shanghai selected outstanding and willing city talents to support the less developed villages like Yaojing Village. Song, who used to be a principal of Songjiang Yongfeng Experimental School, was sent to the village as an instructor to help its development.

"When I came, the party secretary said to me earnestly, 'You will be in charge of the poetry society'!" Song said, with a smile.

The Egret Poetry Club, founded in 2016, was the first village-level poetry club in Shanghai. Actively responding to the initiative on revitalization of rural culture, the party secretary at that time, Jiang Qi, decided to take the village mascot egrets as the cultural calling card of the village and named the society after it.

Before Song came, the Egret Poetry Society was just an empty name. The key reason was the lack of leadership. "Village officials and club members used to come and go. And it was almost impossible to hold regular meetings," Song said.

Therefore, when she first took over the Poetry Society, she didn't know what to do. On the one hand, some poets in this society had stopped writing poetry for a long time; on the other hand, if she invited her colleagues from the education field to participate in the poetry society, the value of it for the local farmhands would be lost.

In order to rebuild the club, Song made full use of her resources to gather local poets and rural culture lovers to write together and communicate with each other. "I also joined another formal club called Huating, which is supported by Shanghai government," Song said. "The two clubs can collaborate, providing an opportunity for the folk one in our village to grow."

Last November, the First Idyllic Art Festival was held in Yaojing Village, which aimed to show and promote the beauty of rural culture. Song invited poets from Huating to experience rural life and versify together with those from the Egret Poetry Society. In the end, they produced 24 pastoral poems for exhibition at the Art Festival.

The members of Huating Poetry Society came to Yaojing village to hold an activity called "Stroll in the Poetic Countryside."

Zhang Meng, the founder of the Poetry Society, believed that the participation of Huating, the urban poetry club, helped enhance the professionalism of their society. "A dozen members of Huating are from the Shanghai Writers' Association and even a few from the Chinese Writers' Association. With their help, the quality of our poetry has improved."

After the poetry club halted publication in 2017, Zhang left the village to start his own cultural and creative company in Songjiang District. Hearing about the revival of the poetry society last year, Zhang returned as a rural poet and was responsible for the editing of their poetry collection. "We have a WeChat official account called Dao Xiang Yao Jing, which has a column for poems. Every week, I will select five high-quality poems and post them at 9 a. m. Friday."

In addition to the Egret Poetry Club, Song also built an Egret Lecture Hall in the village, and regularly held activities every week, such as poetry reading, martial arts, and sinology. To Song's delight, these activities are welcomed by both the children and the elderly members of the village.

10.3 The last note

This last chapter follows our rambling around Songjiang in reporting and writing about the local life. Some of the stories produced are good. Some are slightly weaker, inflicted by the various mistakes that beginning writers often make. But all in all, it was a learning experience that was both valuable and rewarding. We worked in the best possible fashion to learn the essential elements of English feature writing: the newsworthiness of feature stories for international audiences, the importance of sources and interviews, the meaning of digging deeper, accuracy, the indispensable background information and, most important of all, expertise and knowledge of the reporting subject.

Bibliography

[1] Louis Alexander.Beyond the Facts，a Guide to the Art of Feature Writing [M]. 2nd ed. Houston：Gulf Publishing company，1982：1-2.

[2] Brendan Hennessy. Writing Feature Articles，a Practical Guide to Methods and Markets [M]. 3rd ed. Oxford：Focal Press，1997：Preface，7.

[3] Bruce Garrison. Professional Feature Writing [M]. 4th ed. Mahwah：Lawrence Erlbaum Associates，Inc.，Publishers，2004：6-7.

[4] William E. Blundell.The Art and Craft of Feature Writing based on the Wall Street Journal Guide [M]. New York：Plume, the Penguin Group，1988：x-xii.

[5] William Zinsser. On Writing Well [M]. 5th ed. New York：HarperPerennial，1994：63.

[6] Bill Kovach & Tom Rosenstiel. The Elements of Journalism：what newspeople should know and the public should expect [M]. 3rd ed. New York：Three Rivers Press，2014：64.

[7] Bill Kovach & Tom Rosenstiel. The Elements of Journalism：what newspeople should know and the public should expect [M]. 3rd ed. New York：Three Rivers Press，2014：212.

[8] Yao Minji. Wild days of newspapering and print battlefield of ideas[N/OL]. Shanghai Daily. (2013-11-02) [2021-08-04]. https://archive.shine.cn/feature/art-and-culture/Wild-days-of-newspapering-and-print-battlefield-of-ideas/shdaily.shtml.

[9] Ke Jiayun. Generation Z artists' perspectives of China explode on social media[N/OL]. Shanghai Daily . (2021-08-04) [2021-08-14]. https://www.shine.cn/news/in-focus/2108043122/.

[10] 新华社简介[EB/OL].新华社. [2021-08-04]. http://203.192.6.89/xhs/static/e11272/11272.htm.

[11] About China Daily Group[EB/OL].China Daily. [2021-08-04]. http://www.chinadaily.com.cn/e/static_e/about.

[12] 上海成为外籍人才眼中最具吸引力城市,逾 21 万外国人在沪工作[N/OL]. 解放日报. (2019-01-16) [2021-08-04]. http://www.cnr.cn/shanghai/tt/

20190116/t20190116_524484010.shtml.

[13] ABOUT US [EB/OL]. The Sixth Tone. [2021-08-04]. http://www.
sixthtone.com/about-us.

[14] Merriam-Webster Dictionary [EB/OL]. [2021-08-04]. https://www.
merriam-webster.com/dictionary/context.

[15] Yao Minji. TCM a key player in the war against COVID-19 [N/OL].
Shanghai Daily. (2020-03-26) [2021-08-04]. https://www.shine.cn/news/
in-focus/2003265075/.

[16] William Zinsser. On Writing Well [M]. 5th ed. New York:
HarperPerennial, 1994:97-98.

[17] Zhang Kun. Shanghai Literature and Art Translation Awards now
accepting submissions[N/OL]. China Daily. (2020-05-07) [2021-08-04].
https://www.chinadaily.com.cn/a/202005/07/WS5eb3b0a2a310a8b241153
fbe.html.

[18] Yao Minji. Shanghai Translation awards open for submissions[N/OL].
Shanghai Daily. (2020-07-14) [2021-08-04]. https://www.shine.cn/news/
metro/2007142108/.

[19] Translators — The First Shanghai Literature And Art Translation Awards
Are Waiting For You! [EB/OL]. ShanghaiEye. (2020-07-15) [2021-08-
04]. https://www.shanghaieye.com.cn/translators-the-first-shanghai-
literature-and-art-translation-awards-are-waiting-for-you/.

[20] Yuan Tianyun. Chinese Green Dumplings: spring delights & poignant
memories.[EB/OL] 上海松江. (2021-03-19) [2021-08-15]. https://app.
sjmedia.net/App/content/detailshare.html? contentId=5354424&appId=
110139&projectId=12&shareAppId=110139&channelType=4.

[21] Wang Lianzhang and Wu Ziyi. From Factory Towns to Facebook, China's
Livestreamers Take On Exports[EB/OL]. The Sixth Tone. (2020-12-21)
[2021-08-15]. https://www.sixthtone.com/news/1006577/from-factory-
towns-to-facebook%2C-chinas-livestreamers-take-on-exports.

[22] He Yujia. Peter Hessler's Last Class[EB/OL]. The Sixth Tone. (2021-7-
19) [2021-08-15]. https://www.sixthtone.com/news/1008025/peter-
hesslers-last-class.

[23] Benjamin Mullin. New York Times to Acquire Serial Productions[N/OL].
Wall Street Journal. (2020-07-22) [2021-08-04]. https://www.wsj.com/
articles/new-york-times-reaches-deal-to-acquire-serial-productions-
11595452716.

［24］Yang Meiping，Song Yiyang. Imaginative ideas to reduce the drudge of garbage sorting［N/OL］. Shanghai Daily .（2020-07-07）［2021-08-04］. https：//www.shine.cn/news/in-focus/2007071630/.

［25］Yang Meiping，Song Yiyang. Imaginative ideas to reduce the drudge of garbage sorting［N/OL］. Shanghai Daily .（2020-07-07）［2021-08-04］. https：//www.shine.cn/news/in-focus/2007071630/.

［26］Yuan Luhang. Coming of age：Protecting the environment becomes big business［N/OL］. Shanghai Daily .（2021-01-29）［2021-08-04］. https：//www.shine.cn/news/in-focus/2101294044/.

［27］Cai Xuejiao and Zhang Wanqing. Middle-Aged' Celebs Are Vying to Become China's Next Girl Group［EB/OL］. The Sixth Tone .（2020-07-20）［2021-08-04］. https：//www. sixthtone. com/news/1005808/% E2% 80% 98Middle-Aged% E2% 80% 99% 20Celebs% 20Are% 20Vying% 20to% 20Become%20China%E2%80%99s%20Next%20Girl%20Group.

［28］Tan Weiyun. Middle-aged sisters make waves in new reality TV show［N/OL］. Shanghai Daily.（2020-07-17）［2021-08-04］. https：//www.shine.cn/feature/entertainment/2007172378/.

［29］Yao Minji. Chinese medicine：defenders and doubters［N/OL］. Shanghai Daily .（2020-04-12）［2021-08-04］. https：//www.shine.cn/news/in-focus/2004126175/

［30］Sunstein，C.. Infotopia［M］. Oxford：Oxford University Press. 2008.

［31］BELINDA ROBINSON. Balanced view urged for parents on digital life［N/OL］. China Daily .（2020-02-25）［2020.07-30］. https：//global.chinadaily.com.cn/a/202002/25/WS5e548092a31012821727a0f8.html.

［32］Zhu Shenshen，Huang Yixuan. Sci-tech companies bask in the glow of the STAR Marke［N/OL］t. Shanghai Daily.（2021-08-13）［2021-08-15］. https：//www.shine.cn/news/in-focus/2108133535/.

［33］2019 年虚假新闻研究报告：专业媒体仍在持续生产错误信息［EB/OL］. 澎湃.（2020-01-15）［2021-08-04］. https：//www. thepaper. cn/newsDetail _ forward_5524167.

［34］Li Shuangyi. How self-media chaos has sparked widespread outrage in China［EB/OL］. CGTN.（2019-03-30）［2020-7-30］. https：//news. cgtn. com/news/3d3d674d77457a4e33457a6333566d54/index.html.

［35］Bill Kovach & Tom Rosenstiel.The Elements of Journalism ［M］. 3rd ed. New York：Three Rivers Press，2014：126-127.

［36］Melanie Magin and Peter Maurer. Beat Journalism and Reporting，

Subject: Communication Theory, Journalism Studies, Political Communication Online Publication [EB/OL]. (2019-05) [2020-07-05]. DOI: 10.1093/acrefore/9780190228613.013.905.

[37] Rachel Barclay. Your memory is unreliable, and science could make it more so[EB/OL]. Healthline. (2013-11-13) [2020-07-30]. https://www. healthline. com/health-news/mental-memory-is-unreliable-and-it-could-be-worse-091313#Now-You-Remember,-Now-You-Dont.

[38] Yao Minji. Redefining what it means to be a man in today's China [N/OL]. Shanghai Daily. (2021-02-09) [2021-08-16]. https://www.shine.cn/news/in-focus/2102094574/.

[39] Yuan Ye and Wang Lianzhang. How Wuhan Cared for Pandemic's Temporary Orphan [EB/OL]s. The Sixth Tone. (2020-04-27) [2021-08-04]. http://www. sixthtone. com/news/1005559/how-wuhan-cared-for-pandemics-temporary-orphans.

[40] Teresa Méndez. Journalism students ask: Why am I here? [N/OL]. Christian Science Monitor . (2004-10-26) [2019-03-01]. http://www. csmonitor.com/2004/1026/p12s01-legn.html.

[41] Joshua Fruhlinger. You may never have to plug in your smartphone again [N]. Wall Street Journal. (2018-05-31) [2021-08-18]. https://www.wsj. com/articles/you-may-never-have-to-plug-in-your-smartphone-again-1527776901.

[42] Susan Faludi. Facebook Feminism, Like It or Not[EB/OL]. The Baffler. (2013-08-23) [2021-08-18]. https://thebaffler. com/salvos/facebook-feminism-like-it-or-not.

[43] John Gravois. A toast Story[EB/OL]. Pacific Standard. (2014-01-13) [2021-08-04]. https://longform.org/posts/a-toast-story.

[44] Ni Dandan. The Latest Front in China's Battle for School Places: Gym Class[EB/OL]. The Sixth Tone. (2021-02-05) [2021-08-04]. https://www. sixthtone. com/news/1006802/the-latest-front-in-chinas-battle-for-school-places-gym-class.

[45] Rick Bragg. All She Has, $150,000, Is Going to a University[N/OL]. New York Times. (1995-08-03) [2018-10-09]. https://www.nytimes.com/1995/08/13/us/all-she-has-150000-is-going-to-a-university.html.

[46] Liu Siqi and Kenrick Davis. Bilibili vs. Bilibili: The Culture Clash Dividing China's YouTube[EB/OL]. The Sixth Tone. (2020-08-07) [2021-08-04]. http://www. sixthtone. com/news/1006027/bilibili-vs.-bilibili-the-culture-

clash-dividing-chinas-youtube.

[47] Ni Dandan. China's Hidden Crisis: A Growing Elder Care Gap[EB/OL]. The Sixth Tone . (2020-08-18) [2021-08-04]. https://www.sixthtone.com/news/1006061/chinas-hidden-crisis-a-growing-elder-care-gap.

[48] Du Xinyu and Wu Yurui. Team China Aims to Conquer an Unfamiliar New Sport: Skateboarding[EB/OL]. The Sixth Tone. (2021-07-23) [2021-08-05]. https://www. sixthtone. com/news/1008029/team-china-aims-to-conquer-an-unfamiliar-new-sport-skateboarding.

[49] Hilary Potkewitz. Quiet! I'm Cramming for Finals —By Watching Some Else Study [N/OL]. Wall Street Journal. (2018-06-03) [2021-08-04]. https://www. wsj. com/articles/quiet-im-cramming-for-finalsby-watching-someone-else-study-1528045886.

[50] Michael McCarthy. Not necessarily signs of the times; Laughing Matter: Messages on roadways and businesses don't always mean what the authors intended[N]. The Province . 2015-01-03.

[51] Alice Steinbach. A boy of unusual vision[N/OL]. Baltimore Sun . (1984-05) [2016-04-25]. https://longform.org/posts/a-boy-of-unusual-vision.

[52] David Kushner. Dead End on Silk Road: Internet Crime Kingpin Ross Ulbricht's Big Fall[EB/OL]. Rolling Stone. (2014-02-04) [2021-08-05]. https://www. rollingstone. com/culture/culture-news/dead-end-on-silk-road-internet-crime-kingpin-ross-ulbrichts-big-fall-122158/.

[53] Wang Lianzhang. Bones of Contention: China's Unhappy Cosmetic Surgery Patients[EB/OL]. The Sixth Tone. (2021-07-05) [2021-08-06]. https://www. sixthtone. com/news/1007902/bones-of-contention-chinas-unhappy-cosmetic-surgery-patients.

[54] Wang Qin'ou, Li Jiaxin and Cao Aifeng. The untrained herdsman who beat Everest[N/OL]. Shanghai Daily. (2020-07-25) [2021-08-04]. https://archive. shine. cn/feature/The-untrained-herdsman-who-beat-Everest/shdaily.shtml.

[55] Sally Hayden. HIV patients suffer as food shortages bite[N/OL]. Shanghai Daily. (2020-05-26) [2021-08-04]. https://archive.shine.cn/feature/HIV-patients-suffer-as-food-shortages-bite/shdaily.shtml.

[56] Rebecca Solnit. Diary: Google Invades [EB/OL]. London Review of Books . [2021-08-20]. https://www.lrb.co.uk/the-paper/v35/n03/rebecca-solnit/diary.

[57] Julie Jargon. Starbucks CEO Turns Focus to Pricier Brew[N]. the Wall

Street Journal. (2016-12-02) [2021-08-20]. https://www.wsj.com/articles/howard-schultz-to-step-down-as-starbucks-ceo-1480626061.

[58] Mae Anderson. Small businesses lifted by return of tourists. Shanghai Daily [N/OL]. (2021-08-04) [2021-08-05]. https://archive.shine.cn/feature/Small-businesses-lifted-by-return-of-tourists/shdaily.shtml.

[59] Yao Minji. Online resources help minds, bodies stay fit amid confinement [N/OL]. Shanghai Daily . (2020-04-28) [2021-08-21]. https://www.shine.cn/feature/wellness/2004287179/.

[60] Hu Min and Ding Yining. Food frugality: empty plates, no leftovers[N/OL]. Shanghai Daily . (2020-08-19) [2021-08-21]. https://archive.shine.cn/metro/Food-frugality-empty-plates-no-leftovers/shdaily.shtml.

[61] Fan Yiying and Zhang Shiyu. For China's Middle-Aged Women, Depression Is an 'Invisible Killer' [EB/OL].The Sixth Tone. (2021-05-20) [2021-08-21]. https://www.sixthtone.com/news/1006992/for-chinas-middle-aged-women%2C-depression-is-an-invisible-killer.

[62] Zhuying. When the chirping stops, a market croaks [N/OL]. Shanghai Daily. (2020-07-11) [2021-08-21]. https://archive.shine.cn/feature/When-the-chirping-stops-a-market-croaks/shdaily.shtml.

[63] Samuel Petrequin. Surgical or homemade, face masks mark a major shift in thinking [N/OL]. Shanghai Daily. (2020-07-14) [2021-08-21]. https://archive.shine.cn/feature/Surgical-or-homemade-face-masks-mark-a-major-shift-in-thinking/shdaily.shtml.

[64] Yao Minji and Maggie Xu. Grounded! International students face hard choices after US policy change[N/OL]. Shanghai Daily . (2020-07-12) [2021-08-21]. https://www.shine.cn/news/in-focus/2007121990/.

[65] Xu Qing. Fitness industry bent into new shape [N/OL]. Shanghai Daily. (2020-07-15) [2021-08-21]. https://archive.shine.cn/metro/Fitness-industry-bent-into-new-shape/shdaily.shtml.

[66] Zhu Ying. Fallen leaves turn over a new leaf in creative artworks[N/OL]. Shanghai Daily . (2020-08-08) [2021-08-21]. https://archive.shine.cn/feature/Fallen-leaves-turn-over-a-new-leaf-in-creative-artworks/shdaily.shtml.

[67] Yao Minji. Audiences face the music again at concert celebrating hope[N/OL]. Shanghai Daily . (2020-07-20) [2021-08-21]. https://archive.shine.cn/feature/art-and-culture/Audiences-face-the-music-again-at-concert-celebrating-hope/shdaily.shtml.

［68］Zhu Ying. The last straw? Never for these traditional artisans［N/OL］. Shanghai Daily .（2021-07-23）［2021-08-21］. https：//www. shine. cn/feature/art-culture/2107232474/.

［69］Jake Coyle. Jim Carry gets real with satirical fictional memoir［N/OL］. Shanghai Daily.（2020-07-08）［2021-08-21］. https：//archive. shine. cn/sunday/book/Jim-Carry-gets-real-with-satirical-fictional-memoir/shdaily. shtml.

［70］Maher al-Mounes. The struggle to keep a dying Syrian craft alive［N/OL］. Shanghai Daily .（2020-07-08）［2021-08-21］. https：//archive. shine. cn/sunday/The-struggle-to-keep-a-dying-Syrian-craft-alive/shdaily.shtml.

［71］Su Jing and Xing Yifan. The Man Shepherding China's Best Zoo Through Its Worst Year［EB/OL］. the Sixth Tone .（2020-02-13）［2021-08-21］. https：//www. sixthtone. com/news/1006844/the-man-shepherding-chinas-best-zoo-through-its-worst-year.

［72］Hu Min and Song Yiyang. Ugh! The city is suffering from an infestation of termites［N/OL］. Shanghai Daily .（2020-07-12）［2021-08-21］. https：//archive. shine. cn/metro/Ugh-The-city-is-suffering-from-an-infestation-of-termites/shdaily.shtml.

［73］Lu Feiran. Lip-smackin' good! Where crayfish lovers turn up at night［N/OL］. Shanghai Daily .（2020-07-24）［2021-08-21］. https：//archive.shine.cn/feature/Lipsmackin-good-Where-crayfish-lovers-turn-up-at-night/shdaily.shtml.

［74］Lisa Rathke and Patrick Whittle. Farm-to-table dining takes on new meaning［N/OL］. Shanghai Daily .（2020-07-11）［2021-08-21］. https：//archive. shine. cn/feature/Farmtotable-dining-takes-on-new-meaning/shdaily.shtml.

［75］Hu Min. Softly，softly，an all-female patrol keeps the east riverbank orderly［N/OL］. Shanghai Daily.（2020-07-14）［2021-08-21］. https：//www.shine.cn/news/in-focus/2007142086/.

［76］Shingo Ito. Grand Theft Auto：90-year-old games her way to fame［N/OL］. Shanghai Daily .（2020-06-14）［2021-08-21］. https：//archive.shine.cn/feature/Grand-Theft-Auto-90yearold-games-her-way-to-fame/shdaily.shtml.

［77］Zhuying. Looms to heirlooms：Artisans weave silk into premium carpets［N/OL］. Shanghai Daily .（2021-08-06）［2021-08-21］. https：//www.shine.cn/feature/art-culture/2108063221/.

[78] Yang Wenjie. There's no place like home in rural tourism [N/OL]. Shanghai Daily . (2020-06-23) [2021-08-21]. https://archive. shine. cn/ district/minhang/Theres-no-place-like-home-in-rural-tourism/shdaily. shtml.

[79] Hu Min and Song Yiyang. One year on: We've bin there, done that! [N/ OL].Shanghai Daily . (2020-07-01) [2021-08-21]. https://archive.shine. cn/metro/One-year-on-Weve-bin-there-done-that/shdaily.shtml.

[80] Tian Shengjie and Li Anlan. Airlines in the doghouse over bringing pets back to China [N/OL]. Shanghai Daily . (2020-08-02) [2021-08-21]. https://archive. shine. cn/sunday/Airlines-in-the-doghouse-over-bringing-pets-back-to-China/shdaily.shtml.

[81] Thomas Adamson. Champagne losing its fizz as pandemic puts a cork on consumption [N/OL]. Shanghai Daily . (2020-08-06) [2021-08-21]. https://archive. shine. cn/feature/Champagne-losing-its-fizz-as-pandemic-puts-a-cork-on-consumption/shdaily.shtml.

[82] Lu Feiran. Nose prints offer the purr-fect way to ID your pets [N/OL]. Shanghai Daily. (2020-08-08) [2021-08-21]. https://archive. shine. cn/ feature/Nose-prints-offer-the-purrfect-way-to-ID-your-pets/shdaily.shtml.

[83] Ming Que. The Unbearable Likeness of Being: The Story of 'Little Jack Ma'[EB/OL]. The Sixth Tone . (2021-03-18) [2021-08-21]. https://www. sixthtone. com/news/1006988/the-unbearable-likeness-of-being-the-story-of-little-jack-ma.

[84] Tan Weiyun. A wave or not a wave, that is the question [N/OL].Shanghai Daily. (2021-07-30) [2021-08-21]. https://www. shine. cn/feature/art-culture/2107302896/.

[85] Yuan Ye. The Chinese Students Stuck in Fake Majors[EB/OL]. The Sixth Tone. (2019-08-270) [2021-08-04]. https://www. sixthtone. com/news/ 1004486/The♯.

[86] Yao Minji. Consumers smart over new smart locker fees [N/OL]. Shanghai Daily. (2020-08-14) [2021-08-04]. https://archive. shine. cn/ feature/news-feature/Consumers-smart-over-new-smart-locker-fees/ shdaily.shtml.

[87] Zhu Ying. When the chirping stops, a market croaks. Shanghai Daily [N/ OL]. (2020-07-11) [2021-08-04]. https://archive.shine.cn/feature/When-the-chirping-stops-a-market-croaks/shdaily.shtml.

[88] Hu Min and Ding Yining. Food frugality: empty plates, no leftovers[N/

OL]. Shanghai Daily . (2020-08-19)[2021-08-04]. https://archive.shine. cn/metro/Food-frugality-empty-plates-no-leftovers/shdaily.shtml.

[89] Wu Haiyun. Temples for the masses[EB/OL]. The Sixth Tone. [2021-08-04]. https://interaction. sixthtone. com/feature/2020/Temples-for-the-masses/.

[90] Kenrick Davis. The Bard of Yuyuan Road. The Sixth Tone[EB/OL]. (2020-07-03)[2021-08-04]. https://www. sixthtone. com/news/1006002/ the-bard-of-yuyuan-road

[91] MICHAEL BLASTLAND & ANDREW DILNOT. The Tiger That Isn't: Seeing Through a World of Numbers[M]. 2nd ed. London: PROFILE BOOKS LTD，2008：131.

[92] MICHAEL BLASTLAND & ANDREW DILNOT.The Tiger That Isn't: Seeing Through a World of Numbers[M]. 2nd ed. London: PROFILE BOOKS LTD，2008.

[93] Best Newspaper Writing 1991[M].St. Petersburg：The Poynter Institute for Media Studies，1991：109.

[94] William Zinsser. On Writing Well [M]. 5th ed. New York：Harper Perennial，1994：63.

[95] Don Fry and Karen Brown. Best Newspaper Writing 1990 [M]. St. Petersburg：The Poynter Institute for Media Studies，1990：56.

[96] Zhu Yinghong，Qin Yiling. Restoration of newspaper magnate's former residence almost finished[EB/OL]. Shanghai Songjiang APP. (2021-04-07) [2021-08-21]. https://app. sjmedia. net/App/content/detailshare. html? contentId ＝ 5444308&appId ＝ 110139&projectId ＝ 12&shareAppId ＝ 110139&channelType＝4.

[97] 朱颖宏.匠心修复延长建筑"生命"，史量才故居修缮基本完工[EB/OL].松江融媒体中心.(2021-03-27)[2021-08-21]. https://app. sjmedia. net/App/ content/detailshare.html? contentId＝5388510&appId＝110139&projectId ＝12&shareAppId＝110139&channelType＝4.

[98] Yuan Ye. The Chinese Students Stuck in Fake Majors[EB/OL]. The Sixth Tone. (2019-08-270)[2021-08-04]. https://www. sixthtone. com/news/ 1004486/The♯.

[99] Lu Feiran. Meme's the word：How Eggman struck a chord[N/OL. Shanghai Daily]. (2020-07-10)[2021-08-04]. https://www. shine. cn/ feature/lifestyle/2007101900/.

[100] Ma Yue. Meet a music composer who never sleeps[N/OL]. Shanghai

Daily . （2020-09-05）［2021-08-04］. https：//archive. shine. cn/feature/ Meet-a-music-composer-who-never-sleeps/shdaily.shtml.

[101] Lu Feiran. If it looks like a duck and quacks like a duck，it may be a pet ［N/OL］. Shanghai. Daily . （2020-07-15）［2021-08-04］. https：//www. shine.cn/feature/lifestyle/2007152225/.

[102] Don Fry and Karen Brown. Best Newspaper Writing 1990 ［M］. St. Petersburg：The Poynter Institute for Media Studies，1990：92.

[103] William Zinsser. On Writing Well ［M］. 5th ed. New York：Harper Perennial，1994：117.

[104] Li Cathy，Ding Yijie. A pig raising rehab story［EB/OL］. Shanghai Songjiang APP . （2021-06-25）［2021-0822］. https：//app. sjmedia. net/ App/content/detailshare. html? contentId ＝ 5749423&appId ＝ 110139&projectId＝12&shareAppId＝110139&channelType＝4.

[105] Ni Dandan. The Lasting Pain of China's Identity Theft Victims［EB/OL］. The Sixth Tone . （2020-07-13）［2021-08-21］. https：//www. sixthtone. com/news/1005911/the-lasting-pain-of-chinas-identity-theft-victims.

[106] Ni Dandan. The Silent Victims of China-India Travel Bans：Cancer Patients［EB/OL］. The Sixth Tone. （2020-09-02）［2021-08-04］. https：// www. sixthtone. com/news/1006136/the-silent-victims-of-china-india- travel-bans-cancer-patients.

[107] Wang Qin'ou，Li Jiaxin and Cao Aifeng. The untrained herdsman who beat Everest ［N/OL］. Shanghai Daily. （2020-07-25）［2021-08-04］. https：//archive. shine. cn/feature/The-untrained-herdsman-who-beat- Everest/shdaily.shtml.

[108] Chen Huizhi. Age is no barrier to achieving body fitness［N/OL］. Shanghai Daily. （2020-09-09）［2021-08-06］. https：//archive. shine. cn/ metro/Age-is-no-barrier-to-achieving-body-fitness/shdaily.shtml.

[109] MaYue. Gritty documentary focuses on miners with black lung disease［N/ OL］. Shanghai Daily . （2020-05-080）［2021-08-06］. https：//www.shine. cn/feature/art-culture/2005087714/.

[110] Ma YueMa Xuefeng. Dancer inspired by his revolutionary role［N/OL］. Shanghai Daily. （2021-06-28）［2021-08-06］. https：//www. shine. cn/ news/in-focus/2106281209/.

[111] Zhang Jiaqi. Village entrepreneur and her Happy Elderly Village［EB/ OL］. Shanghai Songjiang APP. （2021-04-10）［2021-08-23］. https：//app. sjmedia. net/App/content/detailshare. html? contentId ＝ 5459230&appId

＝110139&projectId＝12&shareAppId＝110139&channelType＝4.

［112］杜希双.服务业发展提质增效［EB/OL］. 中国经济网.（2020-01-19）［2021-08-06］，http：//www.stats.gov.cn/tjsj/zxfb/202001/t20200119_1723779. html.

［113］China sees 97 million domestic tourist trips on National Day［EB/OL］. Xinhua.（2020-10-02）［2021-08-06］. http：//www.china.org.cn/business/ 2020-10/02/content_76773131.htm.

［114］China's rural tourism revenue tops 850 bln yuan in 2019［EB/OL］. Xinhua .（202012-07）.［2021-08-06］. https：//www.chinadaily.com.cn/a/ 202012/07/WS5fcd9a4ba31024ad0ba9a44f.html.

［115］Yao Minji. Desert kingdom of contradictions is opening up tourism［EB/ OL］. Shanghai Daily.（2020-05-29）［2021-08-06］. https：//www. shine. cn/feature/travel/2005299145/.

［116］Lu Feiran. As tourist stops go，one village is a different kettle of fish［N/ OL］. Shanghai Daily.（2020-11-04）［2021-08-06］. https：//archive.shine. cn/feature/As-tourist-stops-go-one-village-is-a-different-kettle-of-fish/ shdaily.shtml.

［117］Lu Feiran. Beds empty，small innkeepers turn to stop-gap measures［N/ OL］. Shanghai Daily.（2020-04-15）［2021-08-06］. https：//archive.shine. cn/feature/Beds-empty-small-innkeepers-turn-to-stopgap-measures/ shdaily.shtml.

［118］Xu Lin and Liu Kun.Hubei's tourism resumes，cautiously［N/OL］. China Daily.（2020-05-19）［2020-08-06］. http：//www. china. org. cn/travel/ 2020-05/19/content_76063230.htm

［119］Lu Feiran. 'Tis the season to venture out and relish 'the year's last， loveliest smile'［N/OL］. Shanghai Daily.（2020-10-28）［2021-08-06］. https：//www.shine.cn/feature/travel/2010288605/.

［120］Yu Hong. Sanya a tropical paradise packed with scenic delights［N/OL］. Shanghai Daily.（2020-11-05）［2021-08-06］. https：//www. shine. cn/ feature/travel/2011059053/.

［121］William Strunk JR. and E.B. White.The Elements of Style（illustrated） ［M］. New York：Penguin Books，2005：114.

［122］Belinda Robinson. Wuhan film tells stories of hope and kindness［N/OL］. China Daily.（2020-10-08）［2021-08-06］. http：//www.chinadaily.com. cn/a/202010/08/WS5f7f364da31024ad0ba7d84b.html.

［123］Xu Wei. Latest festive films ready to be unleashed［N/OL］. Shanghai

Daily. （2019-12-07）. ［2021-08-06］. https：//www. shine. cn/feature/ entertainment/1912077548/.

[124] Britannica［EB/OL］. ［2021-08-06］. https：//www. britannica. com/art/ visual-arts.

[125] Shi Hua. Traditional Chinese bird-and-flower art with a modern twist［N/ OL］. Shanghai Daily. （2020-08-28）［2021-08-06］. https：//www.shine. cn/feature/art-culture/2008285000/.

[126] Tan Weiyun. Capturing motion when beauty strikes a chord［N/OL］. Shanghai Daily. （2020-09-05）［2021-08-06］. https：//www. shine. cn/ feature/art-culture/2009055470/.

[127] Donia Bijan.The last days of Café Leila：a novel ［M］. Chapel Hill： Algonquin Books of Chapel Hill，2018.

[128] Li Anlan. But does it go well with rice? ［N/OL］.Shanghai Daily . （2020- 11-04）［2021-08-07］, https：//www.shine.cn/feature/taste/2011049015/.

[129] Pang Yuxia，Yuan Tianyun. A Day in the Life of a Census-Taker［EB/ OL］. Shanghai Songjiang APP . （2020-12-03）［2021-08-26］. https：//app. sjmedia. net/App/content/detailshare. html？ contentId = 4952833&appId =110139&projectId=12&shareAppId=110139&channelType=4.

[130] Yu Peixin，Wang Zizhen. A young man on track in community work［EB/ OL］. Shanghai Songjiang APP. （2020-12-01）［2021-08-26］. https：//app. sjmedia. net/App/content/detailshare. html？ contentId = 4941507&appId =110139&projectId=12&shareAppId=110139&channelType=4.

[131] 第七次全国人口普查主要数据情［EB/OL］. 国家统计局.（2021-05-11） ［2021-08-07］. http：//www. stats. gov. cn/tjsj/zxfb/202105/t20210510 _ 1817176.html.

[132] Zhang Chenjia，Zhou Yao. Family farmers in Songjiang enjoy prosperity working in tandem［EB/OL］. Shanghai Songjiang APP. （2020-10-19） ［2021-08-26］. https：//app. sjmedia. net/App/content/detailshare. html？ contentId = 4775796&appId = 110139&projectId = 12&shareAppId = 110139&channelType=4.

[133] Chen Yufan，Liu Yuhang. Young people follow startup dreams in countryside［EB/OL］. Shanghai Songjiang APP. （2020-10-16）［2021- 0826］. https：//app. sjmedia. net/App/content/detailshare. html？ contentId = 4775943&appId = 110139&projectId = 12&shareAppId = 110139&channelType=4.

[134] Bai Jinshuang，Teng Yutong. Egret poetry society returns to village［EB/

OL]. Shanghai Songjiang APP. (2020-10-13) [2021-08-26]. https：//app. sjmedia. net/App/content/detailshare. html？ contentId ＝ 4761297&appId ＝110139&projectId＝12&shareAppId＝110139&channelType＝4.